Praise for From Impossible To Inevitable

What Readers Have Said About *From Impossible To Inevitable …*

"Over the past 8 years, I decided to become really good at sales and lead generation. I've read and studied everything I could, practicing several different methods of generating traffic and sales. This book made me feel like a dummy. Wow, it's amazing. Really brilliant. Aaron and Jason outline simple solutions with specific methodologies that make it seem impossible to fail. They tell you why, how, and what can go wrong. Their use of case studies clearly illustrates common growth challenges and how to navigate past or through them. It's changed my whole method of working."

— Fraser Morrison, CEO Schiffman Morrison Asia

"At our portfolio company Agility Recovery, Aaron and Jason's '10x Exercise' helped us increase our enterprise deal sizes 4.8x in under 6 months, by enhancing our offering, modifying our sales approach, and implementing value-based pricing."

— Larry Coble, LLR Partners

"I was amazed by this book. Aaron and Jason are unbelievable references for anyone working in the SaaS space. They're not just 'been there, done that' professionals, they're thoughtful leaders in the community. Their sales model math completely changed our business and pricing strategies. For example, it seems obvious in hindsight, but their 'Double Your Deal-size' section nailed it for us: we weren't able to build a big business out of small deals. This book is a must-read for any b2b entrepreneur."

— Leo Faria, Hustler and Founder

"Most business books tend to be dry and dull. Aaron and Jason's informal approach is a refreshing change and much more interesting and better: useful. Details and case studies (like the one outlining HTML versus personal, plain-text email campaigns) made it easy for me to put the ideas to work right away. I can see anyone who wants to succeed getting remarkable insights here, as I did."

— Sabrina Bianchi, Marketing and Social Media Strategist

"I came to this book wanting to see how these people grew 10x, and I did, but what was truly amazing was how much of that could be applied and adapted by even the smallest businesses, like my own. No 30,000-foot view here; this book is straightforward, very hands-on, very in the trenches, and because of that, very exciting."

— Larry Hicock, CEO Sparketers

"The topics within *From Impossible to Inevitable* have brought my own career to new and exciting levels. It's fed the beast of my yearning for useful revenue tactics and sharper business acumen. The book also helped me become a better leader in every aspect of my career and life. By applying these principles in your daily life, not just work, you will see changes happen (for the better) faster than you ever could have imagined. *From Impossible to Inevitable* should not just be a business book but a high school text!"

— Ryan Donohue, Director, Agility Recovery

"I've been a huge fan of Aaron and Jason's ever since I read *Predictable Revenue* and found SaaStr, but they take it to another level in this book. The depth with which they understand the current talent and culture ecosystem in tech (especially sales) is remarkable. I now feel like I know exactly how my boss and my exec team think about my performance, and how to get ahead in my growing career. Before I was totally 'renting' my job as Aaron and Jason put it, but now I realize I have to become an 'owner' when it comes to my role if I really want to get ahead."

— Eric Taylor, Sales, HackerRank

"I have been following Aaron's and Jason's work for quite a while. For example, when *Predictable Revenue* came out, I devoured it during a flight to London. Upon landing, I sent an email to my team to have Aaron interviewed for our blog. That interview had the highest measurable traffic, stickiness, and time on page of any other piece of content at the time. And I'm a devout SaaStr reader. Their new book is even better. Its approachable style, with easily identifiable actions that any company could take, makes it my go-to present for any new executive I meet. As someone who's been working in sales and marketing for 20 years, my favorite quote from the book is 'Your VP Sales has a quota—why doesn't your VP Marketing?'"

—Erik W. Charles, Incentives Expert, ErikCharles.com

"*From Impossible to Inevitable* helped me see exactly how to focus on what I am best at. The Sales Specialization section inspired and showed me how to rework my sales system. It's unlike any other sales methodology I've encountered. Most trainers are helping you improve phone or email techniques, but those are a waste of time if the underlying system isn't efficient. I'm already recommending this book to all my sales and marketing friends."

— Mike Smith, Director of Partnerships, Touchpoints

"My previous job was running my first subscription business and I learned the hard way in the new economy that you can't just sell a customer and walk away. I haven't seen a better case for investing in Customer Success than the way Aaron and Jason lay it out in Part 2 of this book. They demonstrate why Customer Success is about revenue growth, not customer satisfaction. They include useful details on how to structure a team, including examples of tiered levels of service. I bought this book for my whole team, and many extra to give to customers."

— Nick Mehta, CEO Gainsight

"If you have ever had a conversation with Aaron about his personal life you know he is a simple man focused on what is truly important. The same holds true when he writes about how to be successful in the business world. 'Don't let your exciting vision get in the way of taking the daily baby steps needed to get customers today.' Such a simple but important truth."

— Trish Bertuzzi, CEO The Bridge Group and Author, *The Sales Development Playbook*

"Aaron and Jason are rare experts, who combine real-world (not theoretical) expertise as keynote speakers with an ability to skillfully teach the complexities associated with conquering Big Revenue Goals in a busy world."

— Barrett Cordero, President, BigSpeak Inc.

"I thought the book would be the same old ideas (invest in people, embrace failure, etc.) I've heard over and over again, but as I pushed through I discovered how many new ideas were here, old ideas were revitalized and combined with useful details demonstrating how to actually implement them."

— Kyle Romaniuk, Partner, The CHR Group

"As we worked through the Niche Matrix (in Part 1) for our key verticals, it was amazing to watch the team learn how to truly value sell our service to solve our customer pain points and significantly increase our deal sizes in the process. The Embrace Employee Ownership section was also powerful. By asking who owns upgrades and how, our account management leader took ownership of up-selling our base, committed the team to double monthly upgrades (a Forcing Function), and worked with the team to decide on key activities to drive results. Within 2 months, they doubled our monthly upgrade revenue."

— Larry Coble, LLR Partners

FROM IMPOSSIBLE TO INEVITABLE

FROM IMPOSSIBLE TO INEVITABLE

HOW HYPER-GROWTH COMPANIES CREATE PREDICTABLE REVENUE

AARON ROSS AND JASON LEMKIN

WILEY

This book is printed on acid-free paper. ∞

Published by John Wiley & Sons, Inc., Hoboken, New Jersey
Published simultaneously in Canada

For general information about our other products and services, please contact our Customer Care Department within the United States at (800) 762-2974, outside the United States at (317) 572-3993 or fax (317) 572-4002.

Wiley publishes in a variety of print and electronic formats and by print-on-demand. Some material included with standard print versions of this book may not be included in e-books or in print-on-demand. If this book refers to media such as a CD or DVD that is not included in the version you purchased, you may download this material at http://booksupport.wiley.com. For more information about Wiley products, visit www.wiley.com.

Library of Congress Cataloging-in-Publication Data is available:

ISBN 9781119166719 (Hardcover)
ISBN 9781119166726 (ePDF)
ISBN 9781119166733 (ePub)

Cover Design: Wiley
Cover Image: Aaron Ross

Printed in the United States of America

10 9 8 7 6 5 4 3 2 1

Contents

PART II Create Predictable Pipeline

PART III Make Sales Scalable

Preface: Systematizing Success

There's never been an easier time to grow a business. Ironically, though, while everyone else around you seems to be crushing their goals, does it feel like a struggle for you?

If you needed to triple your revenue in the next year or three, would you know exactly how you would do it?

Tripling isn't magic. It's not about the school you went to, luck, or working harder. There's a template that the world's fastest-growing companies follow to achieve and sustain hypergrowth.

Whether you want to add $1 million or $100 million, the fundamentals are the same. You can grow your business 2x to 10x faster in honorable ways that feel good to you, your employees, and your customers. (In fact, the truth is the best form of sales and marketing.)

This book shows you how to break growth plateaus and get off the up-and-down revenue rollercoaster, showing you how to answer:

1. "Why aren't you growing faster?"
2. "What does it take to get to hypergrowth?"
3. "How do you sustain it?"

LESSONS FROM THE WORLD'S FASTEST-GROWING COMPANIES

The Internet's filled with advice on how to grow your company. Some great, some harmful, mostly outdated, or just nice to have. How do you sort through the clutter to figure out the few, big things that will change and sustain your growth rate?

Whatever your business is, rather than a 2% or 20% increase in sales, we want you to find ways to get a 200–1,000% increase in growth by learning from companies like:

- **Zenefits**, growing from $1 million to $100 million in revenue in ~two years

- **Salesforce.com,** the multibillion dollar, fastest-growing big software company
- **EchoSign (now Adobe Document Services),** growing from $0 to $144 million in seven years
- **HubSpot**, growing past $100 million in revenue, and valued at more than $1 billion
- **Acquia**, named a #1 fastest growing private software company in 2013–and made breaking $100 million in total revenue a "when, not if" challenge
- **Avanoo,** growing from $1300 to $5 million in about a year, in the uber-crowded corporate training space

Now if you're like us, you want to know *how the heck did they do that?*

It wasn't from posting a video that went viral or anything else that would make you say "oh, they got lucky." Instead, there are repeatable lessons any company can learn from.

Success can be a system, not random. Revenue and growth can be (mostly) predictable. And has to be, to take *impossible goals* and turn them into *inevitable success* for your business and team. Successes far bigger than you can imagine from where you're sitting today.

The Seven Ingredients of Hypergrowth

1. *You're not ready to grow* … until you **Nail A Niche**.
2. *Overnight success is a fairy tale.* You're not going to be magically discovered, so you need sustainable systems that **Create Predictable Pipeline**.
3. Speeding up growth creates more problems than it solves. Things will actually get worse until you **Make Sales Scalable**.
4. *It's hard to build a big business out of small deals* … so figure out how to **Double Your Deal-size**.
5. *It'll take years longer than you want* … don't quit too soon or let a Year Of Hell discourage you. Be prepared to **Do The Time**.
6. *Your employees are renting, not owning their jobs.* **Embrace Employee Ownership** to develop a culture of taking initiative beyond a job description.
7. If you're an employee, *you're letting frustrations stop, not motivate, you*. Stop waiting for someone else to fix it, and turn your frustrations to your advantage to **Define Your Destiny**.

Follow the recipe and kick off your biggest growth spurt yet.

PART I

Nail A Niche

The Painful Truth: You're not ready to grow.

CHAPTER 1

"Niche" Doesn't Mean Small

How do you know whether or not you're ready to grow? Don't let a big vision, or wanting to serve too many kinds of customers, trap you into sounding vague or confusing.

ARE YOU SURE YOU'RE READY TO GROW FASTER?

You're excited about your business, your ideas, products, and services … and you're ready to grow faster. You might be a startup, a consultant, or a Fortune 100 brand.

And you know that lead generation is *the* #1 lever that drives revenue growth, and can create hypergrowth. You've been trying to grow your leads, and thus sales, but it's been harder than you expected … maybe a lot harder.

Are you *sure you're ready* to grow faster?

Because when it feels like you're swimming upstream every day to generate leads, or to sign new customers from the ones you do get, you usually have a bigger problem. All that time, energy and money invested in growing new leads and closing sales can be poured into a black hole—if you haven't Nailed A Niche.

You can be a Fortune 100 company, or the greatest expert at organization design, or have a killer SaaS (software as a service) subscription model app for managing employees. But, if you can't *predictably* go out and generate *leads and opportunities* where you're *needed*, *win* them, and do it *profitably*, you're gonna struggle. It's frustrating. But there's no shortcut here, whether you're a business or an individual. Struggles often mean there's a niche problem, either at the company, marketing department, or salesperson level.

Clues You Aren't Ready to Grow (Regardless of What the CEO or Board Expects)

- You've grown mostly through referrals, word of mouth, and up-/cross-selling.
- Inbound or outbound lead generation has been disappointing … or abysmal.
- You realize, looking back, that you're dependent on preexisting relationships or a recognized brand to get in the door, even if your product or service is amazing.
- You're good at too many things, and struggle focusing on the one best opportunity to sell and deliver over and over again.
- Even when you get quality appointments, too few people buy.

> **If you can't *predictably* generate *leads and opportunities* where you're *needed*, *win* them, and do it *profitably*, you're gonna struggle.**

Most Frequently Seen When …

- You hit a plateau between $1 and $10 million in revenue, and you start trying new kinds of leadgen programs.
- When you launch a new product/service, or enter a new market.
- In getting your first 10–50 customers, getting to product-market fit or a minimum sellable product.
- You're in consulting or professional services.
- Your company offers a wide range of products and services (Portfolio Attention Deficit Disorder).

Everyone Hates to Admit They're Not Ready to Grow

Swallowing the "we're not ready to grow yet" pill is bitter. Especially when you have a board or CEO breathing down your neck, a payroll to meet, or big family bills.

No one likes admitting they're a nice-to-have rather than a "need-to-have." Or that the elevator pitch the CEO came up with is totally off-base and confuses prospects. Or that you can't yet measure or document other customers' results.

Companies with a large portfolio of products face the same problem. Do your salespeople or customers get confused by all the product options? They don't know what to buy or sell first, and so they struggle along trying to buy or sell a little bit of everything. Confusion stunts growth. A lack of focus distracts you from being "insanely great" at just one thing.

HOW TO KNOW IF YOU'VE NAILED A NICHE

When you're a startup getting to your first million, or launching a new product, lead generation program, or market—one of the indicators that you've Nailed A Niche is that you are able to find and sign up unaffiliated customers. Unaffiliated. Paying. Customers.

One of the indicators that you've Nailed A Niche is that you're consistently able to find and sign up unaffiliated customers.

We don't mean friends of your investors, or your old coworkers or boss. They aren't past customers, partners, or part of your LinkedIn network. They weren't referred to you; they didn't hear about you from a group. They started out "cold" without the advantage of prior relationships.

Whether they found you by coming in through the either, or whether you went out and pounded the (physical or virtual) pavement to source and close them.

And now they're paying you—profitably.

Because here's the thing. Ten customers may not seem like much. We called these guys "beer money" in the early days at EchoSign. Ten customers was $200 a month, which didn't come close to paying the bills on four engineers and three other guys—it barely paid for beer. But 10 clients are actually amazing. Yes, you may still fail, of course, because of cash-flow issues. But 10 is a first sign of pre-success—even though it's very likely that more than one will turn out to be a dud, while you're learning which customers you can make successful or not. Because it means three things:

1. Since you have 10, you can definitely get 20 … and then 100. If you can get 10 unaffiliated customers to pay you (no small feat), I guarantee you can get 20. And if you keep going at it, you will get at least

to 100. And then 200, at least. At a minimum, you can keep doubling and doubling. I'm not saying it's easy, but it's possible.
2. More important, it's amazing you got those 10. Ten is not a small number! Because why the heck should they trust you, and pay for your product? It stands on its own without you needing a prior relationship. It's a huge vote of confidence. Maybe you were on TechCrunch, Reddit, Bob's Insurance Newsletter, or some blog—great. But in the real world, with Mainstream Buyers, no one has ever heard of you. You're not "the thing" all their friends are buying, making them feel that without it they're being left behind.
3. This means you built something real. Something valued. Most important, it's something you can build on. These 10 customers will give you a roadmap, feedback, and indeed, the path to 1,000 more customers—if you listen carefully. You won't heed all their advice, of course, but the feedback from these first 10 customers won't be from outliers. It will be transformational. I guarantee it.

   Because your 1,000th customer most likely will be just like your 10th, in concept and spirit, in category and core problem solved.

At EchoSign, the first unaffiliated customer was a distributed sales manager of a telesales team. The exact industry she was in was unusual (debt consolidation), but digging deeper, the actual use case was exactly the same, in spirit if not in workflow, as 80% or more of the customers that came later. The same as Facebook, as Twitter, as Groupon, as Google, as Verizon, as BT, as Oracle … the same as all of them.

The same core "goodness" that you've built attracts all of them. Of course, you're going to need to build tons more features, mature your product dramatically, and so forth. But the core will be the same goodness as customers 1–10 experienced.

Trust us. Ten customers may not pay the bills. But if you got them from scratch, you have the start of organic leadflow or of some leadgen process that you can replicate. That's really special, and something you can actually build on.

So this is your first time to double down, after Customer 10 … even if it seems way, way smaller than your goals and vision. Forget 1,000: Double them to 20, then to 40, and so on. Compound that 10 month after month, year after year, get the flywheel cranking, and you'll make your big vision inevitable.

ACHIEVE WORLD DOMINATION ONE NICHE AT A TIME

Let's address a misperception right now about the word "niche." When you Nail A Niche, you're *not* "thinking small." You're not limiting your dream. You're not permanently shrinking your addressable market.

Niche here means *focused*. On a *specific* target customer with a *specific* pain. Regardless of how many types of customers you *could* help, or how many of their problems you *could* solve.

Don't let your exciting vision or big, hairy, audacious goal get in the way of taking the daily baby steps needed to get customers today.

Hypergrowth doesn't come from selling many things to many markets, covering all your bases (really, dividing your energies). Hypergrowth comes from focusing on where you have the best chances of winning customers, making them successful, building a reputation of tangible results, and then growing from there. For example:

- Salesforce.com started with Sales Force Automation.
- Zenefits started with Californian technology companies of 100 to 300 employees.
- Facebook began with Ivy League schools.
- PayPal took off with eBay users.
- Amazon started with books.
- Zappos focused on shoes.

Where's the easiest place for you to build momentum *now*? What's the *path of least resistance to money* for you?

Focusing on specific industries or types of customers—like banks, software companies, or large businesses—is part, but not all of it. It also means focusing your *unique* strengths (not *all* your strengths) where they can create the most value (not any value), and:

- Solve a specific *pain* for
- An *ideal* target customer in
- A *believable, repeatable* way,
- With predictable methods to a) *find* and b) *interest* them.

Any kind of specialization that helps you to break through the clutter, stand out, be the best, win, or be unique is valuable.

For example: If you're a company that creates customized solutions for every client, and you need to recreate the wheel from scratch each time, you're going to struggle with a double whammy. First, it'll be harder to market yourself, because really—what problem do you solve? Second, unless you have some kind of repeatable solution, framework, or system—growth is going to be *hard*. You have to be one stubborn S.O.B. to grow that kind of company. Or lucky—but luck doesn't create sustained success.

If you focus on solving a single problem really well and can adapt as the market evolves, the sky's your limit.

If you focus on solving a single problem really well and can adapt as the market evolves, the sky's your limit.

THE ARC OF ATTENTION

Why is there a niche problem in the first place? It has to do with how people's brains and attention spans work. The *Arc of Attention* and *Trust Gap* ideas are vital to understanding why there's a problem, and what to do about it.

When you start a business, most people begin with Early Adopters, as they should. These include networks, friends, friends-of-friends, and people whom instinctively "get it." Then, once you hit $1–$10 million in revenue, you usually hit a wall as word-of-mouth and referrals start to plateau. Or, as a large company you might plateau when your new leadgen program, product launch, or market struggles. At some point you will run out of Early Adopters, and will need to figure out how to click with Mainstream Buyers, who don't already know you and don't intuitively "get it" like Early Adopters.

There's a painful difference to evolve from selling to Early Adopters who trust you, to Mainstream Buyers who don't. Geoff Moore called this "crossing the chasm." We call it bridging a Trust Gap. Whatever it's called, when you understand why this gap exists in the first place, you'll better know how to cross it.

There's a painful difference to evolve from selling to Early Adopters who trust you, to Mainstream Buyers who don't.

Enter the Arc of Attention (see Figure 1.1).

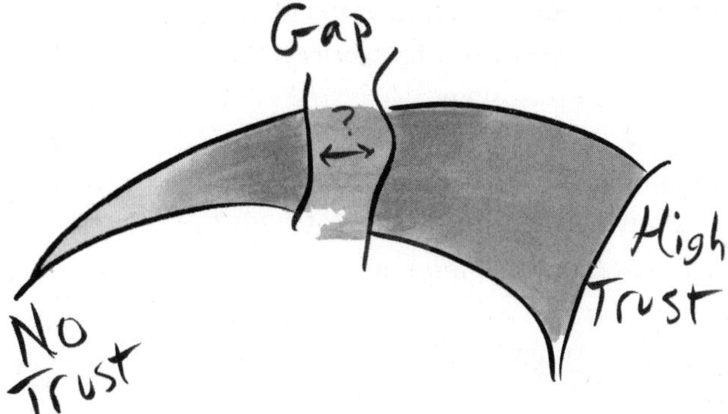

FIGURE 1.1 Arc of Attention

The Right Side—High Trust

On the right side of the spectrum are "Mom/Dad/Best Friends"—the people who know and trust us (or your company/brand), and are therefore willing to give you a big slice of attention just because you asked for it. If you call up a best friend and ask them to meet with you for two hours to review a demo, product, blog post or talk, they will—even if it makes zero sense to them.

This side of the arc also includes the few people who somehow run across your product, as crappy or obtuse as your website is—and just "get it." You don't need to explain anything to them, because intuitively they know what you can do, why it matters and how to use you service. All of these Early Adopters are willing to invest a lot more mental energy to figure out what you're doing and how they can benefit. They give you a *lot* of leeway—which is invaluable in getting a new company, product, or leadgen program off the ground.

But it becomes a liability—and often a rude awakening—when you start expecting everyone to give you that same leeway.

The Left Side—No Trust

On the opposite end, there are the people who have never heard of you or your company. When people don't know you, they'll only give you a tiny sliver of their attention to figure you out. If they don't click with you within that window, they move on.

The more connection you have with them right away, the more leeway they'll give you. The less you have, the faster you lose them. Some sample (nonscientific) windows:

- A cold email or online ad: a 0.3- to 3-second window before they engage or move on.
- A cold call: a 3- to 30-second window.
- Walking door-to-door: a 3- to 60-second window.

Compare these to:

- A referral: 15 minutes–1 hour
- A best friend or parent: Unlimited (In fact, you may be the one who wants to limit the time!)

This is the Trust Gap: The difference between marketing to people who already know us or our brand, and people who don't, and aren't willing to invest anything to figure us out. And the difference between being able to market to Early Adopters (15% of the market) versus Mainstream Buyers (85% of the market). It affects everything related to how you market and sell.

This difference between Early Adopters and Mainstream Buyers can be *huge* and easily underestimated. You may expect jumping the gap to be doable, like crossing a river from one side to the other. But it's more likely to be the Grand Canyon. Or if you're completely dependent on relationships, it's an Earth-to-Moon-sized gap.

The whole point of Nailing A Niche is to help you cross the Trust Gap, moving from depending on buyers on the right side (trust) to being able to better market and sell to buyers on the left side (no trust).

You have to either (a) find a way to fit your message into that slice of attention, or (b) expand the amount of attention they're willing to give you.

Everything we're doing in the Niche part of the book is to help you cross this Gap.

Assume You Are Marketing to Fourth Graders

With those tiny slices of attention that "cold" people are willing to give you, it's similar to the mental investment of a 3rd or 4th grader. So your message has to be simple for them to both *understand* and easily *act* on, or else they'll move on before ever giving it a chance.

Your message has to be simple for them to both *understand* and easily *act* on, or else they'll move on before ever giving it a chance.

This is why short and sweet emails and videos tend to work better than long emails and videos as first touches with new people. People see a long email or video from someone they don't know, and they just aren't willing to invest in consuming it.

Perhaps if you're a genius copywriter, you can make them work, but for us regular people, shorter is better—at least for first contact. The more your messages are *simple to understand* and *easy to answer*, so that they'll fit into your prospects' window of attention, the more effective they'll be.

You can watch this in yourself: what goes through your head when you get a long note from someone, even someone you know? What about a short one? Do you see how the effort you're willing to give that messages changes so dramatically depending on who it comes from, how simple it is, and what they are asking for?

It's also why appealing to their dinosaur brains—rather than the purely logical brain—works.

Speak to The Dinosaur Brain

Reptiles think with their eyes, not their brains—and so do we! Dinosaur-brain thinking (the same thing, but dinosaurs are cooler than reptiles) isn't about thinking consciously and making logical decisions—it's about *reacting*.

There are different reasons something appeals to us at the dinosaur brain level, before our conscious minds have time to process it, such as:

- Newness
- Contrast ("There's a bucket of blue pens with one orange pen on the top")
- Movement/speed
- Surprises
- Details
- Visuals

This is why you'll see banner ads with a color that's different from the page background and with moving pictures, to combine the attention-getting elements of visuals, contrast, and movement. Or why video-sharing sites have so many videos titled like *He Hated His Boss for Two Years until This Happened* with a picture, combining visuals and anticipated surprise and detail. And it works, at least until you learn from watching several that the videos are rarely as interesting as the titles, and you start ignoring them.

So, be intriguing and attractive, without overpromising—at least not too often.

Learning how to reframe your ideas to appeal to people's dinosaur brains makes sense when you consider the tiny window of attention you get. Even if it's frustratingly hard to do at first, or feels sales-y. You can't fight the Arc of Attention, even if you believe "My stuff is so amazing and necessary that it shouldn't need to be sold. Plus we're donating money to save trees, so there's no reason anyone won't want to buy!"

CHAPTER 2

Signs of Slogging

If growing is harder than slogging through mud, it's probably because of one these reasons.

ARE YOU A NICE-TO-HAVE?

Do you believe your intended buyers *need* what you're offering? Or are you a nice-to-have? One clear sign that you're a nice-to-have: Everyone you show your product to say "cool!" but no one buys.

Consumers don't buy what they need; they buy what they want. How much do consumers spend on Porsches and ice cream compared to broccoli and psychotherapy?

But businesses don't buy "nice-to-haves." For example:

- Marketers *want* a beautiful website—but they *need* a website that converts visitors to outcomes such as leads or purchases.
- CEOs *want* "happy employees"—but they *need* people to show up and do their jobs, for products to be released on time, or for cash flow to be improved.
- A VP of Sales *wants* "increased sales productivity"—but they *need* and *buy* what contributes to it, such as leads, accurate reporting tools, and training.
- Venture capitalists *want* to invest in honorable founders—but they *need* to generate above-average returns, which may or may not come from companies with honorable founders.

It takes a lot of energy to buy *and use* something new, so if you're a nice-to-have, it won't stick. Nice-to-haves fall to the bottom of the "must do" list.

If the buyer doesn't *need* your solution, they won't be motivated to go through all the work to convince their people, justify the purchase, roll it out, and get people to use it.

- What problem is painful enough that a team of people will spend both their money and time to fix it?
- If you are solving a need, how can you describe what you do differently, so prospects also see it that way?
- What differentiates the customers who *need* you from the ones who don't?
- Where can you create the most financial value?
- Where can you get permission to create case studies or get references? (With some types of markets or customers these are almost impossible to get.)
- How can you "sell money"?
- How can you sell "things"?

"Sell money" means proving to customers that your product will help them make more money, spend less of it, reduce the risk of losing it, or stay compliant (avoiding fines and legal risk). Demonstrate how spending money with you will make them more money.

Make money by proving to customers that your product will help them make more money, spend less of it, reduce the risk of losing it, or stay compliant.

If you say you'll "increase revenue" or "decrease costs," you sound just like everyone else. What's equivalent to money in their mind—leads? Close rates? Social activity? Collections?

Employee engagement or fulfillment? Although we know engaged employees and fulfillment are vital, how do you prove to customers that you can help them make money with better employee relations, or with better resources and tools for their employees? How can you make the case that your product is *needed*?

Example: What ACME Learned from Failing at Outbound Lead Generation

A $15 million SaaS company, let's call them ACME Corp., came to us and said, "We need to grow, we need more leads!" ACME had grown to that point by being a partner of Salesforce.com and getting referrals from them. These referrals closed at a high rate, quickly. Clearly it was because they were referrals. ACME was growing, but wanted to grow faster, to double their rate with paid lead generation. Referrals and organic growth weren't enough. But ACME assumed that if they just got twice as many leads, they could grow twice as fast.

- *Trouble Clue #1:* They'd been trying different online and offline marketing campaigns for the past three years, with results ranging from abysmal to crummy.
- *Trouble Clue #2:* They started an outbound prospecting program (with Aaron's help) and totally failed. A total *zero*. It took four months (well, on top of the prior three years), but the key learning was that *ACME wasn't ready to grow faster*.

This company hadn't Nailed a Niche. The signs were there before. But they didn't want to accept it until they tried outbound marketing and hit a wall. Any kind of paid or nonorganic lead generation (like marketing or prospecting) can be a forcing function that makes you confront the reality of whether you've nailed a niche or not. If it doesn't work, you need to rethink your target customer ... and possibly your solution.

ACME was in a noisy, commoditized market. All of ACME's target prospects already had something "good enough." Their targets' pains weren't ones ACME could credibly solve. To the prospects, anything ACME could offer beyond what they already had was just a nice-to-have, and not worth the pain of switching systems. However excited the ACME team was about their own stuff, prospects didn't get it. They didn't *need* ACME's solution

Target, Pain, and Solution

Your niche isn't just picking an industry vertical or target, though being selective about whom you're targeting is important. It also sits at the intersection of the *pain* they have and your *solution* (Figure 2.1).

FIGURE 2.1 Where is your sweet spot of Target, Pain & Solution?

Now, if you're in the same situation, do you blame the prospects for not getting it—or do you admit you have work to do?

BIG COMPANIES SUFFER, TOO

A top-five global software company hired us to help the salespeople of a particular division improve their prospecting. These salespeople, with limited time, were spending too much time researching rather than campaigning. When they did call or email people, they rarely got responses. The salespeople were as frustrated as the execs: "We *want* to prospect, but what we're doing is just a waste of time."

Ideally they should create a specialized sales team of junior prospectors to do most of the outbound prospecting, but that was impractical. They needed to do something *now*.

This team of salespeople sold to $1 billion-plus companies, like Bank of America, who often had multiple divisions. The company had a product list of at least 10 or 15 respected technology solutions they could pitch, to pretty much any kind of executive: IT, sales, marketing, finance, HR … basically anyone.

Their email, phone, and time management techniques weren't the main problem. They suffered from selling too many things to too many targets, and bouncing around instead of focusing.

They'd target the CEO of a bank on marketing, then a CTO for databases, HR for people management, and so on. It's the same Nail A Niche problem we've discussed, just in a different format.

The point is, Nailing a Niche (Figure 2.2) isn't just a problem for startups and small businesses. You don't solve it once. It becomes a *recurring* problem as you expand your lead generation programs, geographies, teams, and product portfolio. Your CMO, division, or individual salespeople may need to repeatedly nail down who is being targeted, who *needs* (not wants) you most, why should they buy, and for how much money And to make it *about helping them*, not just about you closing another deal.

How do you make it all about them, not all about you?

It's hard to resist going on and on and on ... to buyers about all the wonderful ways you can help them. But if you keep doing that rather than specializing, you're more likely to confuse buyers than excite them.

CASE STUDY: WHERE AARON WENT WRONG

My income increased 10x over four years, from $67,000 to $720,000, while I (usually) worked 20–30 hours a week. And, at the same time, my family grew from zero to 12 kids. I couldn't have done any of this without Nailing my Niche, specializing 100% in an opportunity where I had the easiest time making money—that is, the easiest time creating tangible results for others—and eliminating all my nice-to-haves.

After working at Salesforce.com for four years, most of which was spent creating and building the inside sales team that did all the outbound prospecting, I left Salesforce.com in late 2006. I'd been telling myself I didn't want to do sales consulting, but some projects came up through friends that sounded interesting, and I could use the income. I started early at Salesforce.com, when there were about 150 employees, but not early enough to make much money there, beyond a nice bonus that paid off my divorce debt.

These friends, my first clients, were my Early Adopters. They hired me because they knew me, not because I had a crystal-clear program and value proposition at the time—because I didn't.

I then spent a while at venture capital Alloy Ventures, researching business-to-business lead generation ideas. This led to a bunch of ideas and possibilities I could pursue. The result: choice paralysis. I had a lot

FIGURE 2.2 Nailing A Niche is the first step of turning struggle into success.

of exciting ideas, and didn't want to pick "just one." When I felt like I could do *anything*, what did I want to do? I had no idea.

I left to visit a friend in China for a couple of weeks, to get away and reflect. At some point during the trip, I still had no idea what I wanted to do next, but I realized:

- I didn't want to start a software company anymore.
- I didn't want to raise money to start a company.
- I wanted to be able to work on what I wanted, when I wanted, and with whom I wanted.
- I wanted to make as much money as I wanted, doing what I loved. I had no idea what that was or how I'd do it, but I'd figure it out along the way.
- What I loved to do most was partnering and working with people I trust. In other words, *what* I did, didn't feel as important as *with whom* I did it.

> ***What* I did, didn't feel as important as *with whom* I did it.**

So, for the next three years, 2007–2010, I tried different niches, bouncing around like so many companies I've seen—software or services—trying different combinations of who to go after and what to offer. Nothing seemed to "click" into the breakout success I'd hoped for and wanted. I wanted people to get excited about what I had to offer, line up to buy it, and then love it. I tried a number of products.

- *Selling "money":* I started BlackBox Revenues with a partner, Erythean Martin, to consult with companies building outbound prospecting teams. Responsys (sold to Oracle in 2014) was a first client, and the system helped them grow 10x in five years, from $20 million to $200 million.

  But I saw the sales consulting role (mistakenly, it turns out) as just a "day job" to pay the bills while I developed two ideas I was more passionate about. So, I didn't triple down here to figure my model out. Instead, I spent more attention on …
- *Selling "fulfillment":* Under UniqueGenius.com I tried personal coaching, to help people find a life purpose and make money from it, combining meaning and money.
- *Selling "freedom":* With my first book, *CEOFlow: Turn Your Employees into Mini-CEOs*, I tried organizational design and CEO- and team-coaching.

Need versus Nice

While at the time I felt more innate passion for the ideas behind Unique Genius and CEOFlow, both were much harder to market and sell than my sales consulting. In both cases, I worked on these ideas part time over a few years, slowly turning them from blogs into events, and then into a series of Unique Genius videos and the *CEOFlow* book.

Along the way, I remember having conversations with people who I thought clearly needed and would benefit from the ideas and the coaching—but they didn't buy. And I just got so frustrated in going through this time and time again, iterating new programs, messages, and proposals, bouncing along making around $5,000–$7,000 a month. Hey, it wasn't bad money, but it wasn't anything close to what I believed was possible, or what I saw other people doing online. "Compare and despair" was a close friend of mine.

I'd bought into the "If you build it, they'll come" fairy tale. I had misguided expectations of what it'd take to grow an expertise-based business. I vastly underestimated the focus, energy, and time it would take to get either brand off the ground.

Neither venture took off the way I'd expected or hoped, even though I believed they were killer brands and ideas. In a parallel universe, if I'd picked one and tripled down, going *all in*, it could have taken off faster. But it would still have been more of a slog than I wanted.

Looking back, my biggest mistake was that I hadn't Nailed a Niche. I wasn't ready to grow.

A distinct learning from this is that while people were *interested* in purpose and freedom, what they wanted to *buy* (at least from me) was *money*, which at the time was through outbound sales consulting. One was a *need*, the others were *nice*.

When people felt that they didn't have enough money (revenue), they couldn't focus on anything else. It was money first, second, and third—then freedom or purpose after that. It's hard to think about much else when you're struggling to pay the bills.

It's hard to think about much else when you're struggling to pay the bills.

Then Came a Forcing Function

When I remarried in 2011, everything changed. I went from being single with low expenses to having a wife and two children. And within a few weeks, we also had a new baby on the way. We needed a bigger apartment.

We could uproot our kids and ourselves and move from (relatively expensive) Santa Monica to a cheaper area. Or I could grow my business. I chose growth. And I kept choosing growth as we continued to add children to our family, year after year, and had to move to bigger and bigger houses.

But to grow, I had to pick the niche that would be the easiest to make money with. I couldn't afford the luxury of avoiding the truth that what I was most passionate about creating was, painfully, still a nice-to-have to others. Given more time, I could figure out the who, how, and where in order to make them need-to-haves … but I didn't have that time.

I made money easiest when I helped other companies grow sales with outbound prospecting, through PredictableRevenue.com. I finally published the *Predictable Revenue* book, and took the plunge—to specialize in helping companies build outbound prospecting programs.

Something I'd held back from doing 100%—not so much in time, but in commitment and focus. I put *every* other business or fun idea, all my nice-to-haves, on the backburner indefinitely.

> When people ask me how much work it took to write and publish *Predictable Revenue*, I don't have a simple answer. It took:
>
> - Six years of baby steps of blogging
> - Two days to put a full draft together
> - Three months to edit, design, and self-publish

I'd been denying or ignoring the skills that made me the most marketable, where I had a unique expertise to create results for customers, just because I wanted to do something new and sexier than the "sales" or "prospecting" work I'd already done for years. Having a family forced me to change my attitude from *sales is boring* to *results are sexy*.

> **I'd been denying or ignoring the skills that made me the most marketable.**

Once I specialized in serving business-to-business companies with at least $1 million in revenue, who needed to grow, who wanted predictable lead generation, but who weren't doing outbound prospecting yet (see? being specific!), business picked up. My rates went up by 10x, too, when I specialized. I mean, who do you think earns more, a general practice doctor or a neurosurgeon?

Ironically, besides going through it myself, it's been talking or working with so many product and services companies who *thought* they were ready to grow, but weren't, that I learned this lesson. I've seen how common this problem is, and why without nailing this down first, spending money on lead generation and sales is going to feel like pushing a string.

PS: If you're a parent juggling career and family, I have details on my style of parent-entrepreneurship in the very last section of the book, called "Aaron, How The Hell Do You Juggle 12 Kids And Work?" *So, stay tuned.*

YOUR CURRENT STRENGTH CAN BE A FUTURE WEAKNESS

Services businesses (especially custom development shops, consultants, design agencies, or anyone who does a lot of custom work), and "utility player" employees who are great at everything, have a special struggle with nailing this. Being great at many things so far has been your strength, because you could take on any challenge and deliver results.

But your strength has now become your weakness.

Because the *Fear of Missing Out* holds you back from picking *One Thing* to specialize in and be the best at. "What do I pick? I can be world class at x, y, z ... " (And that One Thing has to be specific—not "We're the best in the world at custom software development." Vague.)

"But if I'm going to be the best in the world at training public speakers, then I'm going to miss out on being the world-class artist I want to be. Or we'll miss out on the financial services market. Or this mobile app we could do, or . . . ."

Here's why picking One Thing is better than trying to pick the Best Thing: *you can't predict* where your big opportunity or $100 million exit will come from. So pick One Thing and figure out how to win at that. Where can you be a big fish in a small pond? Get momentum winning in that small pond, then expand into the next bigger pond, and so on. If you learn how to win at One Thing, you'll know how to win at the *Next* Thing.

If your One Thing struggles, then learn and pivot, until you learn how/where to win. Let go of knowing what the answer is ahead of time—just get to the next step. And re-evaluate. And repeat. Guaranteed, though—if you're spreading yourself across multiple things, you're just diluting yourself.

Yeah, easy to say. Hard to do. That's why you need to be able to ignore any expectations of quick success. Just keep taking baby steps to keep moving.

The problem is especially hard if you've been in services, because it requires a total mindset change. To go for growth, you need to switch your whole sales attitude 180 degrees:

From: "*What's your problem? We can solve it. Whatever your problems are, we have many capabilities. There's something we can do for you if we look hard enough.*" You end up solving different problems in different ways, making it virtually impossible to scale.

To: *"Here's the problem we are the best at solving ... with our repeatable solution we have delivered 100 times. Do you have it? No, you don't have it? Do you know anyone else who might be interested?"*

We're not saying you don't find out about the specific situation and pains of a customer, but there's a difference between understanding exactly how your solution can help them, and creating a solution from scratch that will help them. It's the difference between configuration and customization.

Be Specific

The more targeted you are, the easier for people to "click" with what you do, and immediately tell if (a) you're relevant or (b) someone they know is relevant.

Hi, I'm Aaron. I'm in financial services.

Hi, I'm Aaron. I'm a CPA, for Los Angeles-based media companies with at least $10 million in revenue.

Special Orange Unicorn Pens

Let's talk pens. Orange ones. Imagine you manufacture pens of all colors, customized to what a customer wants. And you decide to specialize on a growth opportunity. "We're going to stop selling all colors of pens, including 'design your own color,' because the market's full of pen makers. We're picking one thing to be the best at, to be known for. We are only gonna sell orange pens, special ones that draw unicorns. And we're only selling them to those companies who need orange unicorns drawn on their sales proposals in order to close big deals. Because we've seen that's where the growth is going to be, and we can be the best in taking advantage of it."

It's easy to feel the loss of all those customers you can't sell to anymore. It's hard, until you see it working, to feel the success of focusing on selling only special orange unicorn pens.

Be willing to lose the people who want all colors of pens, because ultimately you'll sell more pens, at higher prices, to the right people—the ones who value those special orange ones.

CHAPTER 3

How to Nail It

Maybe you already know your best target. Perhaps your head's still exploding with options. Let's narrow it down with a step-by-step approach to prioritize your best bet(s), and how to get more from them.

WHERE CAN YOU BE A BIG FISH IN A SMALL POND?

It's better to pick a focused market that's "too small," but where you can find and win deals, than it is to stick to defining your target market so broadly that you get lost in it. Why is this?

- It's easier to make the pond smaller than make the fish bigger: it's easier to retarget, refocus, and reframe yourself than to change your products and offerings.
- To grow past word-of-mouth marketing, you have to stand out. It's easier to stand out and win deals in a smaller pond.
- When you share too many things that you excel at (too many ponds), it's more likely to confuse prospects than impress them.

Five Aspects of Your Best Niche

Let's look at what helps determine how ripe a niche is for you.

1. *Popular Pain:* So what if you do custom application development, analytics, mobile-enablement, or sales training? Those aren't pains; they are solutions. What main *pain* do you solve? Missed product launch deadlines, inaccurate forecasts, high customer attrition, lead generation struggles, low conversion rates from demo to proposal? Those are *pains*.

And the pain has to be common enough: You want to specialize in a specific pain you solve, but not get so narrow that you can't find anyone that has it. Within the niche you're targeting, what pain can you solve that's common enough to allow you a fair shot of finding customers? You know that a pain is common when you see that people are willing to pay money to solve it, repeatedly.

Specialize in a specific pain you solve, but don't get so narrow that you can't find anyone that has it.

2. *Tangible Results:* Where can you show concrete or detailed results? How can you answer the question "What do I get?" For example, if the answer is "Peace of mind or a better night's sleep," how do you make that tangible? "Grow leads 217%" or "Shorten month-end closing to 12 hours" are much more concrete offers. If you struggle with hard numbers, you can use visual examples or detailed customer stories and testimonials.
3. *Believable Solution:* It's easy to make claims of "more revenue, lower costs, blah blah." Buyers hear this every day. Why should they *believe* you and your claims? There are two sides to this: (a) They have to believe you can deliver, and (b) they have to believe it'll work for them, including their own ability and capacity to do it. Detailed case studies of similar companies are powerful—they make your solution highly credible. Honesty, expertise, confidence, simplicity, authenticity, from both the person and business they work for, all help.
4. *Identifiable Targets:* If you can't build a list of prospects or channel partners or marketing options to get access to them, you can't very well go after them! How would you build a list of "technology CEOs suffering from severe depressive episodes at least once per quarter" or "companies that need to change the software they're running their website on"?
5. *Unique Genius:* To find or be found, to close deals, to avoid commoditization—you must be *different* or unique. Every business (and individual) has unique strengths, weakness, and superpowers—whether or not they realize it. A talent for making money, focusing, creative writing, art, service, engineering, relationships, innovation, a passionate community, celebrity employees, an interesting personal story or history …

   Sometimes it's clear, like the customer service and culture of Zappos. Sometimes it's hard to put your finger on, or it needs developing. But it's always there. What makes you stand out? What are your special advantages? If you can come up with nothing else, you have the personal stories of the founders and employees. Personal stories—like "I struggled, I wanted to help others avoid the same struggle so I did X, Y, Z"—can in themselves be very compelling.

To find or be found, to close deals, to avoid commoditization—you must be *different* or unique.

WORK THROUGH THE NICHE MATRIX

The next steps are going to help you list out, prioritize, dig into, select, and act on a primary and secondary niche. Do this with your team, and give yourself half a day to thrash it out. Don't worry: thrashing's part of the process. You can also download a workbook at FromImpossible.com/niche.

Step 1: Make a List

List your top 5 to 10 customers and/or types/categories of projects by size of deal or impressiveness of results. The best predictor of future success, or at least the best place to begin, is with the history of where you've been most successful.

1. What was the pain or problem they wanted to solve?
2. Why did they decide to solve it—what triggered them to decide to buy?
3. Specific results they desired?
4. What was the solution they wanted?
5. Deal size or financial results (how much money did you make, or not make?)
6. On a scale of 1 to 10, how much do you want more projects like these ones?

Keep listing other possible market opportunities in order to identify (a) where the easiest sales/most demand comes from, (b) where the most revenue is coming from, and (c) where the most passion or excitement is:

- Interesting/weird/compelling/exciting outlier customers that you'd want more of

- Other new exciting opportunities.
- What market or type of project has been the most successful?
- What are you the best at?
- What's been the easiest way you have been able to make the most money so far?
- If people hired you for just one thing, what is it or would it be?
- Review other customer patterns:
  - What *should* you win at but haven't because you haven't invested in it?
  - Categorize your biggest projects, types of project, problems solved, benefits/results.
  - What's your best proof case from the past?
  - Which projects created the biggest financial benefits for customers?
  - Where is there detailed proof that you're allowed to publish?
- Best competitive position? Where are your best chances for winning?
- Where is the best future opportunity: What's in demand? Is there a rising tide?
- Where/with what kind of project can you get measurable results?
- Where do you have passion? (Or will *success* be your passion?)

Make a "Stop Doing" list

- Which projects failed—and why?
- Which markets, customers, or projects do you need to stop pursuing?
- What kinds of customers are impossible or not worth helping?

Step 2: The Matrix

Once you get a broad list together, rate or rank them across five aspects (Popular Pain, Tangible Results, Believable Solution, Identifiable Targets, Unique Genius). Don't overanalyze things (yet); we want you to narrow down to a few best options (two to five) to dig into next. Sometimes it's easy. Sometimes this is very frustrating, and you go round and round in circles. They don't have to be perfect at this point. You're not getting married.

Next we're going to break them down into a more detailed matrix. It will help you find blind spots—especially with the "Pain-Solution-Result" breakdown we'll get to.

Niche/Use Case	Popular Pain	Power Person	Specific Pain	Solution	Results	Proof	Validate
Retail chains	Slow store-over-store annual growth	Retail Operations Exec	Sales data reporting unfriendly, out of data	Mobile, real-time reporting for buyers and sales teams	Improve \$/ft^2, speed turnover, reduce breakage	None yet	Interview two more buyers in this space

Download the Nail A Niche workbook at: FromImpossible.com/niche

Everyone adapts this approach to their own unique situation, but essentially this is the model.

Niche: Which opportunity or use case from the list are we talking about? "Cashflow Management," "Financial Services HR," "General Electric," or "Mobile Advertising"?

Popular Pain: A general label of the problem customers need solved. "Content Marketing Reporting," "Sales Team Attrition/Costs," "Inaccurate Executive Reports," "High Employee Costs," and so on. The detail comes two steps later.

Power Person: Who are the people you aim to help, and who have the most power over buying your stuff? What roles are the typical decision-maker and influencer/helper? To keep it simple, begin with just one or two roles.

Who are the people you aim to help, and who have the most power over buying your stuff?

Business or Personal Pains: What *specifically* does that one person deal with on a day-to-day basis? Not the company as a whole, but that one person. This is where the pain gets detailed. "Embarrassed in front of board because forecast was off," "Overwhelmed with time spent interviewing because there's no way to filter candidates early," "Goals are going up, leads are staying the same." Start with one to three specific pains for the main decision-maker, and do it again for one other influencer on their team.

Solution: What do they need and want in order to solve this? Customers want to buy solutions, not products or services. How can you position your solution to them? It's possible what they want to buy is different or "more than" what you currently offer. Usually, this is the easy part for you, since you know your solution so well.

Results: What are the identifiable outcomes that customers get? What can you measure, track, or gauge? "Everyone feels good" isn't specific enough. "Employee satisfaction increased from X to Y" is better. How can you demonstrate financial benefits? (Make money, save money, reduce risk of losing money.)

Proof: To charge based on value, or to market and sell to Mainstream Buyers, your lead generation and sales teams need proof. If you don't have proof, you can still sell to people, but this will require more relationship-building, or sticking only to Early Adopters. Examples of proof:

- Free trials
- Case studies with details
- Testimonials, especially in video
- Lists of logos or brand names
- Stories
- Demonstrations

It's always better to "show" rather than "tell" (stop talking and prove it).

It's always better to "show" rather than "tell" (stop talking and prove it).

People need practice differentiating pains from solutions and from results. Filling out these three columns can be an education in itself, because people often confuse pains with solutions. "Their pain is a lack of automated payroll" or "payroll is manual" aren't pains. Automated payroll is a solution. Manual payroll is just a description of how it works today.

Break it down: Why does that matter? So what? "Manual payroll creates errors every month, meaning employees get frustrated, reducing selling time (pain #1), and finance teams spend 10 hours a month fixing silly errors (pain #2)."

Usually the "Solutions" box fills up fast. That's the easy one.

- Do your people keep wanting to fill the "Specific Pains" box with solutions?
- Is your "Results" box frustratingly blank?

Spend the time to nail these down—pains/solutions/results—even if it takes 10x longer than you think it should. Because it can help open up a whole new way of thinking for your team, so they can catch themselves when they skip over digging into customer pains, leap too fast into pitching solutions, or are unsure of the results they can promise.

Step 3: Choose

Now pick a primary opportunity to pursue. If you have more than one great one, you can pick a secondary opportunity to test and compare against the first.

If you have more than two that you're excited about, remember that by digging deep into a first-niche opportunity, you'll learn so much more—and you can always go back to evaluate and test other niche ideas later. You're not going to miss out on anything by putting the others on hold.

Step 4: Validate

- *If you're ready to jump in:* By this point, you may be ready to jump into going after that first choice, such as with a lead generation campaign. Even so, get started by finding a couple of prospects in that niche(s) to interview, to fill out and update your niche with details—especially the Pains and Results. Find people who either don't know you too well, or a customer who's not afraid to give you brutally honest answers. And then move on to Step 5.
- *If you're not ready to go after it:* Sometimes you realize that although your top niche seems like a great possibility, something important is missing. It may require a different product, research into regulations, licensing, research, or another kind of validation. Before going on here, skip ahead to "Jason's 20-Interview Rule" on page 37.

Step 5: Campaign to Learn Now and Grow Later

If you feel like you are ready to start targeting that niche, you should be clear enough by this point to start a lead generation program around it. Spending effort on a lead generation campaign of some kind (any kind) forces you to jump in and keep iterating who you're going after, why they should care, and what they're interested in.

It's not the leads here that are important—yet. It's the learning. The faster you learn how to generate leads, the faster you can get ready to grow. Give yourself 90 days as the learning or beta-test period before counting your growth chickens. Essentially, what you're doing here is four things:

1. *Define a target list*, usually of prospects, partners, or marketing outlets.
2. *Decide on how you want to reach out*, that is, cold emailing, calling, referrals, social, mail, blogging, and so on—and what you'll say and ask for. Remember to write from the reader's point of view: What's in it for them?
3. *What's the minimum required preparation needed* before you can start campaigning? Don't over-plan here on creating the ultimate marketing or outbound plan, building a ton of content and then … nothing works. For example, if you're prospecting, ideally you have a case study or short introductory video you can use. But if you don't—don't let that stop you from getting started. It's more efficient to learn and create any other tools or content along the way.
4. *Finally: Stop procrastinating and just send* the first campaign. Even if it's just one phone call, letter, tweet, or email. Send more. Measure results. Adjust. Try again. Act, learn, and adjust. Fire, ready, aim. The more tests you run, the faster you learn. Speed of learning creates speed to growth.

Speed of learning creates speed to growth.

The learnings are more important than the results in this step. If you get 10 sales right away but you don't know why, you can't repeat them. If you get two sales, but know how to replicate them, you're golden and can ramp things up.

Once you get something working, you'll be able to step back and have a better sense of when and how fast you can grow next, in what niche, and with what kind of lead generation. Or, you'll realize you need to revisit your matrix again (back to Step 3).

CASE STUDY: HOW AVANOO NAILED IT

Avanoo is a company hitting the hypergrowth track early, going from a few thousand in revenue to $5 million in a bit more than its first full year of selling. Avanoo delivers video-based training to improve employee performance. Corporate training: talk about a busy, noisy market!

Daniel Jacobs and Prosper Nwankpa founded Avanoo in September, 2013. Daniel distinctly remembers Prosper saying as they began,

"The key to this first phase is to never be afraid of blowing something up. It'll get us quicker to where we want to be."

In the first seven to eight months, they came up with, and then threw away, four different product approaches. By March 2014, they had a core product. It was a service offering 30-day educational programs, with one three-minute video a day.

This one was a winner, yet it still took the company a few more swings and misses before it nailed its own sales niche and actually made money.

Niche Try #1: Consumers

They began with four programs: Happiness, Focus, Life Purpose, and Weight Loss, all created by Daniel. They ran a "Name your own price" deal, and by getting some top posts on Reddit, they managed to sell 2,000 programs in the first two months for $10,000 (average of $5 per course).

What They Learned in Launching

- *The product worked.* People used and consumed the courses, and they were reporting improvements. Great. It's a huge accomplishment. But …
- *A great product wasn't enough.* Even though people used and loved it … they didn't share it. Avanoo was going to have to find other ways to grow besides creating great product. And going on Reddit again and again wouldn't work—they'd mostly tapped out that audience. As Daniel put it, "You can only do so many #1 posts before the Reddit people want to throw pitchforks at you."

You can only do so many #1 posts before the Reddit people want to throw pitchforks at you.

- *They needed to expand their content.* Daniel wasn't a recognized expert in these areas. They decided they needed more experts and variety in the topics beyond the first four courses.

The Hunt for Sustainable Lead Generation

They tried all kinds of lead generation programs to find one that would sustain growth. "By July 2014, besides Reddit we'd also tested Google/PPC ads, Facebook ads, SEO, Twitter, and Pinterest techniques—but none of that was doing anything for us."

They also contacted various experts in fields that were interesting to them personally, like leadership, stepping outside your comfort zone, and happiness.

In a working session, one expert said, "This would be perfect as a follow-up program to my corporate speaking engagements." This was an "a-ha!" moment: could this be a way to reach customers?

From July to September 2014, Avanoo worked hard to make this happen—to help speakers create courses, and to see if speakers could sell them to their clients.

They landed their first sale that way, to Kaiser Permanente, for $1,300.

Then, for the next four months, Daniel worked tirelessly with speakers to help them sell their programs. Unfortunately, he saw that "they could sell, but it was ad hoc and unrepeatable. We couldn't depend on it for growth. We realized that we have to own this process, of marketing and selling directly to companies. If we own the process, we can scale it. If they own it, we'll never scale."

By now it was December 2014. It had been 2.5 years since Daniel had the initial idea, and almost 18 months since they legally founded the company. They have just $2,000 in monthly revenue.

Daniel said he had "no idea what he was doing" but he started learning about direct sales—the difference between a problem and a solution, and between benefits and pains. He learned how to sell to businesses, especially when the sale involves multiple people instead of a single buyer. How to put together a sales team of outbound prospectors to drive new leads, and how to create Customer Success after the initial sale.

They initially thought their niche was consumer sales. When that didn't work, they moved on to the next niche . . . .

Niche Try #2: Growing Businesses with 50–300 Employees

"When selling to consumers didn't work as we wished, we thought the next best target to go after would be businesses with 50–300 people that were growing quickly. We figured they wouldn't have put in much training yet, but now that they were growing, they should have the resources and the desire to do it easily."

They started reaching out to their networks and through outbound prospecting to get appointments, but …

"It turned out we were massively wrong. It turns out that if they've had no experience with training, with nothing to compare it to, it was incredibly hard for them to decide to do anything. There wasn't a concrete pain that they felt yet."

If prospects had no experience with training, with nothing to compare it to, it was hard for them to decide to do anything.

Niche Try #3: Fortune 2000

After that first corporate sale of $1,300, just months later they hit a run rate of $1 million, mostly comprising four- and five-figure deals. They plan on continuing to move upmarket to be able to close six- and seven-figure deals. So how did they get there?

They retargeted their outbound prospecting and network outreach, pointing their efforts towards bigger companies. And they were able to get appointments. In these companies, it turns out being able to offer a *guarantee* of employee improvement proved to be invaluable in building trust with buyers.

"Surprisingly," Daniel says, "the people who jumped on us were big companies like NBC, KMPG, and Cisco. No one was more surprised than us to find out that the first niche we nailed was selling to senior Human Resources executives in the Fortune 2000".

"In fact, the pain we addressed wasn't one I ever would have understood until we were solving it: VPs of HR at those companies spend millions on training, and they had inadequate measurement tools to see the benefits. They didn't get much beyond participation, completion data, and employee reviews. As employees move through our programs, we measure data that HR departments don't have access to—data that goes well beyond participation and completion numbers, and measures performance in quantifiable ways."

Here is an example of a conversation they would have to get past what a prospect was merely interested in, to what they needed:

Prospect	"We want leadership programming."
Avanoo	"Sounds wonderful. Why?"
Prospect	"Because we want better leaders."
Avanoo	"That makes sense. Why do you want better leaders?"
	[Fast forward, more "whys," to …]

Prospect	"Okay, here's the deal. We just did a merger, and both cultures are wonderful. But when they merged we lost a lot of people. We think leadership programming might help stop the bleeding."
Avanoo	"Okay, great. We can measure employee course consumption related to employee retention changes."

Sold.

"Creating repeatable, sustainable way to find new customers sometimes felt like we were moving a mountain. It's grueling. But there isn't anything I'd rather be doing. For as that mountain gets moved, we're paving a road that can get us lifelong traffic."

JASON'S 20-INTERVIEW RULE

I know everything can't go according to plan in any startup. It certainly didn't for me. But if it's early days, let me make one suggestion: If you are planning to sell to an enterprise/businesses of any meaningful size: *Don't forget the 20-Interview Rule*.

The 20-Interview Rule is simple: Before you write a line of code, finalize your niche, or take some other kind of leap, interview 20 *real* potential customers.

Not your friends. Not people you know. They have to be real potential buyers; that is, if you hope to sell to sales managers, you can't interview a rep. You have to interview a VP or a Director of Sales or Sales Operations. And you have to do 20 of them. I know it's hard to get to 20, but it's the right number:

- You need the *first five interviews* just to truly understand the white space and the current opportunity. Yes, you probably think you already understand it. But you are the vendor, not the purchaser. You need to understand your prospective app from the purchaser's perspective, for real.
- You need the *next five interviews* to confirm your pattern recognition. You *learn* from the first five; you *confirm* in the next five.
- You need *interviews 11–20* to nail your pitch and hone your thesis. Once you truly understand the white space from a buyer's perspective, and you've figured out the nuances and challenges, it's time to nail your pitch. And by doing this, you'll also hone your thesis and

> strategy. That's what interviews 11–20 are for: To filter out all the "nice-to-haves'" from the "must-haves" in your pitch. To dig in on what is really 10× better, not just two times or five times better.

And let me tell you, at least from my experience, don't expect all 20 interviews to be positive. Many of my 20 interviews, in both my startups, were very critical. Or worse—lukewarm. Lukewarm is worse because it says, "Yeah, it's sort of interesting, but no way I'd buy" and, implicitly, "Your idea is a huge waste of time." I'd rather get the negative feedback.

I get the Steve Jobs thing. You just have to build it. You do. But when you're solving business problems, not consumer problems, research matters. They don't know how to solve it, or what you should build for them. But they *do* know how to express their problem. Acutely and thoughtfully. So even if the specific feedback on your product and idea is off point, the learnings on the *true* pain point you're solving will be perfectly *on* point.

By way of example, here are two seemingly similar SaaS startups. Both are at about $1 million in revenue. Both have happy, enthusiastic customers. Both have really great products and are organically growing. Both have great founder CEOs. But even though both are now at $1 million revenue, one is just so much better positioned for success getting quickly to $5 million and $10 million annual run rates. And, at least in this case, in this case study, the difference is clear: the better-positioned $1 million SaaS startup *knew its customers from Day One*. The other one at $1 million, figured it out on the fly—and, really, is still figuring it out.

They both got to the same place, at the same time, more or less, so what's the difference? The difference is architecture. Not just software, but the whole company. The startup that didn't know who its core customer would be is behind on team, behind on market presence, behind on how to market and sell to its core customers, and behind on visibility at the prospect level. And the startup that *did* know its target customer has a more appropriate team for those customers' needs, and for accelerating visibility at the prospect/market level.

So if you haven't started yet, as fun as it is to just build the wireframes and get a-codin' without having to talk to people, do the 20 interviews. For real. Don't skimp here. And listen. And if nothing else, force yourself to make key changes to your assumptions based on those learnings. It will pay off.

CHAPTER 4
Your Pitch

We've identified your best target, and perhaps a backup. And you know their pains. So when you meet a prospective customer at a conference, or email one, what do you say or write? How do you tune your elevator pitch and messaging?

IF YOU WERE A RADIO STATION, WOULD ANYONE TUNE IN?

Imagine you're clicking through radio stations. You have jazz or classical, classic rock or easy listening, and then you hit one called KALL—"we play jazz, hip hop, rock, classics, oldies, dance, holiday music, and anything else you want—you tell us what to play!" It'd be a confusing mishmash. Don't be a mishmash!

Get smaller. Get to that one thing people want from you, at which you're the best. Remove the clutter to make it easier for the right customers to see why they need you. We know, this is easier said than done. If it were easy, everyone would do it.

Going Narrower Simplifies Everything

Do you have too many good opportunities in front of you, in your radio station? You have to narrow it down to make it easy for people to tune into your frequency. And when you do, it vastly simplifies many of your challenges, like whom you're going to go after and what you'll say to them to see if they're interested.

As the world gets busier and people's mental inboxes get more crowded, what you need to do to stand out from the crowd and connect with your customers will also change.

The simplest way to do this is to *go narrower*, that is, to further specialize and simplify. Remember, you can try this as a whole company, for a product, for a project, or for a marketing campaign, or even as an individual working to advance your career.

Let's say you're a part-time CFO. Is it easier to write an elevator pitch as "a part-time CFO" or as "a part-time CFO who lives in Los Angeles and works with media companies with $1–$10 million in revenue"?

Or you *can* serve healthcare, financial services, and technology companies, both small and large. Where's the most money coming from? Writing emails or blog posts that speak to all those businesses would be a lot harder than zeroing in only on large financial services companies.

Maybe you refocus the whole business that way. Maybe you refocus individual case studies, blog posts, web pages, or outbound campaigns that way. But narrow in. How?

It can be by type of target customers. Or where you work. What you offer. What you're fixing. The results you create. Anything that makes it simpler for a prospect to tune in and see why they need you. A few examples are:

- Instead of "North America," which states or metropolitan areas are you strongest in? "San Francisco," "Los Angeles," "Chicago and New York."
- Instead of "pipeline management," what standout function do you have? "Proposal conversion," "demo mastery," "15-minute executive pipeline reviews."
- Instead of "author coach," how about "business author coach" or "e-book author marketing coach."
- Instead of "employee learning," how about "salesperson onboarding."
- Instead of "crowdsourcing," how about "support ticket translation."

Hey, broad categories can work, too. We're just saying that if they aren't working, try thinking narrower, then test it to see if it clicks with customers, because a sexy, fancy, or grandiose message that doesn't click with people is useless.

A sexy, fancy, or grandiose message that doesn't click with people is useless.

Specificity—in target, desires, or message—doesn't limit you; it makes it easier for customers to "get it."

Why It's Harder for Services and Superstars

American Data Company was a Salesforce.com implementation and development partner that wanted to grow. But as a services company, they'd grown up doing anything for anyone. In starting an outbound prospecting program, initially nothing worked in looking for companies that needed help in improving their marketing, sales, or services results.

It turned out they'd created a mobile application for Westfield Shopping Centers used by their leasing agents. When they focused on running outbound campaigns just to shopping mall management companies, they started getting appointments right away.

Going narrower helped them figure out how to make it easier for prospects to tune into why they mattered.

ELEVATOR PITCHES ARE ALWAYS FRUSTRATING

With an elevator pitch, you're not trying to *sell* people on buying something or get them incredibly excited and jump up and down. You're only giving them a quick sense of whether they want to find out more or not.

Most people deliver an elevator pitch that's too long and too much about them: *We're the leading scalable networked social media platform innovator … blah blah blah.*

A tight elevator pitch can tell someone quickly whether they are a prospect or not. You're not trying to engage everyone, just the people to whom you're relevant. Here are a few tips.

- Avoid jargon.
- Keep it simple.
- Simple is better than accurate.
- It's always frustrating: You'll never be 100% satisfied, so stick to "good enough."

No doubt you can find a million formats and templates for elevator pitches on the Internet. Here's one sample format that's worked for us: Start by saying, "You know how some people have [problem]? Well, we [solution and/or benefit]. For example, [one sentence case study]."

> *You know how some retail chains struggle getting mobile users to redeem coupons? We have a way to increase redemption rates*

by 50%. For example, Bob's Tacos saw redemptions double in 30 days.

You know how some retail chains turn over employees as fast as they can hire them? We can tell you the top five fixable reasons your employee attrition is too high. For example, Walsmartz halved their retail store staff attrition, so they're turning over the whole staff only every two years, instead of every year.

Notice it's not about the steps you take to help them—it's about the results they want and desire. If it's interesting, they will naturally ask you more questions about how you do it.

One Moore Format

Geoff Moore (author of *Crossing the Chasm*) has another template you can also try:

For [target customers]
Who are dissatisfied with [the current offerings in the market],
My idea/product is a [new idea or product category]
That provides [key problem/solution features].
Unlike [the competing product],
My idea/product is [describe key feature(s)].

You can find more—many more—of other formats and templates online, easily, if nothing yet feels right.

Pro Tip: Add a Pause When Speaking

You know how on your mobile phone when you pull up a Maps app, sometimes you need to hit a button to have it recenter on your position, so it can be ready to map directions? Anything you type in beforehand you'll just have to redo.

People's minds work the same way. When most people introduce themselves, they dump too much information, too fast, on the listener.

Their minds need to orient first, before you can throw more "directions" at them.

Do this by adding a simple pause whenever you're speaking in person, on the phone, or in video. Pause after your first sentence, or after about 10 words. Try it out on some strangers—not coworkers—to refine your use of the pause. Give them a second to orient mentally, then keep going.

It gives their minds a chance to get ready to process what you say next, like hitting the "center" button on that Maps phone app. If you don't pause, their minds won't be ready to receive more, and much of your pitch will go in one ear and out the other.

THEY DON'T CARE ABOUT "YOU": THREE SIMPLE QUESTIONS

When they're first meeting you, they don't care about what you do or what stuff you sell—whether you're SaaS, services, an auction site, mobile, whatever. They only care about what you do *for them*.

If you get stuck pitching solutions rather than results, try these three questions to hone in on what people care about. You can ask them about each sentence, slide, or point of whatever you're creating. They automatically help you reframe your thinking in terms of results for customers:

- How do you help customers?
- What's so great about that?
- So what?

I'm an accountant in Los Angeles.

"How do you help customers?"

I help businesses stay compliant.

"What's so great about that?" Or "So what?"

A business that's not compliant in ___ can face fines of $150,000. I help businesses stay in compliance to have zero risk of big fines.

Whether you have a fancy pitch ready or not, the next time someone at a party asks you what you do, pretend instead that they asked, "How do you help people?"

People Like to Buy "Things": Details Make the Difference

You're figuring out how to describe your stuff in ways that *click* quickly with customers. You see yourself as a need-to-have, but others don't. Maybe you're being too vague.

For example, choose which of these resonates more:

- "Transportation" or "a BMW 3-series sedan"
- "Sales process consulting" or "an eight-step sales process"
- "Freedom" or "self-managing teams" or "being able to take a two-week vacation, unplugged, and enjoy it"
- "Premium support" or "24/7 access to our support center, via email, phone, or chat."

People like to buy "things." Their minds are asking, "What do I get for my investment?"

Whether it's a $10 or a $10,000 purchase, they'll want to know exactly what they get. Spell it out as much as you can as "things," with concrete details.

"Should" Is an Evil Word

Focus on those customers with a burning need you can solve—not on the ones that think you're "cool" or who *should* or *could* need you.

It might be easier to refocus your niche instead of rebuilding your product/service. Rather than thinking, "What can we do to make our product compelling?" try, "What kind of person/company most needs what we have to offer?"

What kind of person/company most needs what you have to offer?

If you decide to change direction in a significant way, the next step isn't to build a whole new website and redo all your marketing and sales collateral. The next step is go back to the 20-Interview Rule. Go talk to real prospects (not friends or partners) to identify which of your assumptions are wrong.

Most people are afraid to get brutally honest feedback about their offering. Don't hide from the truth that you may not be where you thought you were, and it may take a lot more work and time than you expected or wanted to get it dialed in for growth.

Create Predictable Pipeline

The Painful Truth: Overnight success is a fairy tale.

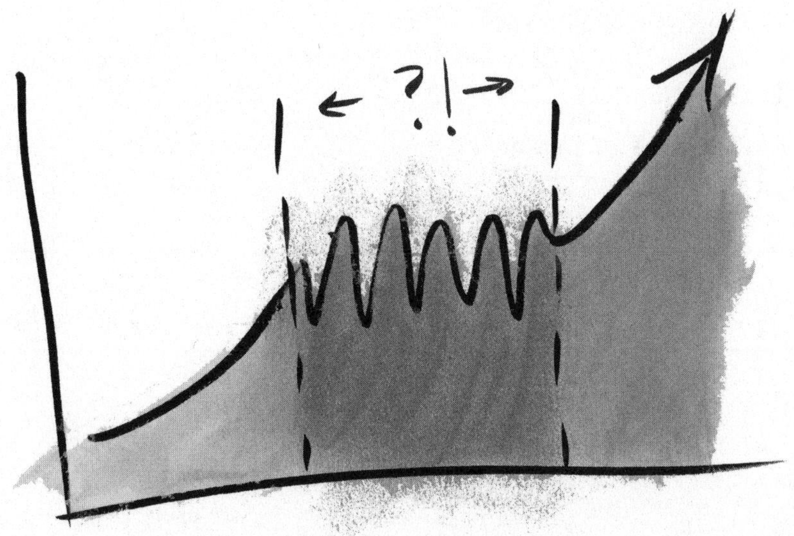

INTRODUCTION: LEAD GENERATION ABSOLVES MANY SINS

You can have the best product, investors, or sales process, but without predictable ways to fill your revenue or sales pipeline, you're going to struggle. Predictable lead generation is *the* lever to creating hypergrowth. And it's more than throwing marketing campaigns online or on billboards, cold calling, or pumping out free stuff to give away.

Many aspiring and first-time founders have the idea that "if we just create an amazing thing [app, video, ebook, blog post …], it'll catch fire online and we'll be inundated with people excited to follow us or buy from us." This works just often enough to create the fairy tale for everyone else. Just like the lottery.

Without predictable ways to fill your pipeline, you're going to struggle.

Assuming you're not a VC, how many people do you *personally* know that had a true overnight or viral success—and could keep it going? The Reality Distortion Field we live in now—being inundated in social media about quick-results stories—makes it seem more common than it is, because it's just the kind of story that makes the rounds. The usual story of success, of working for years slowly building up an audience or business, baby step by baby step, is much more boring. "Exciting" plays better than "sustainable."

So go for being "discovered," but don't bet you or your company on the fairy tale. Because it's 99% more likely that, whatever you launch, people won't even know or care. And you'll have to work your ass off to first get them to come, and then again to figure out how to help the right people buy in any meaningful amount.

Yes, you do need a great product or service and some happy customers, but that's not enough. Can you drive pipeline and leads predictably—whether from new prospects or current customers/users?

> We used these techniques to grow more than 500% in one year, from a $360,000 to $2 million run-rate."
>
> —*Jeb Ory, CEO Phone2Action*

Are you experiencing any of these?

- Unpredictable lead generation and sales
- Salespeople complaining about the amount or quality of leads they get

- A revenue rollercoaster of up and down growth results (either as a company, team, or individual)
- You're beating your lead volume goals, but are missing your revenue goals
- More than 30% of your salespeople are missing quota
- Unexpectedly low close rates
- Unmotivated salespeople

Rather than chasing piecemeal solutions—like trying to improve your demo process, hiring approach, or salesforce.com setup (though all are important)—more often than not, sustainable, predictable lead generation solves a lot of sales problems.

When you struggle generating enough decent leads for your salespeople, everything else needs to be perfect:

- You need a perfect product.
- You need perfect salespeople.
- You need a perfect sales process.

Because *you have no buffer to get anything wrong*. But when you have a predictable lead generation machine, you can get pretty much everything else wrong, and still do really well.

The best way to triple new sales isn't by tripling your salespeople (the traditional method for sales-driven companies) but by growing your qualified leads. You can have a Ferrari, but it doesn't move an inch without gas. Lead generation is your gasoline for growth.

Yes, you do need a great product or service and (some) happy customers, but that's not enough. That won't sustain growth if you can't proactively drive new leads that can turn into customers.

Even if your funny YouTube video or app download goes viral, how are you going to keep the party going after that initial burst of success plateaus? If you can't, you'll be a one-hit wonder.

What's Important: There Are Three Types of Leads

1. *"Seeds" are many-to-many leads, created from word-of-mouth, networks, and relationships*. Usually grown through creating happy customers who refer others, and who remain as customers for years. Salesforce.com, Google, Facebook, and Slack have all ignited initial hypergrowth through Seeds.
2. *"Nets" are one-to-many marketing campaigns,* including the now-popular approaches of content and inbound marketing.

3. *"Spears" are targeted outbound prospecting or business development campaigns*. Usually a human is involved, working through a targeted list, calling, emailing, or using any other technique that helps them make contact and get appointments.

Peanut Butter and Chocolate

Too many companies obsess over a single form of lead generation and ignore the others, often because of a philosophical belief. You'll see marketing snobs: "We don't want to interrupt prospects, we only want them to find us," and "Inbound good, Outbound bad." And product snobs: "If you have to market and sell your product, it's not good enough." And sales snobs: "Marketing's a waste of money. Only direct sales works."

You're missing out on bigger opportunities by thinking this way. Because, for example, like peanut butter and chocolate, inbound marketing and outbound prospecting are two great tastes that go great together – especially when served up with a fantastic product.

Too many companies obsess over a single form of lead generation and ignore the others.

To build a house you need multiple tools: a hammer, a saw, and a screwdriver. Likewise, Seeds, Nets, and Spears are complementary. Know why, how, and when to use each tool. They each have different funnels, conversion rates, expectations, sales cycles, average deal sizes, ideal target customers, and methods of increasing them. The important thing is to know which type(s) will work best for your business, in what mix or ratio, and what investment of time, money, or resources are required by each to grow.

What about Partners?

Partners aren't a fourth kind of lead. They are a different type of customer.

Whether they are channel partners, resellers, marketing partners, or anything else, you're acquiring and supporting them as customers—or should be.

Partners can be acquired through Seeds (word of mouth/Partner Success), Nets (mass marketing for partners), and Spears (prospecting into a targeted list of ideal partners).

CHAPTER 5

Seeds—Customer Success

Seeds are *many-to-many* campaigns; they're based on word of mouth and relationships. Some companies, like Dropbox, Box, and Slack, have been able to take off by creating products that spread like wildfire through word of mouth. But for most companies, seeds will mostly come through systematizing how you ensure your customers stay happy and get value from your service, and who then generate more referrals and lower attrition rates.

All the great work you do to help others succeed, while building relationships and networks, is "planting seeds"—whether they're with employees, partners, investors, or customers.

It's getting what you want by helping them get what *they* want. In so doing, you can succeed and feel good at the same time. The results look like this:

- Happy customers telling others about your service.
- Getting customers or partners through your own friends, networks, and relationships.
- Launching a product, post, or video that goes viral and creates results beyond views, such as increasing active users or sales.

Seeds in many ways are the best type of lead, but they aren't perfect.

- Pros: Highly profitable—word-of-mouth leads are the fastest to close and have the highest win rates.
- Cons: You have much less control over how fast they grow.

HOW TO GROW SEEDS PREDICTABLY

The best way to methodically grow your seeds is with a repeatable program or with systems that ensure your customers are successful.

FIGURE 5.1 Customer Success is a beautiful way to fertilize growth.

This field is now commonly called Customer Success Management or just Customer Success. It means systematically reducing customer churn, increasing upsells, increasing referrals, and helping capture more and better case studies and testimonials.

But this is really important: Customer Success is not about increasing customer satisfaction, but creating *revenue growth*.

> **Customer Success is not about increasing customer satisfaction, but creating *revenue growth*.**

What Customer Success Isn't

Customer Success is not free help. It isn't glorified customer support. And, like sales, it should be a revenue driver, not a cost center. As with sales, you should make money, or avoid losing it, by investing in this role. Most important, though, Customer Success is a *mindset,* starting at the CEO level—on targeting, creating product for, and servicing the kinds of customers that need your product.

FIGURE 5.2 Turn your revenue funnel into an hourglass by tracking how Customer Success affects revenue.

We believe that the future standard for all executive teams will include a head of Customer Success who's on the same level as the heads of Sales, Marketing, and Demand Generation.

Turn Your Sales & Marketing Funnel Into A Revenue Hourglass

Customer Success is a growth investment just like marketing and sales. Instead of a triangular funnel, think of it as an hourglass:

By investing in Customer Success, you should see:

- *Lower churn:* The easiest revenue comes from keeping the customers you have.
- *More revenue:* More referrals to new customers; more willingness to try and buy your other offerings (upselling & cross-selling).
- *Better marketing:* You can improve *everything* in lead generation and sales with detailed case studies (success stories) and testimonials from happy, successful customers.

Six Keys to Customer Success

Do you retain 95% of your customers month-to-month? That sounds like something to be proud of—until you do the math. That's 5% churn per month, or 60% *per year*. In other words, you have to replace 60% of your revenue every year just to break even.

What if you have monthly 98% retention/2% churn? That's still 25% a year, or a quarter of your revenue.

The best-run SaaS companies can see up to *–2% churn per month* (on a revenue basis). Yes, that's *negative* 2%, which means they make *more* money every month. How? Because the customers who stay with them buy and spend more over time than what the company loses from other customers leaving.

Target Churn Metrics in SaaS

1) Customer churn (or "logo churn") of 15% or less per year, or just over 1% per month, based on the number of customers who leave.
2) Revenue churn of 0% or less per year, based on the revenue that leaves and offset by revenue from the customers who buy more.
3) One Customer Success Manager per $2 million in revenue, to help you gauge the size of the team you'll need.

If you're a CEO, you need to take Customer Success as seriously as marketing, sales, or product development.

Rule 1: Customer Success Is Your Core Growth Driver

All great companies' customers come from one main source—word-of-mouth, whether the leads come via referrals directly, or whether new customers are closed using case studies, references, or testimonials. This is much more measurable in recurring revenue models, where we can track renewal rates, upsell amounts, and referrals. But the principle applies to *every* business, even if you must be creative in applying them.

Rule 2: Customer Success Is 5x More Important Than Sales

Yes, sales is your priority. But sales begins what will hopefully be a longer-term relationship. To function at all, Sales needs Customer Success resources—like high-retention, references, stories, and case studies.

Generally, founders do a good job of whatever it takes to get a big deal closed—but often they do a poor job of everything after that, because they're off to help with the next fire, drama, or big deal. CEOs and founders: don't focus on getting new customers so much that you ignore your current customers.

Rule 3: Start Early, Hire Early

In SaaS, Customer Success is a "single-digit hire"—one of the first 10 hires. Another SaaS rule of thumb is having one Customer Success manager per $2 million in revenue—hired *in advance of that revenue,* not after you have it. Silicon Valley companies with enough funding often now invest big at the beginning, with two to four people on the team right away.

Remember, a Customer Success person, like a salesperson or a marketing budget, is an investment that should make money (a lot); it's not a cost to be put off.

Rule 4: Visit Customers in Person

Unhappy customers don't (always) complain before they leave. In-person visits can make all the difference in identifying their problems and in changing their attitudes. Here's a 5+2 rule on this point for every cofounder, the CEO, plus every Customer Success Manager:

- Must meet onsite with five customers a month (that's 60 per year)
- Get two customer badges every year as a bonus (that is, you visit so often they give you your own ID badge)

A phone call is not a meeting. By visiting in person, regularly, your company will learn more about what's really working or not, earn more trust—and those customers will (almost) never churn. It's much harder to tell a friend you're leaving them than some faceless company. What if you have nothing to say? Just show them your roadmap and ask for feedback on it, and on issues they are having today. That alone will fill the meeting.

Rule 5: Customer Success Needs Financial Responsibility and Metrics

When your Customer Success function doesn't have financial goals, its value can get muddled. One bad assumption is that "a great product will automatically create happy customers," and therefore you won't need to hire people to actively work with your customers. However easy or incredible your product is, *you need humans talking to select categories of your customers*.

One bad assumption is that "a great product will automatically create happy customers."

The whole point of Customer Success is to increase *net negative churn*, so you need tools and processes to measure and improve the function, including how the people on your team perform. To justify investment (such as in headcount or tools), and to create the hunger that a Customer Success leader and team will need in order to deliver *measurable results*, Customer Success needs to own some financial results: usually at least on *retention rates* and perhaps even on *upsell revenue*. (For example, see the Gild case study in the next section.)

Rule 6: Evolve Customer Success Goals and Metrics as You Grow

For example, SaaS companies experience these phases (courtesy of Gainsight):

1. Traction ($0–$1 million): What do customers want, and what do they do with our product?
2. Adoption ($1–$5 million): Why and how should customers include our product in their daily business?
3. Retention ($5–$20 million): Why do customers need to keep on using our product after the honeymoon?
4. Expansion ($20–$100 million): Why should customers expand to more seats, more features?
5. Optimization ($100 million–plus): Automation and improvements driven by data.

Your phases may be different. The point: never assume Customer Success is "done," and won't need extra investment or executive attention next year.

Customer Success Indicators

Most Customer Success efforts still involve a lot of guesswork and manual reporting. But get your data act together—perhaps manually at first and later with the growing category of Customer Success software options—to get smart about gauging who's at risk of leaving and who should buy something else from you.

Some examples:

- *Contract data:* Customers stagnating, or renewal or key dates coming up
- *Support interactions:* Lots of low-priority tickets, or customers that have stopped calling
- *Billing/payment history:* Delayed invoice payments, perhaps due to frustration
- *Product and feature usage:* Which features are sticky and who's using them
- *Marketing engagement:* Unsubscribing to newsletters
- *Survey feedback:* Negative input from key person
- *Sponsor changes:* Exec contact leaves, new CMO
- *Data can't alert you to every problem:* You will always need humans talking to humans to uncover and resolve issues. But this data will help you to:
  - *Develop triggers for when to intervene proactively* before bad stuff happens. Obviously it's easier to save a customer before they send you a cancelling notice! First the team does this based upon intuition, and over time it can be based more and more on historical data and automatic triggers/alerts.
  - *Standardize interventions* so that each Customer Success Manager is using the same set of best interventions; with this consistency you can better measure the effectiveness of each intervention or type of problem/solution.

CASE STUDY: HOW GILD DROPPED MONTHLY CHURN FROM 4% TO 1%

Gild is helping companies recruit engineers more effectively by using data available on the web (including developers' actual code) to help measure their abilities. Brad Warga is their SVP Customer Success. He joined when there were just five people: CEO, CTO, CSO, head of Sales, and head of Marketing (now there's more than 50 people). Brad had been in HR/recruiting for 20 years, including recently as VP of Corporate Recruiting at Salesforce, where he helped organize and execute *thousands* of hires.

The team wasn't exactly sure what Brad would do at first, but they felt he could bring a lot of credibility—and he did. First, he helped bring in new customers.

After the First Year of Selling

During most of the first year of selling, Brad helped bring in new customers, until there were about 50. Churn was artificially low—as everyone was on annual contracts! When the contracts began coming up for renewal, churn jumped to 3 to 4% a month, or over 30% per year—*two to three times their target*. SaaS companies typically want (a) 15% or less churn per year on their total number of customers, and (b) 0% or negative revenue churn.

Gild starting measuring and analyzing churn, and realized many of their assumptions were wrong. For example, it turned out that how often people logged in wasn't a great way to tell who would stay or go. Gild actually needed to look at which parts of the product were being used, and how. How savvy were the users? What were their recruiting needs and methods? By digging into these root causes of churn, Brad and his colleagues at Gild were able to systematize Customer Success and drop churn to lower than 1% per month. (And this made Gild much smarter about targeting the right kinds of customers from the very beginning with their lead generation.)

The Three Methods That Dropped Gild's Churn

1. *"90-day adoption":* The Customer Success team's relationship with a customer starts when the customer purchases the product and starts using it. The team trains the new users how to use the product, what the best recruiting practices are, and resells/re-evangelizes Gild to the users to get them excited.

   Gild found out that if there's successful usage of the product in the first 90 days, *usage will be three × higher for the rest of the year* compared to a customer who didn't adopt as quickly.
2. *Quarterly business reviews:* These reviews are formal and help hold the customer accountable to what they signed up for. Ideally, they're onsite with the right customers.

3. *Using predictive tools:* Gild's main Customer Success application is Gainsight, along with Zendesk (to capture trouble tickets and feature requests), Salesforce.com, and Olark (chat).

> **Gild found out if there's successful usage of the product in the first 90 days, *usage will be three × higher for the rest of the year.***

Team Structure

The Gild Customer Success (CS) team has about 10 people across three roles (out of 50 employees!):

- *Inside CS reps* train, monitor usage, and run analytics; there's one rep per 70 users.
- *Outside CS reps* handle, and are measured on, renewals; there is one rep per 30 users in their relevant customer segment.
- *Executive CS reps* are responsible for upselling, and work mostly with large and fast-growing customer segments.

The teams have dashboards to help spot earlier both at-risk customers and customers who should buy more product, giving reps a reason to call a customer to talk.

C-Level Customer Success

A lot of companies treat Customer Success as an afterthought, or glorified customer support. Companies need to treat it (at least) as importantly as sales or marketing. At Gild, Customer Success owns:

- 90-day adoption
- Feeding usage data and customer feedback into the product roadmap
- Renewals
- Upsells

By owning these functions and being able to clearly articulate them, it's easy for Gild's board to recognize the value of Customer Success.

CASE STUDY: CUSTOMER SERVICE EXCELLENCE AT TOPCON

Frustrated customer support agents help create frustrated customers.

Customer support typically *reacts* to fix problems that have happened. On the other hand, Customer Success works best in *preventing* problems from being created in the first place. They are two sides of the same coin in supporting customers.

For most, companies, support is a hard job: intense work, often dealing with irate customers, with low pay, and (often) low respect. This is unfortunate—because customer support (like sales or sales prospecting) doesn't have to be a burnout, boiler-room job.

Why are the two teams that interact with customers the most (sales, support) so commonly mistreated or unappreciated? That needs to change, since frustrated agents (and salespeople) help create frustrated customers.

Topcon Positioning Systems (part of the $1 billion/4,000 employee global Topcon Corp.) is the world's largest developer and manufacturer of… yes, positioning systems. Topcon's customers are in industries like civil engineering, surveying, and agriculture—where mapping and positioning are vital. Topcon has contact centers around the world. Topcon's Angie Todd supervises the company's 18 U.S. agents in Columbus, Ohio, and in Olathe, Kansas.

Angie spent four years as a support agent and four years as a supervisor. The team handles 25,000 calls per year, which are all recorded and reported on. Angie says their goal is to provide predictably excellent service.

Angie's Expert Advice—Five Tips

1. *Get agents away from the phone:* Spending 40 hours a week on the phone and interacting directly with frustrated customers can be a recipe for agent burnout. Get agents away from their desks regularly for product cross-training and to visit customers at their locations. This will keep agents interested, refreshed, and engaged. It will help develop more experienced and confident agents with better attitudes

and a more skillful ability to help customers, increasing first-call resolution rates.

In the past few years, it's finally easy with Internet-based call center/telephony applications to route calls to any agent's phone (mobile phones, home phones, etc.). Now agents don't have to be chained to their desks, making the job friendlier and more flexible for them.

40 hours a week on the phone with frustrated customers can be a recipe for agent burnout.

2. *Use technology to help customers as well as yourself:* Don't forget that technology is not only about improving the experience for customers but also reducing your costs.

   The last time you called a bank, how many × did you have to enter your credit card or account number before you got to the right person? When a customer calls Topcon, their call center/telephony system, NewVoiceMedia, compares the phone number against data in Salesforce.com (used as their Global Case Management system) and can automatically route that person to the right agent. The customer doesn't have to type anything. For example, if they are marked in Salesforce as a gold-level client (with the best service level agreement), that caller can be automatically bumped to the front of the phone line, with no wait.
3. *Continuously listen to feedback:* In most organizations, the customer support group interacts with the customer the most. Unfortunately, some organizations overlook the support team and all their valuable knowledge. *The support team is the voice of the customer.*

Some organizations overlook the support team and all their valuable knowledge.

4. *Create a career path:* Your best employees won't want to stay in the same job their whole lives; they'll want to grow. At Topcon, agents know they will spend two to four years in Support, learning everything

about Topcon and its products, as a first step in their career path. If you hire right, you can use Support as a great training experience that develops experts to later transfer or promote throughout the rest of your company.

5. *Specialize agent roles:* Topcon has five "first-level" agents who have a basic understanding of all products, and 13 other agents who specialize in a given application or industry. With a variety of support specialists, customers can get better service—and this also creates different opportunities for reps to grow within support.

CHAPTER 6

Nets—Inbound Marketing

Nets are *one-to-many* campaigns to generate leads, with tactics like inbound marketing, in-person and online events, and online advertising. EchoSign, HubSpot, and Marketo have all driven $100 million–plus businesses mostly through Nets.

These leads create quantity over quality, because you're literally "casting a wide net." For example, if 50% of word-of-mouth leads (Seeds) might turn into customers, perhaps just 1-3% or less of marketing-generated leads will convert into customers. So, you usually want *a lot* more of them.

Out of a trillion ways to market, *inbound marketing* (or content marketing) is the most popular kid in school. It works, and it works for *every* company—unlike, say, outbound prospecting. The idea is creating marketing that customers love or learn from, inspiring them to want more from you, eventually buying your stuff.

Every business can benefit from creating content. Beyond creating leads, making your ideas and customer stories public speeds "time to trust." People get to know you faster, better, when they can learn about you, your business, and customers besides just face-to-face or over the phone.

A word on social media: which obviously keeps growing like gangbusters. It may or may not be related to marketing, depending on how you use it. We see social as another medium, like email or video, which can be used for anything—such as in Customer Success or outbound prospecting. If you're passionate about social media—go for it. If not, wait. Rand Fishkin, founder and former CEO of inbound marketing company Moz, says to CEOs, "It's more important to do social only when it makes sense. Don't just jump on the bandwagon because everyone else is doing it."

If you're passionate about social media—go for it. If you're doing it "because you're supposed to," don't be afraid to put it on the backburner.

FIGURE 6.1 What content is loved by your market AND creates measurable results?

Pros and Cons of Marketing-Generated Leads

- *Pros:* Often easy to generate high volumes of leads; some kinds of marketing programs are scalable; content published online can generate leads forever; highly measurable.
- *Cons:* The leads aren't "free"—there can be high fixed costs for generating leads (mainly time and salaries); low conversion rates, since most leads aren't a fit; usually works better at reliably generating leads at small/medium businesses than at enterprises—at least for the first few years.

THE FORCING FUNCTION YOUR MARKETING LEADER NEEDS: A "LEAD COMMIT"

First, don't worry about all the ways you can create inbound leads. Because the #1 place to start with improving marketing is to create a Forcing Function for the leader. Your VP Sales has a quota—why doesn't your VP Marketing? Your sales team has a quota—your marketing team and leader have to have one, too—as a *Lead Commit.*

Everyone hires marketing folks who have squishy goals. Half of startups and probably 90% of other kind of businesses miss this, and don't have any kind of concrete Lead Commit at all. It's the

"We get what we get and we don't get upset" approach. Lead Commit goals "force" marketers to focus on sustainable marketing practices instead of get-rich-quick methods that spike leads briefly. It's not easy—especially when you're creating it for the first time—but it's vital in a function that can generate lots of leads that go nowhere.

In the beginning, when you're so early there's little data to work from, all you can do is start by estimating or guessing. But having a guess is still better than nothing.

Ideally, you can base the commit on a metric related to qualified leads and pipeline being created every month, but if that's not practical, find something, anything, that you can accurately measure as a starting point. Even "total new leads per month" without a quality gauge—as vague as that is, because they could be mostly crap. But again, it's better than nothing to get started.

Once you get the ball rolling, over the months you'll learn how to more confidently set future—yet ever-evolving—targets, just as with sales quotas.

CORPORATE MARKETING VERSUS DEMAND GENERATION

So many companies hire a head of marketing with a strong resume, from another strong company. But they hired someone from *corporate marketing*, rather than *demand generation*. So that hire fails and you're left with nothing more to remember him/her by other than those nice blue pens they ordered with your logo on them.

Traditionally, corporate marketing is the sexier of the two. With branding, positioning, logos, and press releases, it's priority number one at big companies. Demand generation (demandgen) has been underappreciated—left to junior folks slaving away in the backroom. And because of this, you'll find leading companies all spitting out tons of senior corporate marketers.

Corporate marketing (such as at Adobe, Google, or Salesforce.com) is all about protecting and promoting the brand *after you're already big*. In the Fortune 500, demandgen folks are usually second-class citizens. But in growing tech companies, these folks are the Lords of Marketing.

Demandgen folks are all about the numbers: spend X dollars and create Z leads, which should be worth five × X dollars in revenue.

Great demandgen marketers can handle the "squishy stuff" (logos, branding, press releases, etc.) well enough until you're ready to get corporate. Their blue pens may not be as pretty as the ones the corporate marketer gets you, but you'll get *leads*.

For companies that need *leads,* brand marketing is very expensive in the early days—and, frustratingly, generates zero leads. For a company with less than $50 million, corporate marketing is a Nice-to-Have, *after you're already growing fast,* because of your kick-butt demandgen person.

You want someone who's shown a passion for areas like inbound/web demand generation programs, lead nurturing, and metrics—but who will also work hand-in-hand with your sales team. And that's *not* corporate marketing. Demandgen folks can figure out corporate marketing. Corporate marketing cannot figure out demandgen. Ever.

CASE STUDY: ZENEFITS FROM $1 MILLION TO $100 MILLION IN ~TWO YEARS

One of the things Zenefits does differently is lead generation. Not the mechanics so much as how predictable they make it and how hard they push it. How *far* they take it.

Matt Epstein is VP Marketing for Zenefits. CEO Parker Conrad calls him their lead generation genius. Matt figured out how to deliver all the demos the sales team needs to hit their goals. He helped establish the first predictable, repeatable outbound lead generation techniques that powered marketing's ability to generate all the demos the Account Executive sales team needed to go from $1 million to $20 million in 2014, then past $100 million ~a year later.

Matt wasn't some proven super-marketer rock star they brought in early. In fact, Matt says, "Before Zenefits, I hadn't done anything significant."

Well … maybe. You may have actually heard of Matt for a funny reason. He worked at a marketing agency for four years, before leaving to find something new to do. He wanted to get into the tech industry, but after a year of trying, he still couldn't get a job. He couldn't even get people to respond with "no" to his applications. One day he decided to go all in and spend his savings—$3,000—to try some crazy ideas to get Google to notice him. He came up with a "Google Please Hire Me" campaign and created a video and website. (Just search online with that phrase to find it.) Besides the video, Matt flew a plane around their building with a sign, and he mailed in five life-size cardboard cut-outs of himself to Google HQ, directing them to check out the website.

He got a lot of attention in Silicon Valley, and interviews with just about every tech company (except Google). He got several offers. One was from SigFig, a company started by Parker Conrad. SigFig was the company Parker started prior to Zenefits; Matt took the job at SigFig just as Parker was leaving.

Fast-forward … sometime later, Matt was visiting Parker's house; Parker was showing him his neighbor's house, which Matt wanted to rent. Parker threw his laptop up on the kitchen table and had Matt check out what he was working on—an early Zenefits app.

Parker had gone through an eight-week development boot camp, and had produced this application that Matt thought "looked just horrible." But when Parker explained the business concept behind it, Matt said, "Holy shit, you're going to print money. Can I help you get your first 30 customers?"

After a few months of helping Parker part-time, Parker pitched Matt on leaving his cushy, stable job at SigFig and joining him full time. Parker's pitch: "You may not get paid for a year, but you should join me."

You may not get paid for a year, but you should join me.

Generating the First Leads

When Matt started, Zenefits' customers had all been found through pure hustle. Matt's thinking was, "How can I get the most customers in 30 days?"

He started finding prospects and cold-emailing them. "My first month and a half, I sat in bed in my boxers, living off McDonald's. I A/B tested at least five different email templates every week, sending about 100 emails a day. I did it all by hand, tracking it all in Excel, and I found a formula.

"At first I'd thought our message of a free service would appeal to Human Resources. But it turned out it was more compelling, more of a need, to the CEO/owner—C-suite. I figured this out through just lots and lots of A/B testing. And hamburgers."

Once Matt found ways to generate interest and appointments through mass emailing, he began hiring junior inside salespeople (sales development reps, or "SDRs") to take over—either making their own calls and emails, or following up and responding to mass emails that marketing sent for them. They often blended "outbound" and "inbound" together while figuring out what worked. In fact, they went from zero to *300* SDRs in about two years.

Whether the pipeline Matt created was from inbound or outbound, Nets or Spears, or some mutant mix is not the point. The methods could have been through direct mail, Google ads, partners, content marketing, or late night infomercials. It's not about *how* they did it.

The point is that Matt took ownership of figuring out what kinds of marketing brought in revenue, predictably and scalably. He got his hands dirty, experimented to find something repeatable for his product and market, proved it out and made it predictable, then kept doubling down on it (and doubling down again). *The point* is that he and the executive team agreed on specific *Lead Commit* goals that focused everyone on what mattered.

No Hiding

For the first 18 months, Marketing at Zenefits had total ownership of lead generation:

- Marketing was tied to, and compensated on, revenue results. Marketing's goals were determined by working backwards from how many demos and opportunities need to be created for the sales team, regardless of how they were created:
  - "Okay, you have 10 salespeople, so you need to generate 80 opportunities a month" or "We need to generate $50 million in pipeline."
  - They couldn't do this until they had reliable historical data: "The average SDR can do is X, so we need the SDRs to do Y and other sources to do Z."
- Marketing couldn't hide. It didn't matter whether opportunities were generated through inbound marketing (Nets), outbound prospecting (Spears), or carrier pigeon—marketing owned it all.

In mid-2015, with the system defined and scaling, they moved the outbound prospectors under Sales.

Matt Epstein's Advice on Lead Generation

"*Test things fast in the real world.*" You have to get your hands dirty to really understand who the target is and what their pains are. What is a *must-have*? Don't make assumptions—go out and email them and talk to them. Get out from behind your desk, Twitter feeds, and laptops and *try things* in the real world. When you sit around white-boarding all the time, analyzing everything internally until it's perfect, you get stuck on theory. You come up with the perfect idea on "This is how we'll market it." It's beautiful, complicated, and impressive to the CEO. Then you launch the marketing in the real world and it completely flops because nothing clicks with the real customers.

"*You better get your shit together before you scale your SDRs, or else you're fucked.*" Hiring a bunch of SDRs or salespeople before you have a system working is going to be a waste:

- Know exactly who to reach out to
- Your messaging
- All the objections
- 80%+ of how your lead generation and sales funnels work
- How it all flows in your sales systems and tools

"*Look for 10x levers.*" See how quickly you can find a lever to pull to get closer to guaranteeing business, then put your pedal to the metal. For Zenefits, in the beginning Matt says, "Outbound was our ultimate early lever." Maybe for someone else it's product, social media, inbound, webinars, or live events.

"*Don't get distracted by shiny objects.*" Matt says, "In the first year I didn't care about social media, pet projects to enhance the website in minor ways, and any other Nice-to-Haves that didn't create qualified leads. Because what we had worked so well, it made more sense to keep doubling down all our energy on that before diversifying." Keep improving what you have, but don't let it sidetrack you from the 10x thing. What's going to get you a big leap? "I got a hundred emails today—am I going to respond to them or bang out the 10x thing today?" Practice saying no to new ideas and interruptions.

"*I repeat: test, quickly.*" Whatever you are going to launch and believe will work, probably won't, at first. So get it out there and iterate fast. Example: In display advertising, Matt saw people iterate ads internally for three months in pursuit of perfection—before trying real world, real prospect, tests. At Zenefits, with Version 1.0 of everything, they found ways to start testing everything they came up with in the real world, within hours. For example, with PPC marketing, they got first iterations out the door the same day. They learned quickly that while results were decent, they weren't effective enough to Go Big with. And then later, they knew through experience how to prioritize it.

"Go for it." Comfort and caution are the enemies of growth. Matt says, "You want to be running fast enough to be almost tipping over. When something works, invest big." Early on, Parker told Matt, "If one SDR is getting you four demos a day, great—go hire 20 more of them." Matt said his first reaction was, "Okay, that's scary, I have no idea how we'll do that." Take the leap, and find a way to make it work along the way.

Don't get distracted by shiny objects.

INBOUND MARKETING: A FOUR-POINT PRIMER

There is an overwhelming amount of fantastic—and free—"Inbound 101" content on the web. The following are a few ideas to simplify and amplify what you might already be doing. Or, help you kick it off....

Point 1: Start with Your Customers' Buying Stages

Make your marketing content useful to your ideal customers by helping them consider, decide and buy. One size does not fit all. For example, Jon Miller, CEO of Engagio (and Marketo's cofounder and ex-CMO), uses three simple buying stages: early, middle, and late. This breakdown makes it easier for his team to sort out which types of content they need, where they need it, and where there are any gaps.

Early stage: "Why?" These customers are actively learning, but not buying (yet). Why should they care about your category? Why should they change? Your content should be entertaining and useful, whether people buy your stuff or not. Don't make it about you, your product, or its features. For example, at Marketo, Jon created content that taught people how to become better marketers, and he's following the same playbook for Engagio around Account-Based Marketing.

Middle stage: "How?" Your audience wants to learn more about how to implement your product/service in their own business. Your content should help educate them on their options and how they can deliver promised results. It should help people make better purchasing decisions. Marketo created content such as "structured evaluations," which help marketers learn more about a category and the space; multiple "Definitive Guides" (such as the "Definitive Guide to Marketing Automation"); and third-party analyst reports.

Late stage: "Which?" Your prospects are getting ready to buy, deciding, "Which path do we take?" Now your content should be heavily about you—why you're better, different, how you can ensure results, including why you are better than that uber-competitor, "Do nothing."

Your content should educate people to help them make better purchasing decisions.

Point 2: Content Is Still King

Neil Patel is a content genius. He's a cofounder of Crazy Egg, Hello Bar, and KISSmetrics. Forbes has named him a top 10 online marketer.

Five tips from Neil are:

1. *Write content for your readers, not for you*. Try to create content that solves customers' biggest problems. Don't write to make your boss happy; write to make your audience happy. Remember—your boss isn't your audience; also, get feedback from real users and customers.
2. *Use tools to find target customers' interests*. Survey tools (like SurveyMonkey or Qualaroo) and drip email campaigns can help you get smarter about tuning into what your audience cares about.

   You don't need to be fancy. [We (Aaron and Jason) find patterns in people's interests mostly by meeting and talking with people every week. "Meetings," "the phone" and "email" can be wonderfully simple tools.]
3. *Add more details to make content more desirable*. The more helpful your content is, the better. Blog posts that lay out step-by-step instructions on how to do things like implement Salesforce.com, break down inbound marketing steps, create sales scripts, do growth hacking, and so on, all do really well. This may be why you've seen growth in

things like "The Ultimate Guide to ____" and "The Definitive Guide to ____." They work.

4. *You don't need to blog every day or every week.* Make a plan and stick with it, whether that's posting daily, weekly, or bimonthly. Start with less commitment and then increase as you go if it makes sense. (Aaron blogs once or twice a month on PredictableRevenue.com, and "sometimes" on his personal blog at PebbleStorm.com. Jason writes five answers on Quora every week, and blogs at least weekly on SaaStr.com.)

Make a plan and stick with it, whether that's posting daily, weekly, or bimonthly.

5. *Pay close attention to what works for you.* Are you inspired after a run? At night, or in the morning? With coffee, after a meeting, after you journal, with a deadline? Are there conditions that help you create freely? Do you prefer creating through writing, art, video, live events, slides ... ? And what best drives traffic, leads, and sales with your niche? Is it short posts, video, guides, interviews, webinars ... ? Model other people, but pay close attention to what works for you and your customers, so that you can better learn how to repeat it.

Point 3: The Magic of Squirrel-Feeding

It can be easy to come up tons of content.

It can be easy to publish it.

And it's especially easy to overestimate people's capacity to absorb it—especially if they aren't already fans and are new to your stuff.

The world's suffering from content overload. And yet there's always more room for great content, or for new ways to make it more digestible to your audience.

Imagine you're standing in a forest and you see a squirrel (a customer). What usually happens today when a marketing or sales person spots a squirrel is that they load up a bunch of different pizzas (content) and try to dump them on the squirrel's head all at once.

What happens? Of course the squirrel—who doesn't know and therefore doesn't trust this person—just runs away!

But what if that marketing person took just one slice of pizza, or an extra-tasty small bite, put it out there for the squirrel, and then stepped back to wait patiently ("waiting patiently"—a foreign concept to so many salespeople). That means not yelling at the squirrel to eat it, or waving your arms, but just … waiting. And if nothing happens, try a different bite.

Then, when the squirrel does eat it, put out a new tasty bite. Repeat this a few times, and soon the squirrel has built up trust and will be eating out of your hands—and eating more and bigger pieces.

With content, think of bite-sized chunks (like a blog post or short video) as a way to give new prospects an easy taste. For prospects who like it and want more detail, that's when the meatier pieces can be useful like longer videos or white papers.

Don't assume the squirrel will know exactly what it wants next or where to find it. Assume that you need to put the right content in front of them. Make it simple for them to consume it, and easy to take action to get the next bite, such as "Subscribe here" or "Are you free to chat on Wednesday?"

The less they have to *think*—that is, interpret what you're asking them to do and why they should do it—the more likely they'll take another step closer to you and continue building trust.

- Convert PDFs into blog posts that you can share as links, not attachments
- Cut out the fluff in all your content
- Create two-minute video teasers that lead them to longer ones

Our uber-point: People's attention spans are getting shorter, and there is an overwhelming amount of content out there. The simpler and tastier you make your bites, the more likely the right customers will consume them and come back for more.

Point 4: Aaron's Mantra: Don't Worry, Be Human

When people ask me about the future of lead generation, the number one idea I raise is that authenticity, funnily enough, is becoming a business necessity. Truth equals money, because it builds trust and connection. As inboxes and brains get busier over the coming decade(s), authenticity as a person or a brand helps you stand out from the crowd.

People want to hear from people—not machines. For example, in B2B marketing, a lot of newsletters look pretty—with logos, images, colors, and HTML. While they might look "professional," fancy newsletters may not be the most effective way to write to your audience.

Truth equals money, because it builds trust and connection.

Personal or Not? A/B Testing a Webinar Promotion

Monica Girolami, the head of marketing for NewVoiceMedia, creator of a popular cloud-based, global telephony system used by sales and support teams, ran an A/B test for a promotion on a webinar I did with her.

First she invited people with a fancy HTML email that read more like a mass update.

Then she sent a newsletter that looked and read more like a personal email from her. It was in plain text. It was signed by Monica, and the "reply-to" went to her directly. She wrote it as if she was writing to a friend.

Which one worked best? Her more-personal email tripled their results. "Even more astonishing," Monica said, "were all the personal replies I received—like "Sorry I can't make that time, but let me know about the next webcast."

Does this mean you should kill all your HTML emails? No! It all depends on your market and style. But look at ways—including "unprofessional" ones—to make them more authentic, and *test* them.

HTML Invitation:	"Personal" Invitation:
Open Rate: 13.2%	Open Rate: 15.3%
Click-through rate: 1.8%	Click-through rate: 4.1%
New Registrants: 20	New Registrants: 60

Other Ways to Be Human with Your Team, Clients, and Marketing

- *Share personal stories with customers*—including the embarrassing ones, in tasteful ways, when they're relevant, whether in your newsletter or over the phone. The more you share about yourself, the good and the bad, the easier it is for others to find a connection to you. I'm still surprised how many of my friends and clients (like Ken Krogue of InsideSales.com and Kyle Porter of SalesLoft) were adopted or have adopted. No one mentioned it until after they found out that I'd adopted a bunch of kids. (Why would they?)

- *Add your own style or personal flourish* to messages or posts. Don't be afraid to embrace your quirks. For example: *i write all my emails in lowercase, e.e. cummings style. yes, including in my newsletter and to Fortune 500 clients. and i sign off with a simple smiley face and nickname. like this :) air*
- "Flourish" means enhancing something, not turning it into a circus.
- Other ways include using humor, or adding a picture, tagline, or catchphrases.
- Try out more videos and videoconferencing.
- Send handwritten letters—or take a picture of one to send.

P.S.: Almost every time I send a newsletter out, I get some responses from people like these (these are all real):

"Please don't send me emails. I find this tasteless" [Mind you, this person signed up for the newsletter]

"Please fuck off" [At least they had manners.]

"This email is embarrassing."

"I've always wondered, do your newsletter emails have terrible grammar as a way to stand out from all the other emails I get in my inbox?"

I also get:

"You are hilarious Aaron, I really appreciate what you are doing and the manner you do it in."

"I *love* the radical transparency of this email!!! Totally humanizes the whole thing."

"These are the best newsletters I get. You should teach people how to write this way."

And I've gotten many emails from people who've written, "i like this lowercase style, i'm going to try it myself."

When you're authentic or quirky, you'll find some people love you, others hate you—but it's better than being ignored because you're bland!

Don't be afraid to try new styles that better fit you and your ideal customers.

When you're authentic or quirky, you'll find some people love you, others hate you—but it's better than being ignored because you're bland!

HEROIC MARKETING: WHEN YOU HAVE NO MONEY AND LITTLE TIME

If you have to handle marketing part-time, or have a tiny team and budget, this section's for you: how to get the most results with (very) limited time and (no) money. This has worked for me for years, while I'm juggling everything else—writing multiple books, growing a business, growing my family, and maintaining a 20- to 30-hour workweek.

Everyone feels like they aren't doing enough with marketing. The possibilities are overwhelming. *Content, markets, niche, blog posts, videos, messages, webinars, newsletters, landing pages, social media, conversion rates* .... Your head can feel like it's going to explode, until you say @*#$^ this! and give up. Especially when you feel like you're publishing stuff that no one is reading—and sales are slow.

If you're struggling or don't have much to rely on, here's a simpler approach. First, here are some mistaken beliefs in marketing:

- Build it and they will come (a fairy tale).
- More is better (not necessarily).
- Inbound leads are free (an urban myth).
- It should happen fast (an evil expectation).

If you let go of these misconceptions, it'll help you create a marketing strategy that costs relatively little time and money—and works.

Step 1: Pick One Thing As Your "Cake"

If you're feeling overwhelmed about having to run a blog, newsletter, webinars, live events, Instagram, Facebook, Twitter, Yelp, and more—all at the same time—then don't. Pick one thing to focus on as your cake, and think of the rest as icing. Does blogging work for you? Focus on that first, with anything else as a Nice-to-Have. Are you a video person? Stick to posting videos on a channel that works for you. Social media is icing to layer on later, unless it's your primary passion.

Jason's cake is Quora; some of his responses get turned into blogs, which get shared socially (icing). My cake is writing books, part of which gets created through blogging, some of which gets shared through a newsletter and social (icing).

As you grow and get your systems running smoothly, it becomes easier to take on more and more until you've got the 10-layer, rainbow-iced wedding cake.

Step 2: Force Yourself to Clarity with Live Events

There's never "the one secret" to success, but if there were one for me, it would be throwing live events both in person and online (usually webinars). Not because they generated leads or customers, but because they are Forcing Functions to foster clarity and progress.

It can take a lot of work, but there's still nothing like getting people together, live. And people *want* it, to learn from each other and connect in person. Whether in small meetups of a half-dozen people, or huge events as big as Jason's SaaStr Annual conference, which attracts thousands of SaaS executives and entrepreneurs every year.

Events *can* be financially successful, but the main value to you, if your lead generation isn't clicking, is *clarity.*

When you host live events, especially in person, it's a visceral experience to see people show up and get value. Or not. You're forced into clarity, revisiting which niche you're trying to nail:

- Who do you want to attend?
- Why would they come; what will they get out of it?
- What will you teach or offer, and how will you deliver?
- What action do you want them to take afterwards?

When you host live events, it's a visceral experience to see people show up and get value. Or not.

You may or may not get a breakthrough with one event. Keep having them. Ideally they're in person, but they can be online, too, as with a webinar or Google Hangout. You can do events showcasing others' content, but include some of your own. Put your own ideas on the line! It might be one of the best ways to force yourself to figure out how to Nail A Niche, if you're still struggling with it.

Other things to love about events:

- They create reusable content.
- They build your audience.
- They generate leads and revenue.
- Your team connects with real live humans (oh my!).

Pro Tips

1. *First,* pick a date for the live event.
2. Announce the date to people you know (before you have all the details, or even a title or location).
3. It's okay to change it before it happens.
4. No matter what, don't chicken out! Go through with it, even if no one shows (which can happen).
5. What you learn from this is more important than the results (how many people attended or took your Call to Action).
6. Do it again, and again, and again, and again …

Step 3: Partners Make Marketing Easier

Marketing with partners is the simplest way to expose new people to your brand. It's hard building an audience from scratch. Working with partners who already have a relevant audience makes pretty much any kind of project more effective.

> **Marketing with partners is the simplest way to expose new people to your brand.**

Also, partners can push you, give you courage, and make it easier to succeed.

Are you getting started and wondering why would they work with you? Any blogger or company with a newsletter wants to share new stuff with their people. You help them by giving them useful ideas or tools to share with their audience that they didn't have to create. Also, forming relationships with marketers is a big deal. Any CEO or marketer will be more inclined to work with you if they know and like you.

Who do you start with? Start with someone you already know or follow. Find out how you can help them, and then propose an event you can do together. Then move on to bigger, colder fish.

Step 4: To Infinity, and Repeat

Stop, reflect, and do it again, sticking to your "main thing" and getting better and better and better at it.

For example, after you've held an event—what do you do next? Pick a date for another one. This is going to take months, at least, and maybe years, so stick to it.

CHAPTER 7

Spears—Outbound Prospecting

Spears are one-to-one campaigns, such as targeted outbound prospecting or business development initiatives for getting appointments with anyone who's not coming to you—whether customers or partners.

In addition to Salesforce.com, Zenefits and Responsys (now part of Oracle) are examples of companies who've created $100 million-plus revenue machines with Spears.

The original *Predictable Revenue* book outlined the "Cold Calling 2.0" outbound prospecting model, which:

- Proposed that "salespeople shouldn't prospect"—that to create an outbound system that works, companies need to specialize sales roles, with prospectors who only prospect and closers who only close. Salespeople who do everything (prospecting and responding to inbound leads and closing and managing accounts) end up doing lots of things poorly instead of one thing really well.
- Created a friendly alternative to high-volume cold calling, replacing it with sending cold referral emails as a way to make first contact.
- Systematized the entire process into a step-by-step funnel, creating a predictable way to generate qualified leads on-demand from companies who have never heard of your business.

Outbound prospecting was in the doghouse for years as inbound marketing took off. Now it's hot again because all kinds of companies are seeing how it can supercharge growth in highly predictable ways—especially when going after bigger companies that often aren't as responsive to marketing campaigns. Even HubSpot and Marketo, two of the companies that started the inbound movement, have big teams of outbound prospectors to speed up growth, increase market coverage, and teach vital skills to their sales teams.

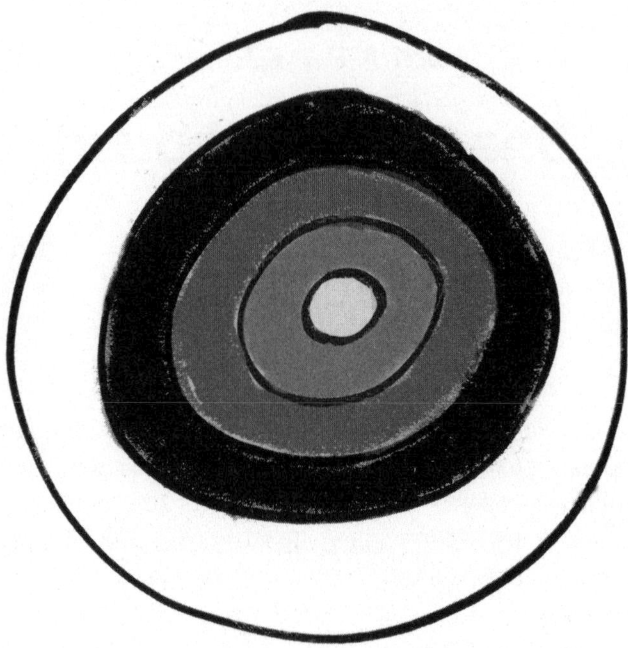

FIGURE 7.1 Careful targeting is the key to outbound success.

If you don't have an outbound program yet, maybe your team still believes that "I don't want to cold call," or "It's a burnout job," or "We don't want to interrupt people who don't know us." These are valid but misplaced ideas about how world-class outbound prospecting works. You don't need to cold call, although you can. Outbound prospecting shouldn't be a burnout job, if it's done right. And it's not about interrupting people who don't need you; rather, it's about reaching out in friendly ways to find the people who do.

What are its advantages? (Even if you already have massive amounts of inbound leads?)

When salespeople have been trained as prospectors, they develop the mindset and skills to be entrepreneurial and make things happen instead of waiting around for something to happen for them.

- *Avoid "inbound dependency" and reactive teams:* Salespeople who get only inbound leads become dependent on them. When inbound leads slow down (through fewer total leads coming in, or if the sales team grows faster than the lead volume), they feel helpless and don't know what to do. On the other hand, when salespeople have been trained as prospectors, they develop the proactive mindset and skills needed to be entrepreneurial—to go make things happen, instead of waiting around for something to happen for them.
- *Easier to double:* After you've figured out the messaging and steps, outbound prospecting is a place where you can double your results by doubling the team.
- *Increase deal sizes:* Your average outbound deal could be 3x to 10x larger because you can specifically target bigger opportunities and avoid small ones.
- *Increase market coverage:* Say you have 10,000 companies in your target market. How long will it take before they all call you? With outbound, you can fill in any gaps left by inbound.
- *Less competition:* There's a leadgen stat that gets thrown around a lot in the B2B space: that "80% of the buying cycle's already done by the time they reach out to you." Usually this is intended to emphasize the importance of inbound marketing or social media and other efforts. This is true—but only for inbound leads, *not outbound-generated opportunities*. So while it's fantastic when someone calls you, they are also calling five or more of your competitors at the same time. Sometimes with outbound prospecting you'll run across an active project, but more often you're going in to help the prospect create a vision and plan for solving their pain. More often than not, that scenario will be much less competitive than if they'd already started a project by researching the top 20 options in the space. You'll still lose 70–80% of the time, but the lost deals will be labeled "Lost—No Decision" rather than "Lost—Competitor" much more often than your inbound deals.
- *Small team, big impact:* You don't have to invest a ton and hire a huge team; even a small number of outbound reps can add another 10% to sales. And even a 10% increase in recurring/SaaS sales per year has a huge impact on your profit and valuation.

WHERE OUTBOUND WORKS BEST—AND WHERE IT FAILS

If you want to go big with outbound prospecting, it works best when you have these four conditions in place:

1. *You can sell deals that are large enough to be profitable*, usually $10,000–$20,000 in lifetime value (bigger is better). Yes, outbound can work with smaller deals, but it gets much harder to do it profitably.
2. *Your value proposition is easy for a prospect to understand* and say yes or no to. If your proposition or messaging is too jargon-ish, not relevant, or if it confuses prospects, you're in trouble.
3. *You're different:* You can't have 100 competitors selling similar stuff and expect to have easy success with outbound. There's too much noise (i.e., confusion) and prospects can't easily tell why you're better than other options.
4. *You're not trying to replace other people's stuff:* If you're trying to call in and compete with DropBox or some financial system, to get a company to rip that out and replace it with your service, it's *hard*. You have to have a damn good reason for them to do it—a reason that you're 10x better. It's much easier to look for opportunities where the buyer doesn't need to replace or trash an entrenched system that works "well enough." Whether you call this whitespace, green fields, blue skies, or magenta flowers, look for that kind of market or way to position yourself.

When It's Harder

Outbound prospecting isn't a fit for every company—sometimes it's easier, sometimes harder. Here are some conditions that make it more challenging or less profitable:

- *It's not a real management priority:* Management hires an intern to dabble, then they forget about it, or they're just too busy to give it time. Or they won't pay for even some basic data or apps you need. (Funny how companies will spend $5,000 a month on paying someone, but not $50 a month on an app that that person needs!)

- *You aren't willing to focus your Ideal Outbound Customer Profile* and you're spraying emails and calls at anyone and everyone with a pulse. Any buyers you run into are encountered mostly through dumb luck. Even a stopped clock is right twice a day, but, really …
- *Unrealistic expectations:* "Hey guys, it's been 30 days—where are our closed deals?" It takes three to six months to go from scratch to consistent pipeline generation—and longer for revenue, depending on how long your sales cycle is (and outbound cycles *will take longer* than your inbound cycles). Stick it out! If you have long sales cycles, you may not see first revenue for a long time, but you will see the regular progress toward it.

It takes three to six months to go from scratch to consistent pipeline generation—and longer for revenue. Stick it out!

- *The CEO believes all prospecting needs to be done only by salespeople,* and doesn't believe in dedicated prospectors.
- *You sell custom or commoditized professional services.* Professional services are harder to market and sell than products. You can improve your odds by going super-narrow with a niche. Be open to doing more testing and it taking longer than you expect. Or accepting that other forms of leadgen will be better, like content marketing or live events.
- *It's Boiler Room 101:* Your outbound strategy involves telling the team every day to "make more calls, send more emails"—whether those calls and emails are working or not. It's all about activity, not about what the activities are accomplishing.

The bottom line, though, is that there are companies in every kind of situation that have made prospecting work. But in some cases it's a lot easier than in others to make it a primary growth engine.

OUTBOUND LESSONS LEARNED SINCE *PREDICTABLE REVENUE* WAS PUBLISHED

In 2011, *Predictable Revenue* came out and helped reignite outbound prospecting and popularize both the Sales Development function and dedicated prospector teams.

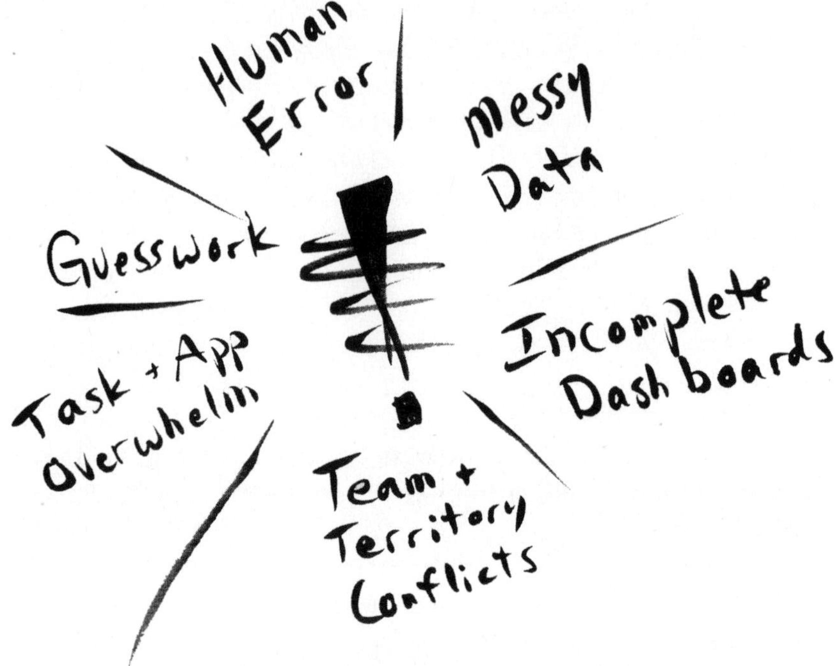

FIGURE 7.2 Common challenges in systematizing outbound prospecting.

Since then, the problems of outbound keep evolving:

1. *Human error is growing*. Email and call automation has increased human error, because more activity equals more errors in response handling, following up, updating sales systems, and territory/account conflicts.
2. *Data is a never-ending problem:* New data sources are constantly being created, but most prospectors still spend two to three hours a day building and fixing lists.
3. *A new knee-jerk reaction to problems* is "send more email!" replacing the old reaction of "make more calls!" Doing more of what's not working isn't a solution.
4. *Overdependence on a single technique,* whether it's researching, or cold calling, or templates, or ... —rather than ensuring prospectors are experts in two to four complementary techniques, and understand the pros and cons of each. No one technique will work all the time, efficiently.

5. *Obsessing over simplistic metrics like email open and response rates* at the expense of understanding how the entire funnel works.
6. *Task, tool, & app overwhelm.* Higher-volume prospecting means more to-do lists, more follow-up tasks, and more apps, overloading prospectors.
7. *Phone calls aren't obsolete:* Don't let reps succumb to "phone fear." Pick up the damn phone! Prospectors should be having live conversations *every day*.
8. *Dashboard problems:* With human error, misconceptions about how outbound should work, and common sales force app configuration errors, it's surprisingly hard for executives to get accurate and complete outbound funnel metrics.

Unsurprisingly, after many years of consulting with companies on *Predictable Revenue* projects to help them build outbound prospecting teams or restructure sales teams, we cofounded a company called Carb.io, a new kind of Pipeline Automation Software, to solve these recurring problems. I wish I'd had it back at Salesforce.com.

For example, an early customer, Agility Recovery, saw:

- *Higher quantity:* Initial calls (called AWAF, or "Are We A Fit" calls), grew from 16 a month per prospector to 15 a *week* per prospector, approximately a 400% increase. Usually the prospector holds the first AWAF with a prospect, confirms a possible fit, then schedules a longer

FIGURE 7.3 Enemy #1: Human Error

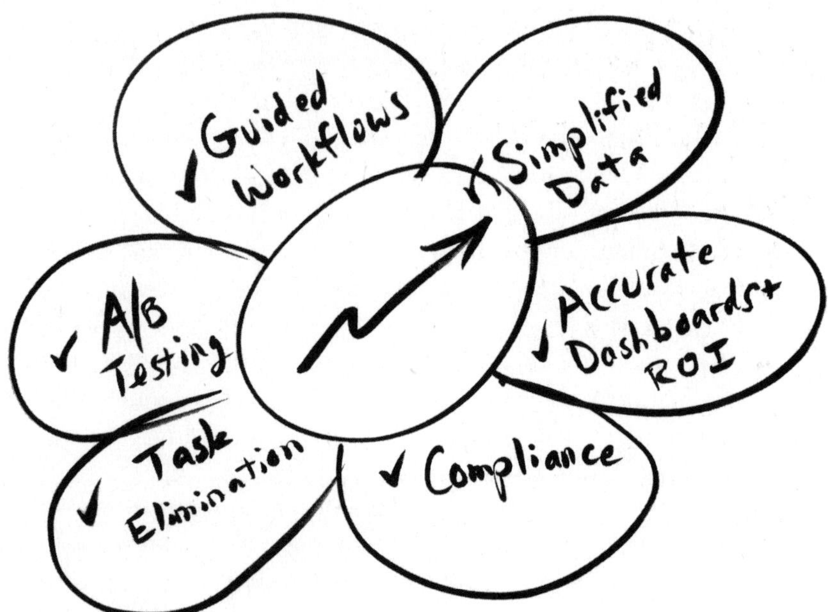

FIGURE 7.4 Modern outbound sales development needs much more than email and phone scripts.

Demo or Discovery call for them with a senior salesperson, who qualifies and accepts or rejects the opportunity.

- *Higher quality:* They raised their AWAF "call-to-close" rate from 4.6% to 12%. So out of 100 initial calls, they about tripled how many deals they closed, with better data and targeting, vastly fewer tasks and to-do's, fewer human errors, and accurate tracking and reporting.

For more, see.

CASE STUDY: ZENEFITS' OUTBOUND LESSONS

Robby Allen joined Zenefits in May 2014 to work for Matt Epstein, just as the company had secured its Series B funding. At the time, a priority was Doubling Their Deal-size (which we'll get to in Part IV), tilting upmarket from very small businesses toward bigger opportunities and deals at companies of 100–300 or more employees.

In his first two months as manager of the outbound prospecting team, Robby doubled the team to 24 people. Two months later, he initiated the outbound operation's move from San Francisco to Scottsdale, Arizona, where overhead costs were significantly lower. Hiring in the

SF Bay Area had become intensely competitive and expensive, and with this kind of role, it's often better to hire less-experienced people anyway, and mold them.

Over the next year, by the end of 2015, he'd grown the team to 300 outbound prospectors—with 30-plus managers and five directors, 80% of whom are based in Arizona.

He gained some the following insights along the way.

The best prospectors have a clear idea of which companies should be a good fit, and which shouldn't. They don't treat all accounts blindly as the same. The best prospectors are also direct, especially on the phone. When calling smaller companies, they can more easily get an owner on the phone. Within 15 to 20 seconds the best reps are telling the prospect that the goal of the call is to set up a demo to show them the product. They aren't pushy, and they aren't trying to be someone's friend. They are just offering the facts.

Hiring: Robby hires for intangibles over relevant experience. Do they have hunger, ambition, initiative? How have they demonstrated that in the past? Lots of prospectors who didn't have sales experience ended up being the best. They didn't have bad habits to change. He wants people with a wide range of backgrounds, who can bring a lot of different skills to the table.

You want people with a wide range of backgrounds, who can bring a lot of different skills to the table.

Prospectors can improve data quality: If you train your prospectors to add, update, and fix the accounts and contacts they own, rather than ignore data errors, they will be the best source of maintaining accurate data in your system.

Thoughtful outreach: The prospectors follow a tailored campaign approach:

- Prospectors build or update a list of prospects, including researching them. For example, they use LinkedIn to gauge a company's speed of hiring, or to look for companies without HR people.
- They group prospects together by probable pain, sending similar messages, but customized to that business. They are looking for the companies most likely to have a pain Zenefits can solve.

- With smaller companies, the emails help open the door to make the call. With larger companies, fewer people pick up the phone and we rely more on email.
- "We don't automate just for the sake of automation."

Organizational switch: In mid-2015, they moved the outbound prospectors from marketing to sales. As we mentioned in the case study on Matt Epstein at Zenefits, launching and growing outbound under marketing created 100% ownership in getting the leads engine cranking for Sales.

Launching and growing outbound under Marketing created 100% ownership in getting the leads engine cranking for Sales.

At scale, though, communication and alignment with account executives became a bigger challenge. By moving the team to sales, the prospectors become better aligned with their salespeople teammates. Zenefits has a pod system, made up of five prospectors supporting two mid-market salespeople and one enterprise salesperson. Robby expects that 5:3 ratio to decrease over time, as other forms of lead generation balance out outbound.

Mistakes and Learnings

- *Impatience with outbound emailing:* The temptation is to load up a big list of names and let it go, but normally this isn't helpful. Slow down and carefully run more, smaller A/B experiments to develop your messaging, results, tools, and important metrics.
- *Too controlling:* "Always empower a subset of your reps, or all of them, to 'always be testing' and trying new things—tweaks to copy, research, calls; never settle for one thing. In the beginning it was a mess. We tightened things up and had everyone doing the same thing. But we went too far, stopping them from trying new email and phone techniques, stifling learning and slowing our evolution."
- *Not always asking "Will this scale?" with every new thing:* Every single thing they did will be tested at scale. If they didn't start with that question, it made it harder in the future. For example, at this hiring rate, they had to do interviews differently, with a "hiring day" approach, to mass-interview candidates without losing quality.

The Last Word from Robby

"Don't stick your prospectors in a basement and forget about them. The more attention you give them, the more likely the system will take off—with both your prospectors and salespeople. And make sure prospectors work closely with their sales teammates—if there isn't regular communication or mutual respect, breakdowns *will* happen."

> **"Developing relationships between prospectors and salespeople is so important to making the system work."**

CASE STUDY: OUTBOUND'S ROLE IN ACQUIA'S $100 MILLION TRAJECTORY

Acquia is a New England–based software company that provides products, services, and technical support for businesses that use Drupal, an open source web collaboration and publishing platform.

With the emergence of the Drupal platform as the platform of choice for millions of websites worldwide, including many of the world's biggest—Acquia grew steadily. In 2013 Deloitte named Acquia "the fastest growing private software company in North America."

$100 Million: Not "If" But "When"

Acquia's sales leaders, including Tim Bertrand (Chief Revenue Officer), decided that in order to hit their aggressive IPO-track/$100 million goals, they couldn't depend solely on inbound leads or on channel partners. After reading *Predictable Revenue*, Tim decided to build an outbound prospecting team to complement all the inbound leads Acquia generated.

Within a year of launching the prospecting team, they almost doubled their growth rate and proved that outbound would help them break $100 million faster and with more certainty. In under three years, they'd added $25 million–plus in recurring revenue from outbound prospecting, almost entirely from new customers, and in 2014 passed $100 million in total revenue.

Here's how their results worked out in the *first 12 months* of their outbound program, while nailing the system down (results not typical):

- Created an extra $6 million in Qualified Sales Pipeline.
- Closed $3 million in recurring revenue.

- The team began adding an extra $2 million in pipeline per ramped prospector per quarter.
- Prospecting went from generating 0% to 40% of all new business sales pipeline (thus almost doubling their new business growth rate).

Like Zenefits, after they started seeing these kinds of results, they decided early to go big with it. They began with three prospectors to get the system working, and then, after about six months, they decided they were going to grow the team by 10x.

By 2015, the team had 56 people worldwide and was still growing: 37 in North America, 9 in Europe, 2 in Asia-Pacific, and half a dozen managers.

What's Expected of Acquia's Prospectors?

- Send 600–800 cold outbound emails a month.
- Make 350–450 outbound calls a month.
- Daily: Mix in some social media touches (LinkedIn, Twitter, etc.) and personalized emails to executives.
- Schedule 20 longer demo/discovery calls between influencers and Acquia salespeople, per month.
- Tally 15 Sales Qualified Leads (SQLs) passed to *and accepted* by salespeople, per month.

The People

They've also used the team as a farm team to develop quota-carrying salespeople, but they've also placed alumni in channel, account management, recruiting, and their technical training program (Acquia University).

Many of the alumni are top performers, and have efficient hires: they're cheaper than hiring from the outside, are less risky, and are preramped.

Four Things That Helped Acquia's Outbound Program Take Off

1. The top management team, including the CEO, was on board.
2. They "just did it," avoiding analysis paralysis. It took Tim Bertrand only 37 days from the time he read *Predictable Revenue* to having

executive buy-in, getting prospector job requisitions approved, and having a signed consulting agreement with the Predictable Revenue team.

3. Acquia initially hired three excellent dedicated prospectors—two in the United States and one in the UK—and their only job was to prospect. Not to close deals. Not to handle inbound leads. Just prospect.
4. They avoided small opportunities: The way the math works out with prospectors, revenue comes faster by finding bigger deals, not by pursuing every single opportunity. Small deals are opportunity costs, taking prospectors' time away from finding bigger deals. "Small" is relative and defined company by company, but usually either 10 or 20% of the average deal size, or a fixed dollar value based on what's profitable.

The way the math works out with prospectors, revenue comes faster by finding bigger deals, not by pursuing every single opportunity.

CASE STUDY: FROM ZERO TO $10 MILLION WITH OUTBOUND AT GUIDESPARK

In 2013 GuideSpark took a less traveled path, focusing exclusively on phone-based outbound sales. No free trials. No freemium. Almost zero inbound leads. No customer advocacy program. No SEO, no SEM. A barely passable website. Nonexistent public relations. Limited investment money.

Despite bucking the generally accepted "norms" for SaaS startups, they grew *fast*—tripling revenue, and then tripling again. Here is the winning formula from CEO Keith Kitani and SVP Sales Shep Maher:

- *Hire a great VP Sales*: More on this in the next section, Making Sales Scalable.
- *Hire fast, hire right:* Growing outbound sales does require that you double your people to double sales, so you need to find the right hunters—salespeople with ambition.
- *Bring the noise:* GuideSpark created an open sales floor without cubicles or offices. It can be noisy, but they wanted their people to learn

faster and push each other faster by hearing each other every single day. It helped ramp people fast.

- *Break the rules:* GuideSpark had salespeople who did their own prospecting, breaking a cardinal "predictable revenue" rule. They figured out how to make it work because it was a company priority, not a side practice.
- *Public metrics:* Easily visible and understood metrics speak for themselves. Everyone knows what's expected and who's delivering. Novices knew who to emulate and veterans knew who could help them develop even further.
- *Test and iterate:* In your exploratory stages (less than $1–2 million revenue), you're still figuring things out. Stay nimble and flexible. Try different messages until you find something that works and then triple down on it. GuideSpark tried many messages during their first year of outbound, and kept the team informed about what worked and what didn't.
- *Avoid travel except when required:* GuideSpark found they could close six-figure deals over the phone. While nothing beats face-to-face for building relationships, it is expensive in time and money, so make sure you travel wisely.

Why Outbound Worked So Well for GuideSpark

- *Fast speed-to-learning:* With outbound sales, you learn *right away* if your messaging is resonating with prospects—like getting email responses (or not) or phone hang-ups (or not). You can change ineffective tactics that day—or triple down on what *is* working.
- *Focus:* Instead of chasing many different leadgen ideas, GuideSpark was laser-focused on one approach—and got very good at it.
- *Cash efficient:* Each salesperson was paid on performance: low performance means minimal expense. As a result, GuideSpark was able to get very far without outside investment.
- *Identifiable prospects:* Their customers span every size and industry, but the buyer in each company spans only a few different titles. So they could know who to call across a huge sea of prospects.

Then … Inbound Marketing

For Act II, once the outbound team was running and growing smoothly, GuideSpark raised more money and invested in marketing (Nets). They always believed in marketing, and of course wanted to grow inbound leads, but they knew that for them, outbound got them off the ground faster. And made them smarter about marketing when they were ready to start investing in it. They could build on the customer profiles, messages, and ideas they had already proven out in outbound campaigning.

CASE STUDY: HOW TAPSTREAM STARTED FROM SCRATCH

Fast-growth companies need to build their own prospecting teams internally: to establish a farm team system, and to have in-house expertise; you will always get the best results with internal experts. But sometimes it can be easier to get started—to launch, scale, or benchmark—with outside support.

You will always get the best results with internal experts. But sometimes it can be easier to get started—to launch, scale, or benchmark—with outside support.

At the end of 2013, Tapstream was a hot startup in the mobile analytics space. They had grown their acquisition platform to 2,000 mobile users in under two years and had just raised a seed investment round in order to grow sales.

While they were growing, many of their new users were coming from small independent app developers; what they needed now was a way to reach out to top app developers.

They had experimented internally with the *Predictable Revenue* outbound system on their own the summer before they raised money, but hadn't had much success. Why?

- They didn't have a dedicated team member who could assume the prospecting role full-time.
- They struggled to consistently find accurate data on the people they wanted to reach.
- They needed to increase low email response rates by simplifying their email messaging.

This time around, Tapstream wanted to build an actual prospecting team in-house, but it didn't yet make economic sense for them. They decided to use an outsourcing service (one through www.PredictableRevenue.com, but there are thousands out there). They wanted to start campaigning right away, before they were ready to dedicate internal people to prospecting.

With outsourcing, Tapstream saw 84 appointments in the first four months. Within seven months they'd closed enough deals to double their key customer base, and had learned enough to decide how to invest and prioritize it internally against other lead generation projects.

Long-term, your own internal people—with management attention—will be more effective than an outside company. Unless you're a company that wants to stay small, entirely outsourcing the outbound function (rather than supporting pieces) is rarely the best long-term solution, but it can be a great interim step to get launched and learn.

CHAPTER 8

What Executives Miss

Are you overanalyzing, or so microfocused on email open rates, webinar attendance levels, or getting your apps configured that you've missed an uber-issue?

When you get so caught up in the day-to-day busy-ness of marketing, lead generation, and app configuration, it can be easy to miss the forest for the trees.

When you get so caught up in the day-to-day busy-ness of marketing, lead generation, and app configuration, it can be easy to miss the forest for the trees.

PIPELINE CREATION RATE: YOUR #1 LEADING METRIC

One great thing about all the new ways to measure marketing and sales is being able to better See the Future (especially in SaaS businesses). You're trying to gauge whether your revenue will keep growing in the future, even though sales results vary a lot, monthly or quarterly, and sales pipelines have big quality issues.

What's worse, *sales numbers are a lagging indicator* of all the hard growth work you've done (right or wrong) in the prior 12 or more months—they can't predict anything.

And what about pipelines? It's fun to list every possible company who could buy, but pipeline reports are crap for predicting the future, since they are more often about hope than truth. Pipeline for this month is useful, but still dependent on how various reps estimate (guess) their probability and close dates. Next quarter's pipeline is only slightly better than a guess, even once you get pretty big.

But there's a better metric, your Key Metric, which you should track and score yourself on—and hold your VP Marketing and VP Demand Generation team(s) to—is Pipeline Creation Rate (or PCR; also sometimes called Lead Velocity Rate).

PCR measures your *growth* in qualified leads and pipeline, measured month-over-month, every month. PCR is real-time, not lagging, and it clearly predicts your future revenues and growth—and, even better—*your growth trend.*

Your Key Metric, which you should track and score yourself on, is Pipeline Creation Rate (PCR, also sometimes called Lead Velocity Rate).

If you created $1 million in new qualified pipeline this month, and created $1.1 million in new qualified pipeline the following month, *you are growing PCR at 10% month-over-month*. So, your sales should grow 10% as well after a period of an average sales cycle length.

Sales (or a lack thereof) are a lagging indicator of what you've done right or wrong for the past 12 months—but tell you nothing of the future.

Once EchoSign hit $1 million in revenue run rate, we set a PCR growth target of 10% per month. Once we hit about $3 million in run rate, we dropped it to 8% growth per month. The goal of 8% per month was to produce enough leads to grow the business at least 100% year-over-year.

We hit the PCR goals just about every month, and certainly every quarter, and every year. And by hook or by crook—enhanced with an ever-improving sales team and an ever-improving product—the revenue growth followed. Not every day. But clearly over time, ever quarter, every year.

One great thing about PCR is that while sales can vary a lot by month and quarter, there's no reason leads can't grow every single month like clockwork: Every … Single … Month. Follow other core business metrics of course—just understand that they aren't as good. Sales and pipeline lag. Monthly sales growth is important, but minor variations can lead to huge forecasting/modeling variances.

Know you will grow.

As long as you're measuring some version of *Qualified Leads*—not raw or unqualified leads—with a consistent formula and process to qualify them, you can begin to See The Future. Hit your PCR goal every month and you're golden. And with practice, you'll see the future of your business 12 or more months out, clear as can be.

THE 15/85 RULE: EARLY ADOPTERS AND MAINSTREAM BUYERS

Has someone from Iowa bought your stuff yet?

You don't get into true hypergrowth mode until you can get beyond your networks (Early Adopters, 15% of the market) and can sell to "regular people" (Mainstream Buyers, 85% of the market).

You don't get into true hypergrowth mode until you can get beyond your networks.

If you find yourself saying "When people *get it,* sales are easy. When they don't, it's hard," then maybe you're stuck selling to Early Adopters, on the high-trust side of the Arc of Attention.

While you want to *benefit* from things like referrals and risk-taking Early Adopters, you don't want to be *dependent* on them for growth, because you'll plateau. You can't scale if you can sell only to Early Adopters. Pay special attention to this if you fall into one of these scenarios:

- You're an early-stage company trying to get to or past your first million in revenue.
- You've been growing through word of mouth and inbound marketing, but now you want to get more aggressive (usually between $1 million and $20 million).
- You're starting a new marketing initiative, even at a BigCo—usually with a new product or target market.

When growing a company, there's a big milestone in getting your first 10–20 paying customers for a new product or target market. Usually these customers are Early Adopters, part of the 15%. They either instinctively get it, or they came through your network and so they're predisposed to give you more credit or attention than a typical "cold" buyer. (Remember the Arc of Attention.)

When you're selling to friends of friends, or you're a startup selling to startups, you're still part of the incestuous 15% club. You haven't "crossed over" until someone from Iowa buys your stuff.

The feedback from these Early Adopters is more positive, and generally does not reflect that of the general masses, which is the other 85%. They are more likely to think like you, be like you, and buy like you. They are willing to jump through more hoops, and tend to be more tech-savvy or risk-friendly, which can give you false positives about the market's reaction to your product. They're willing to push hard within their company to get it done, on their own initiative. But when you depend on these people to land deals, it limits you. They're hard to find.

Mainstream Buyers Are Different

Early Adopters aren't like the rest of the much bigger market—that 85% of the world who don't know you, aren't like you, and don't like risk: Mainstream Buyers.

Early Adopter	Mainstream Buyer
Risk-taker, in your functional area	Risk-averse, in your functional area
Inherently interested in your product/service (sees you as an opportunity/you're interesting)	Only interested in your product/service because they have a problem they need to solve (you are a burden/extra work)
Just "gets it"—requires little guidance	They, or their team, need a lot of guidance, frequently repeated
Finds you through serendipity or word of mouth	You gotta find them (at least while you're still under $10 million)
Impossible to grow fast with, because there aren't enough of them	Hard to grow fast with (at first), because they are demanding
Entrepreneurial, capable at selling internally to their team and CEO or Board	Capable of selling internally, but need to rely heavily on you to help them
Documented, concrete results may or may not be needed	Documented, concrete results are required

Early Adopter	Mainstream Buyer
"I get it, but can you show me some proof before I buy?"	"I don't get it; show me a lot of proof both before I decide whether this is a fit and whether to buy"
"We'll work out the details during implementation"	"We need every question answered before we buy"
Doesn't care much about what other people are doing or what they think.	Cares a lot about what other people are doing, and what others think (especially internally)

The Challenge

You've been selling to people who are extra-trusting in working with your new thing. Then, when you try marketing to Mainstream Buyers, it's incredibly frustrating because *they buy differently* from your first customers. For example, most Mainstream Buyers don't want to do a free trial or read all your blog posts to self-educate.

Mainstream buyers won't buy on faith; they buy concrete "things." They need to sell projects internally, to their VP or the CEO or CFO. To do that, Mainstream Buyers need everything spelled out: what they get, expected results, the timeframe, cost, risks, and steps. It's a *lot* more work for you to figure out all the tools they need to sell and justify the purchase internally. Sales calls and discussions can be very repetitive, repeating the same things multiple times.

> **Figure out all the tools your prospect needs to sell and justify the purchase internally.**

Okay, Early Adopters need some of this as well, but they tend to be entrepreneurial and know how to push and sell internally to make things happen. Usually they aren't nearly as demanding.

"Just Show Me"

Mainstream Buyers often will go to your website and three others, submit "Contact Us" inquiries, and sit back to have you and the other companies educate them about the space.

They want you to explain things to them with a demo over the phone. They can't or won't unilaterally push a new project through; they want more approval and support from more people. They're less risk-tolerant. They work at more complicated organizations.

This isn't bad, just different. Don't fall into the ego trap of thinking that because they don't "get it" as quickly as you that they're dumber or lazier—they aren't.

Stop bitching. Start learning.

Rather than bemoaning, "Why don't they get it?," just accept that it's not their job to figure you out. Start learning how to speak their language and how to help them buy. Especially at bigger companies, where it can be hard to buy and implement new ideas.

When you find ways to do this systematically—seeing six months of month-over-month growth in qualified leads (i.e., your Pipeline Creation Rate keeps going up six months in a row)—you're approaching hyper-growth territory.

WHY YOU'RE UNDERESTIMATING CUSTOMER LIFETIME VALUE

Everyone in tech talks about Customer Lifetime Value, also known as CLTV OR LTV. So they run a magic metric to calculate that their average customer is worth $10,000, and then say you're supposed to spend a certain amount on Sales and Marketing in order to grow—usually some fraction (one-third or so) of your LTV, or about the first year's worth of revenue from a customer.

Sounds fine—as long as you have the money to fund it. But the real problem is that this doesn't go far enough. Standard LTV calculations don't account for the "second order" viral and word-of-mouth customers—the ones that come in later, from the first customer referring their friends.

In other words, your average LTV should be higher, because the first customer should get extra credit for helping bring in their friends to your company. By underestimating the value of a customer, you may underinvest overall in acquiring them. Or, more commonly, you invest too much in Sales and Marketing and not enough in Customer Success, which, as you may recall, we believe is 5x more important.

By underestimating the value of a customer, you may under-invest overall in acquiring them.

Total Lifetime Revenue from a Single Average SaaS Customer

Let's imagine that sales closes its average enterprise customer for $10,000 a year. Nice. Then, in Year 2, average enterprise customer A adds $2,500 in additional licenses, for $12,500 total. Then in Year 3, they add another 25%, or $15,625 total. So direct revenue over the first three years is $38,125 from that first sale. Most customers last longer than three years, but let's stop there for now.

Second-Order Effects

At the end of Year 1, your champion quits Enterprise Customer A, but goes to Enterprise Customer B to do the exact same job, and buys your product again. (This happens about 10% of the time.) So that first sale is actually worth $42,000 (that first $38,000 above times 110%). And then it happens again in Year 2. So it's really $46,000. And at the end of Year 1, your champion tells three of her friends about your company. And one of them purchases. (This happens about 30% of the time.) So now the first sale is actually worth $60,000 with the second-order revenue—*as long as you're making your customers super-duper happy*. So your all-in CLTV, including second-order revenues, could be *two times your current estimate*.

Go ahead and figure out the perfect ratio of sales and marketing costs to CLTV to share with your board. Remember that the second-order effects compound. This is where Seeds become a growth driver. They're *essential* to fast, profitable growth.

Your all-in Customer Lifetime Value, including second-order revenues, could be double your current estimate.

Make Sales Scalable

Speeding up growth creates more problems than it solves.

If you're a small shop or not ready to aggressive expand, you can skip this Part and head to Part IV: Double Your Deal-size.

On the other hand, if you're not thinking about and figuring out what it will take to scale ... it's not going to happen anyway.

CHAPTER 9

Learn from Our Mistakes

What makes sales scalable? Where do people fail? What problems can you solve before you run into them?

GROWTH CREATES MORE PROBLEMS THAN IT SOLVES—BUT THEY ARE BETTER PROBLEMS

A top engineer from EchoSign, who had strong experience in growing both consumer Internet and enterprise technology companies, told me a while back that the number one reason he disliked SaaS/enterprise selling: It never gets easier.

His point was, once you solve the problems for Big Customer #1, then you get 10 more Big Customers, which mean 10x more problems. Then 100 more customers, which is 100x more problems. It gets worse, not better.

A fair point for the development team of a technology company. And especially true if you have a consulting or services business.

But one of my top learnings from EchoSign, going out to all you technology startups and founders out there: it gets easier in other ways. Once you get past 50 employees, it gets a lot easier. Once you break through $10 million in ARR, it gets a lot easier. And once you break through about $15–20 million in ARR, it gets truly, dramatically, a whole lot easier.

It's not that it gets any easier to grow, or hit your plan, or make your investors happy. That stays just as hard. And competition gets harder as you cross this point—your competition sees it, and tries harder. And more enter the space.

But much of the *operational pain,* especially in recurring revenue SaaS companies, seems to go away around $10–15 million in ARR. At that point:

- Your customer base is highly diverse, and not dependent on any whales.

- You have enough reference accounts. You want more—but don't *need*—more logos, as great as they are.
- Your sales and client success teams are working as a team, as an imperfect but effective engine, and not dependent on a single rock star or two.
- You have a brand, maybe a small brand at first, but a real one. This is a key inflection point in the getting-easier process. More leads come in, more easily. Customers still need to be sold, for sure, but at least you don't have to kill yourself to get into the discussion.
- You can't be killed by BigCo entering the space or the competition. Wounded, yes, but not killed.
- Your product may still suck in a lot of ways, but it's pretty rich with features. You have what many customers need.
- You know the market so well, it's pretty easy to see two years out, not only from a product side, but also from a scaling revenue and team side.

Yes, you'll have to put another plate (or two) on the bench press every six months. And for the few companies that go public, it's a whole new level of pressure like you've never seen.

So growth won't magically eliminate all your worries, but it will get easier. And you'll keep coming up with new—and hopefully better—problems to solve.

Growth won't eliminate all your worries. You'll get new ones.

JASON'S TOP 12 MISTAKES IN BUILDING SALES TEAMS

I made all these mistakes at EchoSign, and I've seen founders at growing companies make them again, and again, and again. So here's my Top 12 list:

1. *You hire a sales rep to sell before you can prove you can do it yourself.* You have to prove it's sellable first. And the CEO/founders need to do the initial sales themselves, so that they understand how to make sales work. You can't outsource this.

2. *You hire a VP of Sales to sell before you prove you can do it yourself.* You gotta prove the process is at least just barely repeatable before you hire someone to turn up the volume and spin the wheel faster. You gotta build two reps that can hit quota before you hire a real VP of Sales.
3. *Any of your first two to three sales reps are folks you personally wouldn't buy from.* Because then you'll never trust them with your precious handful of leads, and they will fail, no matter how well they did in the last startup.
4. *You insist reps #4–400 are folks you personally would buy from.* It takes a village.
5. *You underpay.* The best salespeople want to make *money*. If you pay under-market, you get bottom of the barrel. Huge rookie error.
6. *Not (intentionally) going upmarket faster to Double Your Dealsize.* Nothing is an anomaly:
   - If you can get 1 enterprise customer—you can get 10.
   - If you have 1 customer in an industry—you can get 10.
   - The outliers aren't anomalies: They are The Future.
   - Corollary: Target bigger deals as soon as you can—same work, more dollars.
7. *Not firing a bad VPS in one sales cycle.*
   - You should know subjectively in just a few months—just 50% of the way through your average sales cycle
   - Numbers should increase in one sales cycle—with a keen focus on Revenue Per Lead
   - First few hires should be clear upgrades—and should be made quickly and seemingly effortlessly
8. *You ask your VP of Sales to carry a bag for too long.* Her job is to recruit a great deal and hit the overall plan, not to sell herself, not mostly. Have her own the whole number, the ARR plan, not an individual quota, not for very long, at least.
9. *You hire someone who last sold Nu Skin.* This can work later, but not in your first reps. They need to understand how to sell vaguely similar products at vaguely similar price points.
10. *You hire because she worked at Salesforce/Box/DropBox/ABC Famous Company.* Don't hire them because they worked at a well-known or hot company. Hire them because they can and have closed at least vaguely similar products at somewhat similar price

points. Not because they are one of 4,000 reps that sell a product at Salesforce.com, which has $8 billion+ in revenues, a proven brand, and huge infrastructure behind it.

11. *You allow any great reps to leave. You should strive for 0% voluntary attrition,* not to fire the bottom one-third. That's for boiler rooms. Great sales teams stick together. Great sales teams inspire each other. Great sales teams attract higher and higher quality reps as time goes on.
12. *Not doubling the plan.* Once the team was (finally) great, we exceeded the plan, every quarter of every year. Always. But ... I should have challenged us to do Even Better. I should have pushed harder the same way Parker at Zenefits pushed Sam to answer the question in early 2014: "What would it take to do $20 million instead this year instead of $10 million?"

ADVICE FROM THE VP SALES BEHIND LINKEDIN AND ECHOSIGN

If you didn't get a fancy title, would you still work for that CEO?

Brendon Cassidy was one of the first 25 employees at LinkedIn, building their corporate sales team from scratch, and he was the eighth employee at EchoSign, helping to take them from $1 million to $50 million in ARR and an acquisition by Adobe, then spent time as VP Sales at Talkdesk.

Here are lessons he learned from both his success and failures. It's easier to learn from failure. Because what went wrong is obvious and leaves a resounding impression you can't ignore. Learning from success is harder, because success covers up mistakes Enter Brendon:

Lesson #1: Stop Blaming Others

Nobody wants to hear "can't" or "it's not my fault." It's not Marketing. It's not Product. It's not your salespeople. It's on you. There is always a solution, even if it's not obvious. You need to help drive the organization to the solution to the problem. If you are facing disaster, and you tell your CEO what needs to happen and he refuses to do it, then quit. Just don't whine about it. Next time do better due diligence on the CEO before agreeing to work for them.

Lesson #2: Build for the Present, Not the Past

A common theme: You hire a person who won before at Company X, then he/she comes in and implements the exact same methodology in your company that worked before. But nothing is ever the same.

Sometimes changing one thing—lead velocity, Average Sales Price, sales cycle, pricing model, target buyer/market, competition, stage, and so on—might mean you need to take a totally different approach to generating leads and selling. Step back before you copy down the prior playbook, and look at the numbers and funnel. What should work the same? What might need to be changed or adapted or re-created?

Be objective and honest with yourself, because it's hard to admit you might be wrong, need to change your plan/playbook, or even admit that you don't know what to do or sometimes feel lost!

Lesson #3: Hire the Best—Period

Surrounding yourself with superstar talent should be a constant goal. Early in my career I hired the best people I could ... but who were not quite as skilled or smart as me. That's inexperience and insecurity and makes scaling sales much harder.

The reality is that any hiring shortcut you take now means you are going to have to work 10x more later to compensate for any shortfalls, such as running too many of your reps' deals because they can't close them themselves, having to coach too much, having high sales team turnover, or missed goals.

Lesson #4: Pay Well for Success

I don't get CEOs or VPs of Sales who are cheap when it comes to paying their sales people. It's incredibly hard to find great sales talent, much less hire and retain them. Pay them well. Trust me, they can go elsewhere, while the B and C players stay.

Lesson #5: Make Sure the CEO Fits

Don't take a job just for the title, investors, or company. Pick the wrong CEO to work with and you'll be miserable. Be honest about what works for you before you make a decision.

Top Five To-Do's for Great Sales Leaders

To-Do #1: Drive Deal Size Up as Quickly as Possible

Small deals pay the bills, big deals drive growth. Small deals are a fantastic way to get started, get fast feedback, and build testimonials and word of mouth. But fast revenue growth usually occurs with bigger deals.

To-Do #2: Great Reps Perform in 30 Days

At Talkdesk, our first rep closed $150,000 in his first 30 days. That's not luck. You won't always see sales numbers rise that fast, but if you're gut tells you that a person was a mis-hire, your gut is probably right.

> **If your gut tells you that person was a mis-hire, your gut is probably right.**

To-Do #3: Honesty Is Critical, Up and Down the Sales Stack

There's a bias toward being dishonest in sales. You and your reps are too optimistic about deals, and this clouds the truth.

Not knowing where reps and managers honestly stand—with deals, pipelines, or each other—creates uncertainty and anxiety. You can't forecast without coaching reps to be brutally honest about deals. You can't solve problems if you are too busy or nervous to dig into the sometimes painful or embarrassing truth of your situation—and share it with the team and CEO.

To-Do #4: Great Sales Teams Stay Together

Again and again. Folks that know how to make a lot of money together want to continue to do so. You should see very little churn among your top sales team members and managers—if any. If you see material churn, there's a real problem somewhere.

To-Do #5: Outbound (Spears) and Inbound (Nets) Aren't Either/Or, They Are "Yes"

Always be doing both. The question is just the relative ratio, and when to begin or expand each.

CHAPTER 10

Specialization: Your #1 Sales Multiplier

If you haven't specialized your sales team roles yet, *nothing* will make a bigger impact in your ability to increase sales productivity and grow.

If you don't specialize, you're going to struggle.

WHY SALESPEOPLE SHOULDN'T PROSPECT

Specializing sales roles is a cornerstone of *Predictable Revenue*. As a quick review, one of the biggest sales productivity killers is having salespeople do multiple roles: some mix of qualifying their own inbound leads, cold prospecting, closing, and account management into one general "sales" role. Let's look at the case of juggling prospecting and closing, as an example of why it's such a problem:

- *Ineffective:* Experienced sales people hate to prospect, and are usually terrible at it. Plus, why have your *most expensive* people make cold calls?
- *Erratic focus:* Even if a salesperson does do some prospecting successfully, as soon as they generate pipeline, they become too busy to prospect. It's not sustainable, and leads to up-and-down rollercoaster results.
- *Unclear metrics:* It's harder to break out and keep track of key metrics (inbound leads, qualification and conversion rates, Customer Success rates ...) when multiple functions are done by the same team.

Different roles makes it easier to break out different steps in your processes, which means clearer metrics.

- *Less visibility, accountability:* When things aren't working, lumped responsibilities obscure what or who is gong wrong, making it harder to isolate and fix problems.

It's not just prospecting and closing that conflict. These same issues apply if your salespeople are both closing accounts and managing them, or any kind of combination.

Without specializing, your team will struggle. Full stop. Doesn't matter if you have amazing customers, product, and closers—you won't make the most of any of it without the right structure.

In football, rugby, baseball, hockey, cricket, basketball ... well, every sport I know, there are specialized roles. Goalie. Forward. Point Guard. Catcher. There's gotta be a team sport that doesn't have positions, but I haven't found one yet.

Specialization is standard in Silicon Valley. And growing. But still the exception. So why do most companies expect one salesperson to fill all their own "positions" of prospecting, responding to leads, closing, and managing accounts? Usually *because that's how it's always been done*.

Exactly how you make specialization work for your particular situation is up to you. The principle is about helping your people *focus and do fewer things better*—because when salespeople multitask (overtask), most end up doing many things poorly.

When salespeople multitask (overtask), 90% of them end up doing many things poorly.

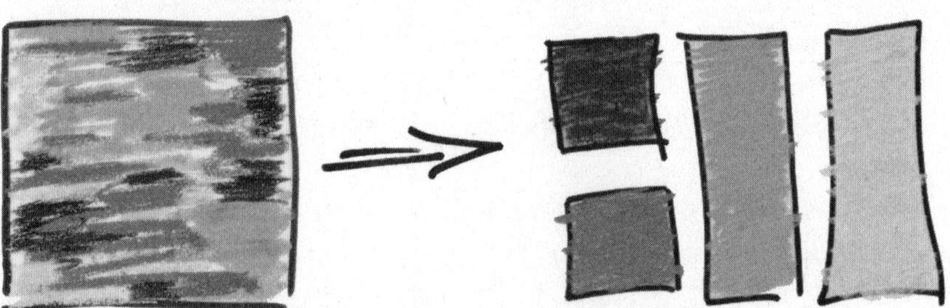

FIGURE 10.1 Specialize people so they can do fewer things, better.

Specializing your roles is the #1 most important thing for creating predictable, scalable sales growth.

Prospectors need to prospect. They shouldn't close; respond to inbound leads, or act as part-time telemarketers when marketing's trying to fill events.

Okay … and when you do need prospectors to juggle tasks, try to have their non-prospecting work fill up less than 10–20% of their time. The same is true of new-business closers: other kinds of work should be a small percentage of their time. Think complement, not distraction.

And, yes, your closers should prospect—we will never tell you that anyone on your team should wait around for business to come to them—but only to a handful of strategic accounts or partners—think special situations, not tons of cold calling or cold emailing.

If you're seeing recurring problems in your team, or some vital function just isn't happening or is weak across multiple people, look first to structure. Maybe changing roles and responsibilities is the Forcing Function needed to deal with it. For example, with the right Sales Development team to help pre-qualify inbound leads or focus on prospecting, any "sales and marketing" divide mostly goes away.

While every team is different and creates different flavors, start with the template of four categories of roles that fit most (but of course, not all) companies:

1. Inbound lead qualification
2. Outbound prospecting
3. Closing new business
4. Post-sales roles, such as account management, professional services, and Customer Success

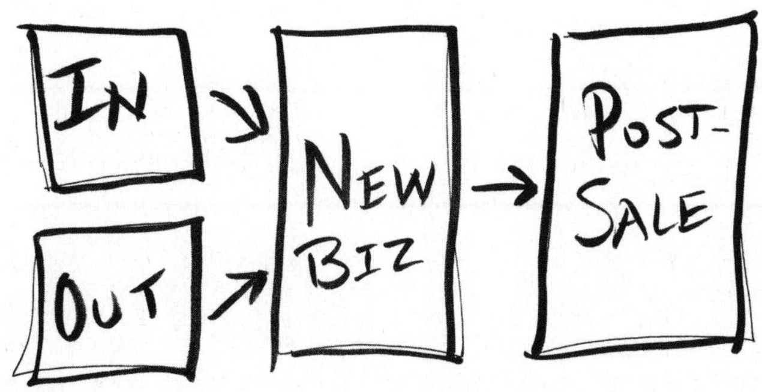

FIGURE 10.2 The Four Core sales roles.

When *not* to specialize, or do it very differently … because exceptions exist for every rule:

- You have a very simple sales process, like a one- or two-call-close product.
- You're in a business or segment currently succeeding with generalized salespeople (like financial services advisors). Don't fix what ain't broken … but also don't be afraid to try new ideas.
- Common sense or proven experience—not tradition—says it just isn't right for you.

CASE STUDY: HOW CLIO RESTRUCTURED SALES IN THREE MONTHS

It can feel overwhelming if you need to restructure a sales team. Roles, quotas, comp plans, territories, Salesforce.com changes … Clio tackled all of this at once.

Clio is a fast-growing SaaS company in Vancouver, whose CEO is Jack Newton (now there's a cool action hero name!). Clio sells practice management software that helps lawyers run their firms better. After growing from 3 to 18 "generalized reps" in less than two years, in 2012 Clio hit some sales team growth problems. Those generalized reps did it all—prospecting, following up on inbound leads, closing new deals, and managing those customers. Around this time, Jack came across a summary of Predictable Revenue called "Why Salespeople Shouldn't Prospect," and he and his cofounder George Psiharis knew they had to finally specialize the team.

The first step toward restarting Clio's sales growth was to transform this team of 18 generalized reps into three specialized teams of 6 reps each.

The three original reps had it easy. "The world was their oyster": they had a lot of inbound interest; they didn't need structure; they could cherry-pick leads and deals to close a lot of business they didn't need territories. By the time Clio had 10 salespeople they'd started feeling growing pains.

- The team was frequently stepping on each other's toes, such as inadvertently starting to work the same deals.

- There was a lot of unhealthy competition on the team, and they wouldn't help each other.
- The reps' success depended wholly on themselves to sink or swim, as there was no sales "system" or support.

Clio went with three, not four, key sales roles. Clio's executive team felt the sales team could do much, much better if they got out of each other's way and worked together to systematically break down and tackle the market. Adapting Predictable Revenue's specialization ideas and customizing them to their unique situation, they created three new roles:

- *Six prospectors:* Tasked with getting into larger law firms.
- *Six closers (Account Executives):* Tasked with closing larger law firms.
- *An "engagement team" of six reps:* Mixing both inbound lead response and closing small law firms/deals (less than $100 in monthly revenue).

To make this transition, Clio had to rework a lot of important sales systems: designing new roles, new quotas, new comp plans, creating a territory system (which they'd never had), figuring out which rep should go into which team, changing Salesforce.com, and a lot more. They dove in headfirst.

Lessons Learned

Lesson #1: *Simplify comp:* Previous comp plans had a ton of rules and regulations around the kinds of deals that would be eligible for quota. Clio was trying to drive the right behaviors with those rules, but they created too much confusion and too many obstacles.

For example: Clio used to have rules and conditions with channel partner deals, and often salespeople didn't benefit at all if a partner closed a deal. Now, $1 of revenue is $1 of revenue no matter where it comes from.

By removing confusing comp goals and triggers, salespeople partner, collaborate, and close much more because everyone's aligned.

> **Salespeople partner, collaborate, and close much more when everyone's aligned.**

Lesson #2: *Overpay salespeople during the transition:* During their restructuring, Clio paid the team a flat fee/fixed bonus for three months while gathering data and figuring out new quotas and goals. Clio wanted the team to feel comfortable helping switch to the new model, without distracting them.

Lesson #3: *Create a collaborative, not competitive, sales environment:* Fun or friendly competition is helpful and energizing. Hurtful or "real" competition kills your team.

By shifting to territories plus specialization, the sales team didn't feel anymore that it was a zero sum game. Jack says they now have an "unbelievably collaborative sales team" that helps each other close deals, that roots for each other, and trades tips, best practices, and sale techniques. Beforehand, this never happened.

CAN YOU BE TOO SMALL, OR TOO BIG, TO SPECIALIZE?

> Everyone is different—you have to adapt this to your specific situation and market.

If You're Big

We spoke to a division of IBM—some people that really liked the ideas of specialization and dedicated prospectors. Yet implementation seemed impossible, even with the head of sales as a believer, because of how complicated things are in a big company. At big companies, meaningful change requires involving lots of pieces: people, politics, legacy practices and systems, all of which make change harder and more complex.

Now, if everyone's struggling and things are dire, you may need a drastic restructuring, breaking your team into the different specialties. But if you can afford some time, if the house isn't on fire, you can experiment with new roles on the side—a skunk works approach. By "doing it before pitching it," you have real experience and credibility to draw from, rather than just guesswork. It's easier to add a prospecting team to your current sales org than to restructure what you have. This can work whether the role's around Customer Success, a new sales segment, prospecting, handling inbound leads, or another position.

If you're going to build your own *Predictable Revenue*–style specialized role system, all you need is a couple of people to start. It doesn't have to be a big deal—just do it and ask for forgiveness later. And if it doesn't work out for some reason, then no one has to know, right?

If You're Small

"*What if I have only one or two people in sales?*" is the most common question regarding specialization. If you're small, start by specializing your *time*, to focus on what needs to get done, but isn't.

- *Block out regular chunks of time* on your calendar—say one to two or more hours, or even a full day—for prospecting or your other top priority that isn't happening. At those times, *turn off* any distractions.
- *Come up with one to three specific goals* for your time, like "Reach out to five prospects through LinkedIn/email/phone," "Make five mapping calls," "Add 10 prospects to my list."
- *Try daily, weekly, or monthly goals*, to see what works for you.
- *Get a buddy system going* with a friend or partner to keep you accountable—and review each other's goals together. Just as if you were starting a new fitness program with a buddy.
- *Get help:* Is there a relative, child, intern, virtual assistant, or outsourcing service you can get help from? If it's prospecting that you're trying to do part time, there are companies that can help take over the parts that you don't like or don't have time for, i.e., building lists of targets and contact information, getting basic research information, sending initial emails and handling email responses and follow-up.

Even if there's some part of your sales process that you don't like to do, it's valuable to do it for a while first so that you have hands-on experience. It'll help you better hire and manage someone else when you're ready.

SPECIALIZATION: TWO COMMON OBJECTIONS

Objection #1: It'll Hurt Customer Relationships

"Doesn't passing off a prospect or customer from one person to another create problems? Shouldn't the same person be building a relationship from day one with a customer, then owning and maintaining it?"

No—not if you have a predefined process to hand off customers thoughtfully, and you set their expectations appropriately. In fact, prospects and customers get *better service* this way. With specialists at each step, prospects are always getting fast responses appropriate to what they need.

> **Prospects and customers get *better* service when you specialize.**

It's hard for a salesperson who's working on proposals, or traveling, to drop everything and get back right away to a new inbound lead, an urgent problem at a current customer, or to focus on much of anything important that's not getting them to their quota this period. So by specializing—in a way that makes sense for your business—you're doing customers a favor, too.

Objection #2: "Those Four Roles Don't Fit Us"

The core roles discussed are not absolute requirements—but a starting template for you to adapt.

Almost every B2B company should have at least three of those four roles, but there are exceptions, as we listed out earlier. Implement the principle behind specialization—*focus*—in your own way. Give people fewer, more important things that they can do better.

Also—the principle works or is already at work in *any* team—marketing, customer support, partners, engineering. Why not do it in sales, too?

Four Important Reasons to Just Do It

We realize some of you still need help convincing your team to go *all in* with specialization. It can be daunting to take a sales team that has been closing and managing their own accounts, and then ask them to change … everything. Here are the four essential reasons for doing it:

1. *Effectiveness:* When people are focused on one area, they become experts. For example, in 10 years, we've never met a team of

generalized salespeople that didn't struggle with generating or responding to leads.

2. *Farm team/talent:* Having multiple roles in sales gives you a simple career path to hire, train, grow, and promote people internally. This creates a much cheaper, less risky, and more effective way to recruit, rather than relying too heavily on outside hires. (A rule of thumb: Over the long term, grow two-thirds of your people internally and hire one-third externally for new ideas and blood.)
3. *Insights:* By breaking your roles into separate functions, you can easily identify and fix your bottlenecks. When everyone is doing everything, it's like having a tangled ball of yarn you can't tease apart.
4. *Scalability:* Specialization makes it easier to hire, train, measure, grow, and promote people across the board.

How you do it may be different than the basic roles we've laid out. Whatever your take on specialization is, find a way to *DO IT*.

For the latest updates, examples, and videos on how to specialize, checkout www.FromImpossible.com

SPECIALIZATION SNAPSHOT AT ACQUIA

In the section on Outbound Prospecting "Spears" in Part II, we laid out how Acquia built an outbound prospecting program to speed up sales growth and ensure that getting to $100 million was a "when," not "if," scenario.

Here's a snapshot from 2014 of how Acquia specialized their sales roles across the company, to show you how far you can go. Your own ratios will vary, they're affected by things like lead volumes, deal sizes, and sale complexity.

- 60 quota-carrying salespeople/closers
- 20 presales solution architects/sales engineers (1:3 ratio to closers)
- 20 dedicated outbound prospectors (1:3 ratio to closers)
- 15 junior reps dedicated to qualifying inbound leads ("Market Response Reps" or "Inbound SDRs")

- 20 Account Managers working with current customers (1:3 ratio to closers)
- 8 Channel Partner Managers
- 5 people in Sales Operations and the Deal Desk (helping process orders)
- 15 in management (SVP/VPs/AVPs/Directors/Managers), ~10% of headcount

Rule of thumb: It's hard for a manager to be effective with more than 10 direct reports.

It's hard for a manager to be effective with more than 10 direct reports.

CHAPTER 11

Sales Leaders

Companies keep "mis-firing by mis-hiring" the most important role on the sales team.

THE #1 MIS-HIRE IS THE VP/HEAD OF SALES

There's a venture capitalist saying (which we hate) that goes something like, "You've got to get past the carcass of your first VP of Sales" or "It's with your second VP of Sales that you really start selling," or variants thereof. It especially bugs us because we're firm believers in hiring and training fewer, more committed people, rather than taking a "churn and burn" approach.

But … those VCs are right. In startups, it seems as though the majority of first VP Sales fail: they don't even make it past 12 months. We've heard that the average tenure for VP Sales of early companies in the valley *averages* 18 months, so that includes the winners—*ouch*.

Let's look at what those VP Sales *should* do. Because most founders/CEOs are looking for the wrong things—especially the first-time founders, or founders who haven't spent much time in or with Sales.

Top Five Things a Great VP of Sales Does at a Growing Company

1. *Recruiting*. You hire a VP Sales not to sell, but to recruit, train, and coach other people to sell. So recruiting is 20% or more of their time, because you're going to need a team to sell. And recruiting great reps and making them successful is the #1 most important thing your VP Sales will do. And the great ones knows this.
2. *Backfilling and helping his/her sales team*. Helping coach reps to close deals (not doing it for them). Getting hands-on when needed, or in

big deals. Spotting issues before they blow up. Seeing opportunities ahead of the horizon.

3. *Sales tactics*. Training, onboarding. Territories (yes, you need them). Quotas, comp. How to compete. Pitch scripts. Coordinating FUD and anti-FUD. Segmenting customers. Reports. Ensuring everyone on the team, including themselves, can get what they need from the sales/CRM system.
4. *Sales strategy*. What markets should we expand into? What's our main bottleneck? Where should our time and money go? What few key metrics tell us the most about the health of our team and our growth?
5. *Creating and selling deals themselves*. This is last of the top five. Important for select deals. But last on the list, because if your VP Sales (or CEO, for that matter) is doing the closing rather than their team, you're bottlenecked. No scaling for you, sir.

So … don't hire a VP Sales *until you are ready to scale, build, and fund a small, growing sales team*. Usually this means you have at least two salespeople—who are not the CEO or head of sales—who are succeeding.

Don't hire a VP Sales until you are ready to scale, build, and fund a small, growing sales team.

And any VPs of Sales who doesn't see this themselves probably isn't a great long-term VP Sales for you. Instead, he/she is either just a great individual contributor, a great builder, or a simply a flawed or desperate candidate.

THE RIGHT VP SALES FOR YOUR STAGE

Early stage and fast-growing companies have a special leadership problem. The head of sales they need today may not be the one they need tomorrow.

What Kind of VP Sales Do You Need?

Type 1: "The Evangelist" (gets you from nothing to $1–$2 million)

The Evangelist is someone who is smart and passionate about your product from day 1. They get it. The Evangelist can immediately go out and

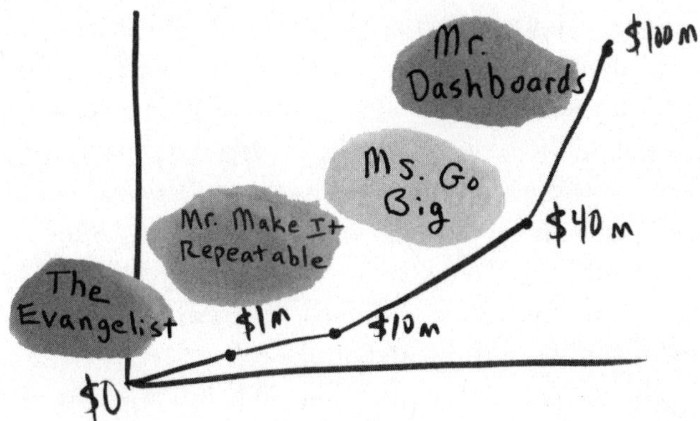

FIGURE 11.1 The type of VP Sales skills you need changes by stage.

just start selling from day 2, and deals will happen simply because of their *passion*. The Evangelist can seem like just who you need to hire—if you've never hired a VP Sales. You'll like the Evangelist—a lot.

The problem with Evangelists? They've never actually built or *scaled* or *systematized* sales. They know how to think creatively and cross-functionally. They're fun to work with. But 9 times out of 10, this is a waste of a hire and your time. *Why? Because the founder/CEO has to be the Evangelist, along with the first one or two reps you hire.*

Type 2: "Mr. Make-It-Repeatable" (go from $1 million to $10 million)

In this phase, you have some customers. Not a ton, but some. You have some in-bound leads. You've hired one to four reps on your own. But you have no idea, or ability, of how to scale and make it *predictable*.

This job is about taking "something is happening here and there and we're not always sure why" to "something is happening over and over again and we *know* why." This VP Sales has to make it happen. He can't pretend or hide behind PowerPoint presentations or "pipeline" dashboards.

This is the lucky find that every early company that's ready to grow really needs. The problem is that most VPs of Sales struggle in this phase, because most got their titles by successfully growing something *that was already regularly working* systematically—not by being the one who systematized it.

Here's what happens with Mr. Make-It-Repeatable: Everything seems much simpler and clearer. Almost immediately, revenue goes up. Because they know how to close, recruit, hire, and coach. And they know how to build the basic processes you need to make it predictable.

The prior two stages were about getting off the ground to having "something," and then turning that into a repeatable system. It's extremely unlikely any VP Sales candidate from Salesforce, from SuccessFactors, from Oracle, from whatever current Hot or Big Company, can possibly fill either of these early stage roles.

They will all almost certainly fail. Why? They just never even remotely did it.

Joining Salesforce when it was at $1 billion in revenue, even as a manager? Yes, it's SaaS … but the sales processes and challenges at $1 billion–plus just are so different from an early company.

When someone has only worked for a Big (or Hot) Company with a Big (or Hot) Brand, they have an unfair advantage in everything they've done there. How much was it them versus the situation? Rising tides and all.

Plus, they are often unknowingly dependent on all the free gifts they got before.... Easier meetings with executives or investors. Easier hiring. More manpower and budget support—for everything: A "real" marketing team and budget, admin support, and lots of inbound leads. Someone to write sales collateral and proposals for them.

It's not their fault, but often they just won't understand how to do either of these early phases. It doesn't mean they *can't* do it; just be very, very careful in hiring them and *don't let a resume blind you—or your investors*.

Don't let a resume blind you—or your investors.

Type 3: "Ms. Go Big" (go from $10 million to $40 million)

Now we're talking about pouring it on. When a VP Sales comes into a decently funded company with $10–$20 million in annual revenue … it's mostly a process already. The main pieces are working, so you mostly do the same things, but more.

Hire the right people. Increase junior hires to further specialize and develop a big talent pool. Make field sales work. Tune your Customer Success programs. Grow outbound prospecting. Get the lead generation engine cranking with the VP Marketing.

It's hard to find these candidates but you can find them. Get them from a company that just went through this phase.

But don't expect 95% of these candidates to be able to do the earlier phase (getting from $1–$10 million), if they didn't do it before.

Type 4: Mr. Dashboards

Unfortunately, this is what you get a lot of when you try to recruit out of the Big Companies. Mr. Dashboard really understands how to sell up. How to make an internal presentation. And he often looks pretty good in a suit. Your board will probably love him. But really, all he does all day is look at and think about dashboards and meet with his managers.

What changes can I make to the team to get the dashboards up? How do I get more resources? More budget? Who can I hire, and who can I fire? How do I get rid of the bottom 10%? Where should the sales kickoff be this year, and what sort of suite can I get? What events can I do behind a secret rope for my top 50 prospects?

Look, at some point, you may need Mr. Dashboard. That's fine. A manager of managers of managers. But whatever you do, don't hire one until you are past Unstoppable. Because unless they did it for real before they were a Mr. Dashboard, they have no idea how to get you to and past $5 million or $10 million or $20 million.

JASON'S 10 FAVORITE INTERVIEW QUESTIONS

Ready to hire a new VP Sales? Let me give you a partial interview script that may help a bit. You'll have to vary it for different types of SaaS businesses—a bit. But it will basically work for all SaaS companies from say $200,000 in ARR to $10 million in ARR or so—a wide range. (After that, you'll probably be looking for a different type of VP Sales. We'll get to that in the next section.)

Before we get there, as a reminder, I strongly recommend that you hire one to two sales reps at a minimum (ideally two) before you hire a VP Sales. And make them successful first. So you can practice what you preach, knowing what success looks like before hiring. And also to get big enough so a VP Sales can actually help, not hinder you.

Practice what you preach, knowing what success looks like before hiring.

Now if you are ready, but haven't done it before in SaaS, here are *10 good screening questions* to see if you have a real VP Sales candidate in hand—or not. These questions mostly don't have right or wrong answers, but will help you determine the quality and fit of the candidates:

1. How big a team do you think we need right now, given what you know? (If he/she can't answer, right or wrong, then pass.)
2. What deal sizes have you sold to, on average and range? (If it's not a similar fit to you, pass. If he/she can't answer fluently, pass.)
3. Tell me about the teams you've directly managed, and how you built them. (If he/she can't describe how they built a team, then pass.)
4. What sales tools have you used and what works for you? What hasn't worked well? (If they don't understand sales tools, they aren't a real VP Sales.)
5. Who do you know right now that would join you on our sales team? (All good candidates should have a few in mind.) Then: Tell me about them, by background if not name.
6. How should sales and client success/management work together? (This will tell you how well he/she understands the true customer life cycle.)
7. Tell me about deals you've lost to competitors. What's going to be key in our space about winning versus competitors?
8. How do you deal with FUD in the marketplace? (This will ferret out the ones who know how to compete—or not.)
9. Do you work with sales engineers and sales support? If so, what role do they need to play at this stage, when capital is finite? (This will show you if he/she can play at an early-stage SaaS startup successfully—and if he knows how to scale once you're ready.)
10. What will my revenues look like 120 days after I hire you? (Have him/her explain to you what will happen. There's no correct answer, but there are many wrong answers.)

Okay, let's make it 11 questions:

11. *How should sales and marketing work together at our phase?* Beyond "blah blah" generalities, and into specifics. This will tell you if he/she understands lead generation and how to work a lead funnel.

These questions aren't magic. None of them are particularly insightful or profound in isolation. In fact, hopefully they are kind of obvious. *But what they will do is create a dialogue.* From them, you'll be able to determine: (a) if this candidate is for real or not, (b) if this candidate can really be a true VP, a leader, a manager—or not—and take you to the next level—or not, and (c) if the candidate is a good fit for your company and space in particular.

If any of the answers are terrible, pass. If any don't make sense, pass. If you don't learn something in the interview, pass. And if you know more about any of these questions than the candidate does, pass. Your VP Sales needs to be smarter than you in sales, sales processes, and building and scaling a sales team.

Your VP Sales needs to be smarter than you in sales, sales processes, and building and scaling a sales team.

CHAPTER 12
Hiring Best Practices for Sales

Your people and culture determine your destiny.

SIMPLE HIRING TRICKS

Predictable Recruiting (with Jon Bischke, CEO, Entelo)

You can take almost all the ideas in this book, especially around Nailing A Niche, lead generation, and sales specialization, and apply them to how you recruit. It's just another form of marketing and selling.

Specialization: Just like the fastest-growing SaaS companies have divided customer-facing functions into roles like outbound prospecting, inbound lead response, closing, and Customer Success, you can do the same thing on the recruiting front. You should have sales development or prospectors (*sourcers*), closing (*recruiters and hiring managers*), and "postsales" (HR or *people ops*).

Measure activities, conversion rates, and elapsed time at each stage of the recruiting funnel. Your outbound recruiting team, the sourcers, focus on reaching out to a set number of candidates each week the same way you have activity metrics for sales prospectors. You can track things like message response rates (whether over email or social), phone conversations per week, how often candidates are clicking on links you send them, which templates are performing best, and so forth.

If you know your hiring plan, your conversion rates at each stage (e.g., phone screen, first onsite, second onsite, offer letter, etc.), average time in each stage, and what's required to close your top candidates, you can back into how many candidates you need to reach out to in order to hit your hiring goals.

Do You Want a "Builder" or a "Grower"?

We find most personality tests too complicated to be of everyday practical use. But the idea of builders versus growers can be useful anytime. When you're in an exploration phase of figuring out how something should work, such as with a new company, sales function, or program, look for people who like to figure things out: *Builders*. When you have a system all figured out and just need to hire more people into it, look for people who are great at following a predefined system: *Growers*.

Both Builders and Growers are valuable. But Growers struggle when the systems aren't defined, and Builders struggle when there's "nothing to figure out anymore."

Develop Reps Who Are "Business People Who Can Sell," Not "Salespeople"

When a salesperson is an *expert* who knows how your product can help customers—and when it's *not* a fit—they will build trust and relationships quickly with the right prospects. There's no better way to quickly ramp a salesperson than to find ways to rotate your new hires around your company, giving them hands-on experience with support, product, or account management. Slowing down their start on full-time selling, so they can get hands-on experience and accelerate time-to-expertise, can speed up their ramp time.

WHEN DOING SOMETHING NEW, START WITH TWO

The time has probably going to come when you have to build a sales team or create a new function; it may be day one if you have plenty of capital and are selling to large enterprises. It may be X months down the road, once you close a few deals that are large enough to justify hiring a sales rep. It might be five years down the road (like DropBox), when you decide to add a corporate/enterprise edition to your freemium app. Or when you decide to create a dedicated outbound/Customer Success/? team.

Now you may somehow have enough capital to hire a VP of Sales and a bunch of reps right then and there. But most likely, you won't have the resources to hire a whole sales team upfront. You'll want to start with one experienced rep.

And there's only one problem with that: *No matter how well that rep does, you won't learn anything. You need at least two to learn.* Here's why:

- *If your first rep does poorly, you'll have no idea why.* The rep will blame you, your crappy product, your crappy company, your crappy lack of marketing, which may all be correct. But if the rep is a bad fit, that may be the real reason. You just won't know.
- *If your first rep does well (our experience), you'll still have no idea why.* Does the product sell itself? Is it the rep's suave phone skills? Is it your deal size, and are your customers representative of the ones you'll really get in the future? Or is this rep only good at a certain type of customer—and are you leaving other potential customers behind? You just … won't know.

At EchoSign, I got this advice from one of our advisors with more experience than me in this area, but I ignored it, because I was focused on saving money and, really, in a mistaken attempt to *keep it simple*. So for our first rep, I narrowed the candidates down to two guys. One was super smart, super eloquent, and explained our product well. The other, well … less sharp, but great at outbound and at prospecting, and never discouraged. He'd make 50 calls a day, 20 days a month, even if he got 1,000 hang-ups.

You can guess I went with the first guy. And he was and is great. I mean, *great*. He let me focus on closing a few key strategic accounts and he just banged out the rest. The engineering team worked well with him; they loved his smarts and insights, and the customers loved him, too. He's still with EchoSign and Adobe to this day, and has done amazingly well.

The only problem was that *I* learned nothing. I didn't gain any knowledge about building and scaling sales processes for our company. It wasn't until we finally had a second great rep that I could learn and that I learned about new segments we could sell into. And about how to sell at lower price points, and in higher volumes. Finally I could compare and contrast. Before hiring the second rep, I could guess and I could squint at data, but I didn't have a well-rounded view on what was needed.

Look, if you've been a VP of Sales yourself for 10 years, ignore this. But most of you haven't built or led an inside sales team before. So you're gonna need to learn. So even if it seems expensive, hire two. To start.

Then learn ... and go from there. It will be better, and thus cheaper, in the end. And the rule of two can apply to any new function, not only sales.

When you do something new, hire two. With one person, you can't tell if what is and is not working is due to the person or to the process.

THE $100 MILLION HUBSPOT SALES MACHINE: RECRUITING AND COACHING ESSENTIALS

Mark Roberge is HubSpot's Chief Revenue Officer and built the sales team from $0 to over $100 million. He's the author of *The Sales Acceleration Formula*. Mark developed a four-part strategy while scaling his team from nothing to hundreds of reps:

1. Hire the same type of successful sales person.
2. Consistently train them the same way.
3. Provide each salesperson with the same quantity and quality of leads.
4. Have the salespeople work the leads using the same process.

If those four things happen, then they'll be successful in achieving their mission. Here are more details on how Mark's sales machine hires and trains....

It's all about recruiting. Especially for small teams, looking to scale is to put the effort into hiring, and making it your top priority. In his first couple of years, Mark spent 40% of his time on recruiting. Interview strategically: Mark developed criteria for hiring for sales success, even if people didn't have a sales background. He wanted to hire people who'd shown past sales success as well as people with untapped potential. After hundreds of interviews and hires, he found five indicators of future success.

Hire people who show past success as well as people with untapped potential.

1. Coachability (#1!)
2. Prior success

3. Work ethic
4. Curiosity
5. Intelligence

Hire people who show past success as well as people with untapped potential. Their prior success doesn't have to be in sales. HubSpot's got an Olympic gold medalist and a professional comic who made it to Comedy Central. These are people who went after something and achieved it. That's what you're looking for.

Invest in running a "real" training program. Too many companies have as their training plan, "Go shadow some people." HubSpot's salespeople spend their first month in a classroom-style setting. To gain an understanding of the product, they create a blog and a website from scratch. They experience the actual pains and successes of HubSpot's primary customers: professional marketers who need to generate leads online ... so salespeople are able to connect on a far deeper level with prospects and leads. After a month, new hires pass a 150-question exam and six different certification tests on the HubSpot product, sales methodology, and the concept of inbound marketing. How can you put your reps in your customers' shoes, to create empathy?

Take coaching seriously. The biggest impact on sales productivity comes from your managers' effectiveness in coaching their people. HubSpot uses a matrix-driven sales coaching model. On the second day of each month, Mark meets with the sales directors, each of whom oversees a few managers and has about 40 sales reps under them. Because Mark takes coaching seriously, these meetings force a coaching culture onto the whole organization. Good coaching is both caring for your reps' success and trying to find out the one thing at a time to work on (not 10 things) that's going to make the biggest difference.

CASE STUDY: HOW TO CUT DOWN ON WASTED INTERVIEWING

Paul Fifield is the Commercial Director at UNiDAYS and former CRO of Ceros. He's built sales and prospecting teams in the UK and United States, even hiring them remotely from another country. We met Paul while he was working in the UK as CRO for Ceros, when he remotely hired their initial outbound prospecting team based in New York. In their first four weeks of prospecting, the Ceros outbound team (all new hires) set up conversations with online marketing departments from over 70 brands, including Chrysler, Cartier, General Electric, and Hugo Boss. Not too shabby!

People always matter, but when you're doing something new, the first hires make an even bigger difference. It's easier to hire people into a system that's already working. Paul wanted Builders, not Growers, to get the team started. He put together a hands-on process to efficiently run recruiting remotely. It took a lot more time than slapping up a standard job posting online, but was worth it. Paul's recruiting process isn't specific to sales; it can be adapted for any kind of role at your company.

> **People always matter, but when you're doing something new, the first hires make an even bigger difference.**

Step 1: *Create a clear picture of who you want to hire.*

Step 2: *Write authentic, interesting job descriptions.* Paul's descriptions read more like a personal letter or invitation than the boring, generic descriptions most companies use.

> **Find the job description and download-able hiring guide at FromImpossible.com/recruiting.**

Step 3: *Include a video in the job description.* The video made it easier for people to get a feel for who Paul is and what he stands for. This helps to better attract the right people and turn off those who won't be a cultural fit.

Step 4: *Spread the word.* Paul didn't need to do a big sourcing project; he got enough applicants (about 400 in total for all three roles) just by posting on LinkedIn and forwarding it to friends and acquaintances. [Note from Paul: "Next time I will spend more time "prospecting" to find the right kind of people in addition to looking via word of mouth."]

Step 5: *Assign homework.* Paul sent an email outlining the steps of his interviewing process to all those who had applied, as well as anyone else he thought had potential, and asked them to write a 300-word essay (a) on any aspect or trend in digital marketing that they found interesting and (b) why they would be a great fit for the role. This helped eliminate the people who weren't serious or qualified and helped Paul quickly get a sense of how/if they'd fit.

Step 6: *Define evaluation criteria*. Paul put his shortlist of candidates into a simple spreadsheet with his criteria and rankings, and any comments or notes. To filter through the candidates, Paul interviewed them first by phone, scoring them on a scale of 1–10 on their first essays as well as in categories such as Voice Clarity, Energy Level, Personality, Vocabulary, Attitude, Listening Skills, Questioning, Cultural Fit, Overall Score.

Step 7: *Interview candidates at least twice—first by phone, then by video or a meeting*. The Ceros sales team works mostly by phone and web meetings, so in the next round of elimination Paul isolated and tested the candidates' communication skills by meeting them either in person or via video. Through the short essays, he was immediately able to remove poor writers. In phone interviews, he'd weed out the ones who obviously couldn't speak articulately. Through video or in-person meetings, he'd see who was an obvious yes or no. Then as a final step, salesperson (closer) and prospecting candidates were asked to do two simple presentations: one on themselves and a second on any other topic of interest.

Step 8: *Set comp expectations*. Paul tends generally to advise companies doing big, new things (new products, teams, markets) to avoid commission-based comp plans as long as they can. You can't put together smart commission plans until you're smart about your sales machine, and that can take a lot longer than you want. While you're learning, it's better to pay salespeople a flat amount per month, or with discretionary bonuses, until you have enough experience and data to put together a practical (not arbitrary) plan that includes commissions. If you put a sales team on a commission-based plan too early, when you're arbitrarily guessing at realistic sales and business goals (even when based on other companies just like yours), you're setting yourself up for a no-win situation. One of two things happens.

- *Either:* Very rarely, the sales team will blow away the targets and you (or your board) will be upset at paying them "too much money" (although everyone agreed to it ahead of time), then quotas will be jacked up and commissions decreased, thus frustrating the reps....

- *Or:* (And this is the one that happens 95% of the time with new products and companies) The sales team totally misses goals because the goals were unrealistic and arbitrary in hindsight. And the sales team is again left very frustrated, and perhaps financially desperate (never a good thing) if they need at least some commission income to pay for basics like rent.

Step 9: *Extend offers and celebrate acceptance!*

Final Advice from Paul Fifield

Having made bad hiring decisions in the past, Paul also had this to say about recruiting and what worked so well this time:

Don't be afraid of doing it all yourself.

- *Don't be afraid of doing it all yourself:* Doing all the recruiting yourself can take a lot of energy and attention, but only you will be the best judge of what you need and who's a fit, so make sure you own it. The right recruiter can be incredibly helpful, but use them to assist you in doing it, rather than hoping they can do it for you.... See the difference?
- *Don't sabotage yourself with impatience:* Don't let impatience trip you into making a bad hiring decision you'll regret later. Better to take longer and get the right person. One bad peach can spoil the bunch.
- *Follow a process:* It will keep you sane, ensure you don't make dumb mistakes, and create a better experience for everyone involved—candidates, you, and your team. Most important, it can help you avoid impulsive, impatient, and/or improper hiring.

CHAPTER 13

Scaling the Sales Team

A bad system will beat a good person every time.

—*W. Edwards Deming*

IF YOU'RE CHURNING MORE THAN 10% OF YOUR SALESPEOPLE, THEY AREN'T THE PROBLEM

Sales culture's different compared to pretty much every other function, in that it expects most people to fail or succeed almost totally on their own. Companies assume "We'll hire 10 salespeople to sink-or-swim and a quarter to half won't make it."

CSO Insights' studies show average sales team's annual turnover of around 25% (it varies by a few points year to year), with half quitting and half fired. That means out of 100 salespeople, 25 are lost every year. So you need to hire (and train, and ramp, and transition pipeline or customer accounts for …) an extra 25 salespeople per year just to tread water.

But—what the hell? Would you hire 10 HR people and then expect to fire 3 to 5? Managers? Supply chain people? Losing a quarter of your engineering team, total employees, or customers would be a board-level catastrophe. But it's accepted, even *expected*, in sales.

Sales team churn is *especially expensive* because of the time required, the lost opportunities, and customer frustration. They are your face to *customers*, people!

At EchoSign, in growing from $1 million to $50 million in revenue, no one quit from VP Sales Brendon Cassidy's team. They were making a lot of money, knew what they were doing, and had fun. Why would you want to leave that?

Imagine you work at a growing company, and you might be hitting or beating team-wide sales goals. But internally the team's struggling with growing pains, such as:

- *Missed quotas*: 30%, 40%, or more of the sales team is missing quota.
- *Team attrition:* Salespeople just keep coming and going … 10 to 50% of the sales team is leaving every year (whether voluntarily or involuntarily).
- *Ramp times* keep lengthening for new sales hires, such as going from two to four months when you were smaller to now six to eight or more months.
- *Rep count is growing faster than leads:* As the team has gotten bigger, each rep is getting fewer leads passed to them. Lead generation isn't keeping up with sales team or goal growth.

And despite all this, and the other reasons, the board is still telling you to keep hiring more salespeople to drive growth! It's pouring water faster into a leaky sales team bucket.

It's Not You, It's Me

Now, if say, 30% of a sales team is missing quota, is it the fault of the people or the system? Was 30% of the team really mishired? If you are losing 25% of your sales team a year (whether they leave or are fired)—is it the people or is it your system? If almost every new sales hire is taking twice as long now to ramp, is it them—or your system? *See the pattern here?*

Who sets quotas and incentives? Who defines territories, roles, and responsibilities? Who's ultimately responsible for hiring and training? Who promotes, hires, and trains the sales managers on the front lines?

It's not the salespeople. Ultimately, it's the responsibility of the VP Sales and CEO to ensure sustainable sales success, not the individual salespeople. Your sales "system" and environment have enormous effects on salespeople, either helpful or hurtful. Until you fix the systems, you're going to struggle getting repeatable success.

Defects in the System

Your ability to scale a sales team depends on making *everything a system*. When salespeople leave for any reason—missed quotas, dissatisfied, bad apple—it means you have "defects" in your system.

> **Your ability to scale a sales team depends on making *everything a system.***

Sales team attrition should be *much* lower—say 10% or less per year overall (and with 0% voluntary attrition). Not only is it incredibly expensive in time, money, and lost opportunities—it also frustrates prospects and customers when their point people keep changing. A commonly accepted estimate of the cost of one lost salesperson is one and a half to two times their annual comp.

At two times their comp, losing five salespeople with targets of $150,000 is a cost of $1.5 million.

A $200 Million Loss?

In 2013, rumor had it that Salesforce.com lost 750 of their 3,000 people in sales (25% attrition). If their average comp was $125,000 (which is probably low), then this was a cool $187.5 million lost or much higher. Studies (ok-usually done by recruiting firms) report the actual cost of an employee's turnover is a multiple of their compensation.

Regardless - that much turnover disrupts *everything* in the sales team and with customers.

Common Sales Attrition Causes

There can be a million underlying causes behind high sales attrition, but the three most common ones are:

- *Lead generation:* The company isn't doing enough to support the reps with quality leads.
- *Specialization:* The company isn't specializing at all, the right ways, or going far enough with it.
- *Management:* Leadership (mostly the CEO & VP Sales) isn't connected with what's going on "in the trenches," or is still very traditional

or conservative. We love this quote: "People leave managers, not companies."

Do Your Salespeople Have a Headwind to Success?

You need to dig and discover the root problems that are making it so hard for people on the team to succeed. Is it that they need more leads? Maybe your products are weak or are targeted to the wrong markets.

Maybe you're an early company with completely wacky sales expectations. Or you're targeting a "slog" market. Maybe some of your sales managers or leaders are doing more harm than good with their management style. Maybe your VP Sales is a bit crazy and is just hiring a bunch of random people into a disorganized system (it happens), and you gotta rebuild it before even leadgen matters.

Don't Make Assumptions

In addition to looking at those areas of Lead Generation, Specialization, and Sales Management, *go talk to your people, one by one*, and identify patterns that lead you to discover the main one or two problems that are causing high attrition.

- Don't just blame salespeople for failing. What else contributes to the systemic problem(s)?
- Keep up the one-to-one coaching, and don't let individual salespeople use team-wide problems as an excuse to give up.
- Great reps with a great (or even good) manager and fair compensation will prefer to stay.
- People leave managers, not companies. Which managers have high churn, and why?
- Voluntary attrition should be 0%.
- Overall attrition should be 10% or less, but but not 0%, because no company has perfect hiring and coaching.

CASE STUDY: SCALING SALES FROM 2 TO 350 REPS AT ZENEFITS

Sam Blond is the VP Sales at Zenefits. He joined January 1, 2014, when Zenefits was at about $1 million in ARR, with 20 employees and just two quota-carrying salespeople (Account Executives/AEs). One year later,

Zenefits passed $20 million in ARR with 80 AEs, and then in 2015 Zenefits passed $100 million ARR, with 350 AEs.

The following sections show a few things he's learned Enter Sam:

Lesson #1: Clarity of Ownership

In the early days, we set things up so that marketing owned *all* lead generation, with a Lead Commit for delivering qualified opportunities to sales. The Sales Development Rep (SDR) team, made up mostly of outbound prospectors, worked for marketing, not sales. Inbound leads went through them. Outbound leads were generated by them.

Marketing isn't measured on just the quantity of new leads created—they can be crap or great. Marketing's measured on the number of leads that get accepted by sales. We have an agreement on how to consistently define and measure them.

It was obvious to everyone who owned pipeline responsibility. If there weren't enough leads, no one needed to waste time and energy pointing fingers. It was a Forcing Function: Marketing couldn't hide from delivering the opportunities. Sales couldn't hide from building a team of reps who can consistently close them.

After the outbound system was proven, and then as we scaled to 300 outbound prospectors on the SDR team, we evolved. We moved the outbound prospectors (but not the inbound-response SDRs) to sales. This created closer teamwork, communication, and alignment between prospectors and their sales teammates.

Lesson #2: Three Key Metrics

In these hypergrowth stages, I'm focused on:

- *Revenue bookings:* In our health insurance system, the people enrolled are referred to as "lives." My main proxy for revenue is the "Number of Lives" signed up monthly.
- *Hiring goals:* In growing 20x one year, and 5x the next, hiring became a chokepoint. Are we meeting the hiring funnel goals?
- *Customer retention:* We watch customer satisfaction like a hawk, because (a) the happier customers increase referrals, (b) they're less likely to churn, and (c) they're more likely to participate in our reference program.

Also on quotas: They should be challenging, but attainable. I like 70% or more of my reps hitting quota.

Lesson #3: Predictability

We started in the beginning thinking, "How quickly can we scale this business efficiently, by hiring sales reps and managers successfully without risking quality?" Planning early on how to scale hiring, training, and the team has gotten us to our targets.

We know to hit X revenue, we need to hire Y salespeople, 0.8Y SDRs, and Z implementation people. There is some seasonality, but our business is very predictable, once we have this machine going. We know what we're putting in and getting out.

Lesson #4: Sales Force Automation

Salesforce is the backbone of our sales team, and we use it heavily, along with miscellaneous other sales, marketing, and data apps. We hired two dedicated people for Salesforce.com: an "architect" and a system administrator who worked in the sales operations department.

A regret: we waited too long to hire in sales ops. We should have built that out when we were 40–50 employees. I didn't appreciate what an awesome sales ops person could do until we had one. I never had to worry about our systems again—Salesforce, our phone systems, all our apps. Our shit just works. And that person owns it.

Lesson #5: Hiring

Resumes lie. I want to know how much money an experienced salesperson has made. W2 history—at least with quota-carrying salespeople—doesn't lie.

We're not hiring only people with an HR background—they can learn the market, and we have a training and certification program for that. We're hiring people from startups, where the culture was more important. As we grew, we had to expand the type of people we're hiring, and adapt our training.

We have luxuries: We've done very well in hiring, but we can afford to pay people very well, and attract top talent. We also got lots of great publicity, so we've been able to recruit many of the top reps from other companies.

Lesson 6: Training

My other regret: We waited too long to create a structured onboarding and training system. In the middle of scaling from 2 to 80 reps in the first year, about halfway through the year, close rates dropped. A serious investment in training fixed it.

I know many companies are successful in hiring great people and teaching them on the job how to sell and close. At our growth rates, we couldn't do that. We had to hire people in these quota-carrying roles who have sold before.

And as a small team, tribal learning worked. New sales reps would begin, get a laptop and phone, and are told to figure it out with their peers. But as we grew, we needed someone who owned training, with a predictable program.

Now we put new hires through four full weeks of classroom training and certification tests for both internal knowledge and health insurance licenses. Reps aren't allowed to take phone calls until they pass them.

This is what I tell other companies now: You can wing it until you have about 10 reps. If you're hiring more than one rep per month, start them in classes, with a real training system and a designated owner.

Lesson 7: Specialization

We're die-hard converts of sales role specialization. It allows everyone to be more efficient. Not every company has the margins to support specialization. If you don't, get creative to find other ways to help them focus—such as specializing time blocks on their calendar.

A team's revenue isn't just the sum of its quota-carrying salespeople. We're not afraid to invest in hiring heavily in nonquota carrying roles, in all the many things the sales team needs to operate at 100%. Training and sales operations aren't costs. Without them, our system breaks down.

Lesson 8: Management Structure

Each closing rep manager should have 8–10 direct reports. We promote from within, when possible, and if it's the best option, but we don't force it. People still have to earn the promotion. We're careful about setting realistic expectations around promotion.

Lesson 9: Going for It—Doubling Down

In early 2014, I met with our CEO Parker to plan out hitting our 2014 sales goal of $10 million. We were getting predictable leads and the team was hitting our goals at the time.

Parker asked, "What would it take to get to $20 million this year?" I told him, "We'd need twice as many SDRs and salespeople." He said, "Why don't we do that?"

"Okay ..."

So we doubled the revenue goal for the year to $20 million for 2014. And ended up beating it.

It's easy to think you're pushing yourself as hard as you can. And setting uber-aggressive goals out of thin air can mean you totally whiff them. But you might be surprised at how much further you can go by going for broke and tripling down on what's already working.

> **You might be surprised at how much further you can go by going for broke and tripling down on what's already working.**

JASON'S ADVICE TO CEOS: PUT NONSALES LEADERS ON VARIABLE COMP PLANS, TOO

How can every single employee that can materially influence revenue have a variable revenue component to their compensation plans?

I know we all agree everyone in sales has to have commissions and a highly variable comp structure. What I mean is that *everyone* that materially impacts the plan should have some variable comp.

- Your VP Product should be incentivized to build the right features, not only to make a great product but also to hit the annual plan. How about a 15% variable cash component, and a 15% bonus for exceeding the plan, and also perhaps some downside for missing it?.
- Your VP Marketing sure better have her comp plan tied to the leads or opportunity commits that make the annual plan work. How about a 20% variable cash component? The leads aren't there, she comes up short. But if the plan is blown out, she shares in the extra revenue.
- Your VP Customer Success sure better have her comp plan tied to hitting the upsell, retention, or negative net churn goals. How about

a 30%–plus variable component? Watch her sweat the lost customers 10x more when money is on the line.

- Your VP and Directors of Engineering need to build the stuff we need to hit this year's plan. How about a 10/15/20% variable comp plan here?
- Your Controller exceeds our collections goals, and you end up with an extra $300,000 of cash in the bank? How about a bonus here?

"Nah, my Director of Engineering doesn't need variable comp," you say. "We're all in it together. She's got plenty of equity."

Maybe.

Revenue is a concrete team goal *everyone* can and should get behind.

But if nothing else, even for nonsales professionals, revenue is a concrete team goal everyone can and should get behind. And paying for performance is just something all of us sort of viscerally understand, even if we've never carried a bag. We hit the '15 plan together, you get a pat on the back, and your equity is worth more, That's great. But if they get another $20,000—just watch how people change. Maybe it doesn't change the life of some of your senior hires. But if the reward is $0—but appreciation in equity—you just won't get the same alignment to your annual revenue plans.

Later, this may get harder. Later, you may need subordinate goals. But for now, I'd suggest tying a bonus plan for exceeding the revenue plan for all your key hires, of every discipline.

Let me share two stories.

Recently, I went through this exercise with an amazing company I work closely with. We added a variable component to the VP of Engineering's comp plan. If we missed the plan, his salary dropped by 10%. If we hit it exactly, he got a 5% bonus beyond base. And if we exceeded it by 10%, he got a 20% bonus.

About 15 minutes after that, he came back. And completely changed the product roadmap for 2015.

Now, you might argue that's a mistake, with too much focus on the short term over the long term. Maybe. But at least it creates alignment, a debate, a discussion. A new sense of shared focus on really, truly, hitting the 2015 plan.

I had a similar experience myself, personally. Back during a Year of Hell when we almost went bankrupt, I waived all my salary. I worked for no cash (though I took equity instead) for about a year *after* we raised venture capital.

And then, in the depths of the Lehman Brothers the-world-is-over-Sequoia-says-Good-Times-R.I.P. days, I did something I was pretty proud of. I got up out from behind my Mac and got two customers to prepay an extra $600,000 in cash upfront. This happened when there was no contractual reason for them to do so, at a time the world was ending. Considering our net burn rate was low, this bought us another nine months of runway.

So I asked for a $10,000 bonus. My salary was $0. But I *needed* the bonus. I brought in the money. I needed a tangible, real pat on the back. In the way only a check can do.

It was a confusing discussion with the investors. You need a $10,000 bonus, but you're waiving your $120,000 salary? Huh? But I *needed* it. To connect my efforts to hit the plan, the $600K extra I brought in when the world was ending … with the plan itself.

So does the rest of your team. They need it, too.

Not just the sales guys.

Get them thinking directly about revenue, and it'll help revenue come.

TRUTH EQUALS MONEY

Anything you're doing to avoid or ignore painful truths, to hide from your weaknesses or avoid embarrassment, will make it harder to scale.

Anything you're doing to avoid or ignore painful truths, to hide from your weaknesses or avoid embarrassment, will make it harder to scale.

You and your company must be impeccably honest. With yourselves and your market. Maybe you already are … or maybe there's more for you here.

First, yes, it of course means eliminating any form of lying or manipulation throughout your community of employees, partners, and customers. Zero tolerance. Unless it's the first-time stupid mistake by someone who has never held a job. And if you work for a lying person or company—one that doesn't want to change—get out.

But it also means being *uncomfortably honest, and transparent*, with employees, customers, and investors. You probably are already … and there's always room for more.

Such as when that high-profile project you're backing starts failing, and may need to be restructured or canned. It's *embarrassing*. Are you so determined to make it successful, or avoiding dealing with the embarrassment, that you're intentionally ignoring danger signs? What are you doing to spot embarrassing problems early in an acquisition, investment, lead generation initiative, new hire, new office or plant, new product or management system?

The best form of marketing and sales is "the truth"—there is never a good reason to lie to your customers or team.

There are many more ways you can expand truth in your company, such as with candid feedback reviews (both up and down) much more often than once a year. You can tell prospects in your sales cycle about what your product doesn't do well yet. Share unhappy sales surprises with investors as often as exciting news. Admit to yourself and your team or board that you're not ready to grow. That a key executive hire that you spent six months finding isn't working out. That customers just don't love the product you built. That you have concerns about your own future in your job.

We're not saying be blindly and thoughtlessly transparent. Whatever you share, do it in a way that helps you *and the recipient*.

Knowing the truth, even if it's painful or disturbing, serves your team and customers better than blissful (and temporary) ignorance. Because it's going to come out sooner or later anyway.

Our business culture teaches us that to be successful we can't be ourselves to succeed, that we have to look good and "position things" to get a job, close a deal, or raise money. Furthermore, we can't share our imperfections or doubts with anyone, and if we are totally honest with ourselves, our team and our customers, we'll put everything at risk. Be strong, be in control, show no weakness—or lose the deal.

Especially in Silicon Valley, where people tell each other they're crushing it in public, but cry in their beer in private. Or present sales pipelines that look busy and full, but are mostly illusion.

Companies, and especially sales leaders, need to set an example of embracing the truth—not only because it's the right thing to do, but also because it will make you money.

The difference between "shady business/sales/marketing" and "honest business/sales/marketing" can be the difference between making money *at the expense of* customers, versus making money *by helping* customers. One is a train wreck waiting to happen, and one is sustainable.

Truth has always been important in business. Truth builds trust, and customers buy from people (and brands) they trust. And when you hold back the truth, intentionally or not, *that* is what jeopardizes the trust and the deal. Just as any relationship (romantic, business or otherwise) that's built on lies has a weak foundation, any business or business relationship built without honesty is at risk of being easily broken.

What's the hard conversation you're holding back from having with your partner, manager, investor, or customer? Even if it upsets people in the short term, and even if some leave, it will build trust and reputation with the "right" people—they're the ones who stay. And an enormous weight will be lifted off you.

Truth and trust help keep your people and customers engaged through rough patches. This includes telling them ugly news as it happens, rather than holding back. Wouldn't *you* prefer to know the bad news, rather than have someone try to protect you from it?

Being uncomfortably honest with yourself and your team helps you spot and deal with weaknesses before they trip you up.

Being uncomfortably honest with yourself and your team helps you spot and deal with weaknesses before they trip you up. It promotes trust in your team and with customers, and the softest pillow is a clear conscience.

PIPELINE DEFICIT DISORDER

If you're in sales or run a team, how do you improve your forecasting? It's always going to be off as long as you or your teams are sliding on maintaining a sparkling clean list of opportunities. There's a reason it's a universal problem.

Okay, you can easily put together a big list or report of all your sales, business, or partner opportunities. Active ones, old ones, possible ones, dream ones.

What's great about having lots of opportunities? When you have a big list of opportunities, it can be exciting! "Yes! I have a lot going on—look at the potential!"

It can help you build momentum and feel progress, which in turn can build your confidence and help you close. Finally, having a bunch of opportunities gives you more shots on goal.

The Problem With Lots of Opportunities

The ugly side of having a lot of opportunities is that being busy working your list can feel productive without actually generating any concrete results.

Also, fighting clutter is an ongoing battle; it's hard for most people to step back and clean out all the opportunities that have gone dead.

Having a long list of opportunities can help you avoid reality, to *dream* instead of *do*. "I've got all these possible sales, *something* is going to have to come through." Well, not necessarily …

Finally, having too long a list makes it harder to give great service to the people who need it—to prioritize where you spend your time, rather than to scatter it evenly or randomly across the list.

The Challenge: Brutal Honesty

It's impossible to maintain a 100% honest and accurate list of opportunities, because (a) people may not respond to your questions, (b) they can be afraid or may not want to be open and honest, and (c) it's easy for you to have happy ears and hear only what you want to hear, not what was said.

How often do you hear a clear "no"? When a prospect does get back to you, often they'll say things like "later" or "send me more information" or "let me get back to you."

Sometimes these are honest answers, but more often they are versions of *not interested*; the person is too nice, or too embarrassed, to say no. Being honest can be hard, and this has nothing to do with whether people are senior or junior, at small companies or big ones.

And "I'm just being polite" or "I don't want to hurt their feelings" can be an excuse for not being honest. If you're polite, you would tell them the truth in a polite way and not hold it back.

This comes from fear of rejection. People want approval from others, and hate being rejected. This means that they don't like rejecting others, either. Yet we confuse rejection with being honest in telling us it's not a fit.

Also, sometimes people just don't know if there actually *is* a fit, and they might be too embarrassed to say so. Especially at bigger companies, where it can be hard to buy things, they might just simply not know where they are in their evaluation or buying process.

Finally, the truth can lead to failure, burst bubbles, and rejection. If you've ever had a crush on someone but hesitated to confront him/her in some way to find out if it's mutual, you know what I mean. It's easier to dream than do, and it can be easier to hold onto hope than to have it punctured with the reality of *No*.

It can be easier to hold onto hope than to have it punctured with the reality of *No*.

Practice Getting to Difficult Truths

Your job with your people and their list of opportunities is to get to the truth, the *why*, and then help them move *on or out* of your pipeline. (Let the dating jokes begin.)

If they're not interested in your product, find out *why*: Not a fit? They don't see the value? Truly not the right time? You don't have the right person? How can you deal with this? Make the truth easier to get to for both parties, so you can stop guessing:

- No guilt or judgment: "It's okay either way."
- Attitude of "just helping": Make it a joint effort, to be successful together at finding out if there is a fit or not, and if so, moving to the next step.
- Make honesty easier with easy outs: "I'll assume this isn't the right time/of interest/a priority/a good fit unless I hear otherwise."
- Ask hard questions–in friendly ways.

- When you come off as challenging someone, you create defensiveness, and that blocks truth.

Four Examples of Challenging versus Curious Questions

1. Challenging: "Do you have buy-in yet from the CEO?"
   Cooperative: "What would it take to get this done by month's end?"
2. Challenging: "Is this a priority?"
   Cooperative: "What else is more important right now?" or "On a scale of one to ten, how important is it to get this done (or done by ___)?"
3. Challenging: "Who's the decision maker?"
   Curious/Investigative: "Who else is typically involved in deciding something like this?"

What's the best part about the painful truth (whether it's about love or money)? You know one way or the other. You can move out of denial and see clearly what needs to happen next.

ARE YOUR ENTERPRISE DEALS TAKING FOREVER?

Back when I was creating Salesforce's outbound prospecting team, I knew I'd cracked the code on prospecting after the fourth month when results jumped 5x. It was obvious to me. But it took Salesforce *eight more months* to finally decide to triple down and invest big in the team. Those were eight frustrating months! I wish I'd known better how complex buying decisions get made, and why they move fast or drag out.

Maybe you're frustrated by a similar thing: Big companies seem to take forever (6–12 or more months) to decide to buy your "no-brainer" service that—to you—they clearly need.

However, if you're an early-stage company, you may not realize that you're still figuring out if you're (a) a need-to-have or (b) a nice-to-have with these companies, and need to Nail A (New) Niche. Or, because you had a few fast Early Adopter buys, you may have totally wacky expectations on how fast your big company Mainstream Buyers can make decisions.

Remember: Big companies usually make *group decisions,* are *risk-averse,* and it can get *complicated.* More people involved means longer decisions. When buying something new or important, a big company might take 6–9 months to buy with more people involved, more complexity, more systems and teams affected and less tolerance for risk. The nature of the beast is *it's harder for them to buy.*

So, in selling to them, one of your jobs is not to "sell," but to *help them buy*. This often means you need to help the primary person at the company—the one who wants your stuff—sell it internally to their peers and boss(es).

One of your jobs is not to "sell," but to *help them buy*.

You may *occasionally* run across an early adopter or a visionary CEO who can push things through faster—but be prepared for the process to take longer than you'd like. Hey, they care about *their timeline*, not yours.

Here are five tips for accelerating big-ticket sales cycles:

1. *Find a champion and help them sell internally:* When you can find someone with influence at a company, rather than selling that person, plan on helping them sell you to their team. Without a champion or coach like that, at least someone who can help you navigate, you're going to get stuck. Dig into your network to get high-level referrals to CEOs and/or board members. If you have a small network, look up top executives at your targets and try a cold referral approach. Your messaging or package needs to appeal to those senior people, not just individual users. What a CIO cares about is vastly different from what an engineer cares about.
2. *Focus on prospects who need you and can buy faster:* Forget all the "speed up sales cycles!" tips and tricks, getting a prospect to speed up a decision-making process is like trying to speed up a traffic jam. You gotta avoid it in the first place. Focus on finding the kinds of prospects who are more likely to buy faster, which is related to the next point …
3. *Clarify your "Ideal Customer Profile"* and identify how this differs from companies who buy from those who just look. Go update your Niche matrix, and figure out what's different between people who buy and "tire-kickers." Be *specific*. Don't fall into the trap of believing "everyone will want this" and scattering your energy marketing to too many kinds of customers.
4. *Confused prospects say "No."* Whatever you wrote up to impress your professors or investors just sounds like bullshit in the real world. If a prospect is confused about what you do or how you can help them, they'll say no—even if you know they need your product. You want your prospects to understand what you're talking about, and the best

way is not to impress them, but to *keep it simple*. Maybe you need to do a new set of interviews to help refresh your messaging.

5. *Show, don't tell.* Why should they believe you and your claims? The less you have to explain, the more you can demonstrate proof, the better. Especially with big companies, people tend to want to see a lot of social proof: other companies like theirs that are getting results. They aren't just risk-averse; they are also bombarded by companies pitching every benefit under the sun, and many are "all hat and no cattle." Suggestions:
   - Case studies prove that you're not all talk: Details on how you helped ACME grow from $10 million to $50 million in two years are more concrete than "We can help you grow 500% in 12 months."
   - References, especially if there's someone in their network who knows your stuff.
   - Can you do some free work for them to prove your claims, rather than have them guess?
   - Start your pitch with a demo or dashboards to show them what they'll get with your product, rather than a long-winded history of your company.
   - Is there a demo or visual you can show, a story you can tell, a picture you can draw, a video you can shoot?
   - Can you get them using your product hands-on—say, with a pilot or free trial? Either can be a double-edged sword. If you run one, don't assume they'll just "figure it out." Define what a successful pilot looks like, and the steps needed to get there, before you begin.

FIVE KEY SALES METRICS (WITH A TWIST)

With Fred Shilmover
CEO, InsightSquared

Use these five classic metrics, but use them more insightfully than you have before:

1. *Number of open opportunities in total and per rep:* Measure the total number of open opportunities each rep is working at *any given time*, and understand how many total new opportunities they should be getting per month—not too few, and not too many.

What to do with it: Your reps should get a sufficient inflow of new opportunities to have a steady number to work in their pipeline, (a) giving them enough opportunities to hit their number, but (b) without overwhelming them so balls start dropping.

A common number for a SaaS rep doing low-five-figure deals to juggle is 25–30 opportunities. Yours may or may not be different. For yours, look to your own history. How many have your best reps juggled? Does it vary much by segment, type of customer, or average deal size? When was it too many?

This metric also gives you a sanity check if you need to grow your open opportunities a lot (by cranking up lead generation), or if your team is overwhelmed (and you need to hire more salespeople).

2. *Number of closed opportunities in total and per rep*: Measure total opportunities closed including both closed-won and closed-lost opportunities.

What to do with it: Your reps should be closing a certain number of sales deals each month (whether won or lost). It's a form of "throughput." If they're not closing enough total opportunities, drill down: Are they light on deals? Not closing effectively? Is their pipeline full of "hope" that never goes anywhere? Are they not updating the sales system?

High win rates aren't good, low ones aren't bad.

3. *Deal size:* Measure the average value of your closed-won deals.

What to do with it: Knowing this metric will make it easy for you to spot opportunities that fall outside the normal deal size (say three times greater than average) and flag them for special attention. Also, if the trend shows an increase in smaller deals won, perhaps some reps are focusing on small fish. Or perhaps your reps are increasing discounts.

If you see a new trend in average deal size, then you need to dig into your pipeline mix or discounting practices to understand why.

4. *Win rate:* Measure the number of closed opportunities, in a specific closing period, that you won *(Closed Won Opportunities)/(Total Opportunities: both Closed-Won and Closed-Lost)*. This won't mean much unless you can watch it trend, or use it to A/B test reps with similar segments, or compare against companies similar to yours.

What to do with it: "High" win rates aren't good; "low" ones aren't bad—either one gives you a chance to get smart about your sales system, to spot areas of success or problems. For example, if your win rate is high, maybe your pricing is too low!

The simplest way to start increasing your team's win rate is to find the one or two most problematic steps in your process, and then look *both* "inside" (e.g., a better demo process) and "outside" the team (e.g., an easier free trial, or simpler pricing) …

It's common for sales teams beginning to scale up to see win rates drop. Is it because of the new people? Has lead quality or management quality changed? Or because of packaging, pricing, or website changes? You need to drill down and see exactly where opportunities are falling off, in order to get to the root cause.

Don't assume—investigate.

Look at your sales funnel and understand conversions through every stage through to closed-won. If most reps are struggling in the same area, then don't blame them; it might be something outside their control. Nominate an investigator to find the truth of what's going on.

If specific individuals consistently have much higher or lower win rates, don't be too quick to jump to conclusions and criticize or compliment them. First look at their data to find out "why" and learn from it. A sales rep with highest consistent win rate may be talented at sales, or talented at sandbagging/cherry picking.

Don't "assume"—investigate. Look at win rates with other data to get the whole story. For example, win rates for word-of-mouth leads (Seeds) should be much higher than leads generated by marketing (Nets) or outbound (Spears).

5. *Sales cycle:* Measure the average duration or time (typically in days) it takes your team to win a deal and, ideally, how long opportunities spend in each sales stage.

What to do with it: The best use of this metric isn't to see how fast you are; it's to get smart about whether your current deals are on track or in trouble. An opportunity has lingered in the same stage three times longer than the average? Uh-oh, flag it!

Faster isn't always better; focus on learning what the "right" time frames are that create successful deals and customers. For example, sometimes customers move too fast for their own good and rush into a deal that later blows up because they didn't do their own diligence.

Our uber-point: Rather than judging these metrics as high/low or good/bad, use them to drill into your sales systems and get smart about what affects them the most.

CHAPTER 14

For Startups Only

Startups are a special breed.

EVERY TECH COMPANY SHOULD OFFER SERVICES

Many companies, especially early tech companies, are afraid to build a professional services team (or do *anything* manually) because "it's not scalable." But you can't scale something that doesn't work yet. And there's no better way to understand what it takes to make customers happy than to work hand-in-hand with them.

Especially if you're doing SaaS for the first time (or even the second), the whole idea of charging for "services" may seem anathema. It sure seemed like that to me at EchoSign.

- If your product is so easy to use that you hardly even need sales people, why in the world would I need to charge for implementation? For support? For training and engagement?
- And isn't it a bit unseemly to charge for services? Doesn't it label your product as old-school, too clunky, inelegant, or complex?
- And isn't the revenue from services a waste? For example, it's not recurring and it's not true ARR. Does it even count? After all, I'm a SaaS company.

Maybe. Perhaps for the 15% of the world of super-engineers or Early Adopters, charging for services doesn't make any sense.

First, let's assume you've nailed your product offering. But you probably haven't, not to the extent you believe. Services gets your people hands-on with customers, and can be the best way to learn the details of which customers find it easy, and which ones find it hard, to get value from you stuff.

Okay, so you've nailed your product and you're following the money upmarket. Let's talk about the money.

Turns out, though, that in the vast majority of six-figure contracts, virtually every seven-figure contract, and quite a few five-figure contracts there's *always* a services component.

And it almost always seems to average out to 15–20% of the annual contract value.

I remember the first time I experienced this confusion myself, on one our first high-five-figure contracts at EchoSign. We had a brutal negotiation over price. And then, at the end, they send us a Schedule for Services. After getting beaten down on the annual contract price … the Schedule for Services they sent us (without me even asking) *guaranteed* us another $20,000 a year in services, with $250 an hour as the assumed price for the services. I didn't fully understand what was going on until I became a VP in a Fortune 500 tech company. But the answer, it turns out, is simple once you get it.

First, in medium and larger customers, *there's always change management to deal with when bringing in a new vendor*. And they not only understand there's a cost associated with that (soft even more than hard) … your buyer wants to do the least amount of change management possible by herself. If you can do the training for her for a few bucks and it saves her a ton of time, that's an amazing deal.

Your buyer wants to do the least amount of change management possible by herself.

Second, in medium and larger customers, *they often have no one to do the implementation work themselves*. So even if you weren't saving your customer money—by helping with implementation, roll-out, support, and so on—they probably have no one to do this internally anyway. You're going to be doing some, a lot, or all of this for them. They are okay paying for this, in the enterprise at least.

And most important, it's *how business is done, and it's budgeted*. When most larger companies enter a new vendor into their ERP system, they typically add an additional budget item or two along with the core contract price. There will be one additional line item for service and implementation, in most cases. And in some cases, an additional line item for other add-ons necessary to make the implementation a success (e.g., an EchoSign on top of Salesforce). Both of these are often line-item budgeted at 15–20% of the core contract value for the product. So …

- You probably can't charge another 15–20% for services and implementation and training for a $99 a month product. Well, maybe you could, but it's probably unprofitable and not worth it.
- But, as soon as the sale gets into the five figures, consider adding 15–20% for services. You'll probably get it.
- And *plan* for charging, and delivering, additional services in mid-five-figure and larger deals. The customers are happy to pay, and in fact, will *expect* it.

And if you don't charge, you're simply leaving money on the table. You'll have to do the work, anyway. You may send negative signals that you aren't "enterprise" enough, that you aren't a serious vendor.

And importantly, this extra services revenue still "counts" as recurring revenue if it's less than 25% or so of your revenues. I don't mean that literally (it doesn't recur), but what I mean is that Wall Street and VCs and acquirers and everyone will still consider you a 100% SaaS company if less than 25% of your revenues are nonrecurring. And you'll get the same SaaS ARR multiple on those extra services revenues: same multiple, no extra work, 10–25% more revenue, extra, nondilutive cash flowing into the business.

Don't leave the services revenue on the table.

WHAT JASON INVESTS IN, AND DO YOU NEED TO RAISE MONEY TO SCALE?

Through my own venture capital fund, I look for two and a half things when I'm investing in companies: great founders, better than average economics (how easily they make money), and a space that may be interesting in a year or two.

1. *Great founders:* Because I've been a SaaS founder myself, I look to invest in founders that are better than I was by comparison. They may not know as much as I do now, but are they better at their age than I was?

2. *Better-than-average economics:* I look for companies with a better use of economics than what I experienced at EchoSign. If you're selling something at $1,000 but can charge $10,000 for the same work, it's just 10x easier.

If you're selling something at $1,000 but can charge $10,000 for the same work, it's 10x easier.

3. *An interesting space:* I look for something that's vaguely in a good space. Markets change, but I want to back a business in a space that's likely to attract someone else's investment down the road.

It's Both Easier and Harder

The best SaaS startups, like the Zenefits, Slack, or TOPDesk, can grow faster than ever when they nail it. The flip side is that product-market fit is harder than ever. There's more noise, with dozens of companies chasing the same space, and user expectations are higher. Great ideas that used to be a dime a dozen, are now, like, a penny a dozen.

Going Big

Professional VCs need $1 billion exits for their funds to be successful. So VCs only care about folks who are at least trying to build something worth billions. Angel investors and investors doing super early stuff have broader goals. But for bigger VCs, you have to invest in crazy-insane people, with seemingly crazy-insane ideas that look brilliant only in hindsight. AirBnB sounded totally wild at the beginning, but now they've done very well.

What Makes You Fundable?

The simplest way to think about it is with a two-by-two matrix: traction and team. The mistake that founders often make is that they don't realize that no team *or* no traction means no check. They think that with only one or the other they can raise money. If you don't have customers in SaaS yet, don't ask VCs or even sophisticated angels for money. It isn't going to happen. You have to have some social proof on your team or *something* to make it happen.

Can Startups Grow without Funding?

To grow without funding, you usually have to focus on the low end of the business first and grow from there. Concentrate on small deals initially and work up to the enterprise level—the most profitable part of SaaS—later.

> **Concentrate on small deals initially and work up to the enterprise level—the most profitable part of SaaS—later.**

If you can regularly close six-, seven-, or eight-figure deals, those are very profitable. But you need a professional sales team. You need a slick brand, a sleek website and materials. You need a development team that can handle extra requests, people in services, and Customer Success professionals. You need to invest money—for example, for people getting six-figure salaries. It's hard to do that without millions in funding.

If you're going to do it without any capital (or minimal capital), you'll almost always have to come up from the bottom. But you don't have to stay in small business deals forever; you can go upmarket once you've started. Box started off with a freemium product and now freemium is less than 1% of their revenue. But for most of us, it's almost impossible without capital when you are true enterprise, because we just need all that headcount.

Advice for People Who Want Me to Invest

Go to SaaStr.com to find out the latest about my fund and how to reach out. Send me the most detailed email you possibly can with a presentation deck, every single metric, and why you are building something that's great.

I only meet with one founder a week max, but I read almost everything. And I can process a lot offline because I've done it before, so the trick isn't a punchy line, and don't send me a pinned document or a teaser.

Key Startup Metrics

A lot of SaaS people actually care more about metrics than I do. I've learned that a lot of them don't really matter in the early days. I don't really care what your customer lifetime value (LTV) is. I don't care what your customer acquisition cost (CAC) is, because if you have a good startup, it's always low in the early days and then it gets high.

If you have true enterprise customers, they're going to last around five to seven years. If you sell to various small businesses on a credit card, they're going to churn out at 3 to 4% per month. Which may not sound like a lot, but 4% monthly churn means losing about 48% of your customers in a year.

All I need to know is:

1. What's your top-line growth?
2. How much money are you burning?

With these two metrics, I know the whole story. I'm interested in one thing: a startup that grows at least 15% month-over-month without hemorrhaging cash after they get to $1 million in revenue. As long as the burn rate is tolerable, if you can grow 15% or more, if you have $1 million in revenue, great founders, and you're in a great space, I'm probably going to write a check.

Exceptional founders who are better than I am, and the ability to go from $1 million to $10 million in ARR in five quarters or less—that's what gets my attention. Beyond that, I don't really care what your SaaS product does.

The Slacks, the Zenefits, and TOPdesks do it in five quarters or less. The best ones find a way. And it's not just because their founders are better (they aren't a lot better, actually), it's because *all* the markets keep getting bigger. The percentage of the CIO's budget that's going to SaaS is higher than ever and growing. And a 1% transition of that budget now being allocated to SaaS is a market size that can fund *many* billion-dollar startups.

Are you going from $1 million to $10 million ARR in five quarters or less?

WHAT THE HEADCOUNT OF A 100-PERSON SAAS COMPANY LOOKS LIKE

Early stage companies (under $2 million) are often a bit shocked by how many people and roles they will need to get to, and past,

$10 million. SaaS requires many functions beyond engineering, especially if it's sales-driven: outbound, SDRs, inbound, field sales, marketing, Customer Success, support, more complex product management, etc. Roughly speaking, most founders will need to hire about *twice* as many people as they'd planned. So let's break it down.

Let's say you are at $10 million ARR and decently funded; you'll probably have 100 headcount by this point, or at least by $15 million ARR. What will it look like, if it's a sales-driven model? You're not "sales-averse," waiting for leads to come in organically, but rather, you are actively investing to grow leads and sales faster.

Let's say sales are growing at 100% annually and you want to hit, say, $20 million ARR the next year.

Don't use this as a hiring roadmap. These guidelines are to help you understand possible headcounts, not tell you who and how many to hire.

On the sales side, we'll need about 40 headcount at $10 million ARR (to grow 100% the following year):

- One VP of Sales, and probably a VP or Director of Sales Ops, and at least one analyst under her (headcount of three). Say 20 sales reps to fully hit the $20 million ARR plan because we're adding $10 million in ARR next year, and more by the end of the year. (That's a yielded quota.) Really, we'll want more than this toward the middle of the year because we'll be adding so many net new bookings/ARR. Budget for 25 in all.
- At least eight SDRs to handle lead generation, outbound prospecting, and responding to inbound leads. Situations vary widely, but a 1:3 ratio is good for modeling purposes. *Many companies have this team in Marketing, so that Marketing can be the sole owner of a lead generation quota.*
- Probably three to four sales directors to manage the 25 reps (8 reps per director is a standard ratio that works well).
- I'm not even breaking this down between small businesses versus enterprise, inside versus in the field. By $10 million ARR, you'll probably want to have two to three people in field sales for big deals.

In Customer Success, we'll probably need about 20 headcount:

- Assume $1.5 million ARR per CSM. So we'll need about 15 CSMs to hit our plan for next year, although we can hire some later in the year, so we can call it 15 for now.
- A VP to manage them, two directors to manage half of the CSMs each, and probably an analyst to support her in data analysis, and so on (four).

In marketing, it can vary based on outside vendors, but I'm guessing four to eight employees:

- VP Marketing
- Director, Demand Gen
- Director, Field Marketing (events, etc.)
- Content Marketing
- Product Marketing
- Probably, Marketing's own Lead Qualification reps to manage the MQLs (two to three).

In support, we want 24/7 support at this point, including phone support. Let's assume that requires five headcount, minimum, ideally six.

Okay, we're up to around 70 people without a single engineer!

Now let's cross over into the product division and engineering.

In product, we're going to need at least four employees, and even that isn't much fat:

- A VP of Product to manage the whole thing
- Two to three product managers to manage segments of the product, integrations, releases, and so on

In DevOps/TechOps, we're going to want probably three to four folks just to ensure 24/7 coverage. Really, four would be a lot better than three. Pager duty is tiring. Maybe it's really six to seven.

In engineering, I think rough-and-tough, we'll want 20 folks. That's two "pizza box" teams plus a few engineers to do crazy next-gen stuff, and a few to just focus on fixing things, back-end, and so forth. We'll want two designers who can work with the front-end team by this point.

And finally, we need QA—probably at least eight QA engineers and one manager. You can use RainforestQA or something else to get the headcount down, but otherwise, best case, assume 1:2 coverage. So with 20 engineers writing code, we're gonna need eight folks on QA team minimum, once things are humming, plus a boss for the team.

So that's about 40 in product and engineering you're gonna want at $10 million ARR or so. Or 110 altogether, plus whomever you need in General and Admin, Finance, and so on.

I went over 100, I know, so cut back from there proportionately. But you'll need those extra heads to hit your growth plan.

Note that I have a lot more in sales, marketing, and Customer Success than your typical model looks like for public comps (around 30% in sales and marketing by revenue). But that's often because they are growing more slowly at that point on a percentage basis than you are, they have larger quotas, and/or they aren't investing as aggressively in Customer Success.

In other words, assume the majority of your headcount at a $10 million ARR SaaS business is not building product, but helping to sell, market, and support it.

Assume the majority of your headcount at a $10 million ARR SaaS business is not building product, but helping to sell, market, and support it.

Double Your Deal-size

The Painful Truth: It's hard to build a big business out of small deals.

CHAPTER 15

Deal Size Math

Push yourself to go upmarket as soon as you can. Here's why.

WHAT JASON LEARNED: YOU NEED 50 MILLION USERS TO MAKE FREEMIUM WORK

Having spent six-plus years building the web's leading freemium e-signature service at EchoSign, I've learned one thing if nothing else: Almost everyone gets the math wrong in assuming how much revenue they can make from giving away a free product and how many users will choose to upgrade to a paying version. It's tempting to believe in the fairy tale that posting free stuff will generate waves of inbound fans who convert to paying customers at a high rate.

But 9 times out of 10, don't expect a freemium model to generate most of your revenue. Especially if you want to Go Big. There just aren't enough businesses in the First World to get to a $100 million freemium business all that often.

Let's do the math:

- Assume you can get $10/month per paid user (many times you can't).
- To build a $100 million business, you'd need almost a million paid seats to hit that.
- Assume a 2% conversion rate, for simplicity's sake of active users converting to paying customers. You'd need 50 million active users—not pretend users and not users who registered and never came back, and not even users that use you once a year, but 50 million active, passionate, engaged users who are using your business regularly. That is extremely tough, but it can happen. Facebook is at 1 billion. Twitter is past it, and Pinterest may be, but in SOHO (small office or

home office) or SMB (small and medium business) apps, 1 million paying customers almost never happens. There are not too many businesses with 1 million business customers, or 50 million active users, beyond Intuit, Microsoft, Adobe, and PayPal. Even if you're trying to create a $10 million business, you'd still need 5 million active (not total) free users. Still tough.

So is freemium hopeless to build a $100 million business? Absolutely not. It can create, build, and seed it.

For example, at EchoSign, pure freemium (i.e., no human involvement, where people started with the free version, then auto-bought some kind of upgrade) never exceeded 40% of our revenue. As we passed the first $10 million in ARR, freemium sales began declining and never exceeded a third of our revenue.

Another great example is Box. Box has grown past $100 million in revenue but "tilted" from a mostly freemium product to an enterprise focus aimed at landing six- and seven-figure annual subscription deals. Today freemium is a minority of their revenue; a big piece, though not big enough to get them to $100 million.

DropBox is past $100 million on freemium, but they have something north of 500 million users. That proves just how many millions of folks you need to be truly, actively using your utility to make freemium scale to the nine-figure level. An exception that makes the rules. Most important, DropBox's growth would be on the backs of consumers, not businesses.

Freemium alone has a ceiling. But it builds your brand.

Freemium can expose you to millions of people, which creates leads, some poor, some qualified, and many of which should go to a salesperson. They've already used the product, love it, and are almost ready to buy … but they need just a couple of questions answered before they do.

Pure, automated freemium—where you put up a website and the money automatically rolls in—is a wonderful vision, when it works. However, it's much harder to achieve than you realize, if you haven't done it yet.

But getting to a big exit, alone? It can happen, but it's highly improbable. The point is, don't buy into some dream that launching some free thing will create a magical growth curve. It's a starting point. You'll need to use it as a launching pad and build on top of it, adding more pricing tiers and helping bigger companies buy bigger packages.

SMALL DEALS GET YOU STARTED, BIG DEALS DRIVE GROWTH

Which is the fastest way to get to $5 million in revenue, selling a million orders at $5 each, or selling 100 at $50,000 each, or selling 10 at $500,000 each?

You can make millions without needing millions of users.

In Part I: Nail a Niche, we mentioned Avanoo, the corporate employee training company, going from a few thousand in revenue to $5 million in a bit more than a year.

They couldn't have done that—at least that fast—if they'd stuck to their first price, selling courses to consumers at "name your price" prices for an average of $5 each.

But in closing $50,000-plus deals now (and on track to sell six- and seven-figure deals), they can grow revenue much, much faster. They're selling to companies that have the ability to pay (Fortune 2000), have a clear need, and have reference-able customers. It's just a question of time before they increase the size of their big deals again. Of course, only time will tell how far they can take this, and still stay competitive and grow fast in a noisy market.

When you're attempting to grow by major leaps, work on doubling your average sale size as much as you work on finding and closing twice as many deals. Or if you already have lead generation machine working smoothly, it's how you can quadruple growth—doubling deal sizes while doubling leads.

> **Work on doubling your average sale size as much as you work on finding and closing twice as many deals.**

You can do it through a mix of targeted lead generation, changing pricing, designing higher-end packages, through premium products with enterprise features, carefully developed channel partners, or whatever. It doesn't happen overnight, but you can take concrete steps to get there.

But start with the question, "What conditions would have to exist to close deals that are 10x larger than we are doing today?"

Many entrepreneurs, especially first-time founders, have expectations of what people will pay that are far too low. It's also easy for experienced executives to fall into a rut with a division or team, through either inertia or habits. Push yourself past those limits, to come up with ways to double or triple your revenue per customer by also asking:

- What would it take to grow our revenue 10x?
- What would it take to grow our biggest sales size 10x?
- How can we find and work with customers to whom our solution would be worth 10x the price we're currently charging?

This works for early-stage companies struggling to get to a million-dollar run rate—companies that need a "sanity check," because they're chasing after $500 or $1,000 customers, but they aren't doing the funnel math, realizing they may need hundreds or thousands of them to hit their revenue goals!

This works for companies who are so obsessed with "getting new customers" that they've taken their eyes off "growing revenue," which is different.

Except for the top ~0.1% of the Apple App Store, most companies struggle to market and sell lots of small deals. How can you think bigger? For example:

- *SaaS products:* What kinds of management features would you need to sell packages of 50, 500, or 5,000 seats?
- *Freemium or cheap products:* What do companies need so badly that they're willing to pay for a five-, six-, or seven-figure annual subscription deal? Or what kinds of channel and distribution partners would have a big audience hungry for your stuff?
- *Smartphone apps:* Is there a way to sell bulk packages to businesses? Or resell the technology or your unique expertise to other business?
- *Books, online programs, or workshops:* Are there partners who can help sell bulk orders? How can these lead to five-figure consulting/services, then six-figure, then seven-figure?
- *Jeans or t-shirts:* What kinds of companies would bulk-buy them, or be a great channel to profitably sell lots of them for you? (For every

successful "Threadless"-type T-shirt success, there are probably 50 other companies that struggle to profitably sell single T-shirts and other small items direct.)

What We Love and Hate about Small Deals

Whether it's software, products, or services, when most people start a business, naturally we all want to get whatever customers we can. This usually means smaller deals, often from "free" to a few thousand dollars. "Small" is a *great* place to start because it's easier to get things going and adjust on the fly. Plus you can get valuable feedback, case studies, and community effects from small customers.

Also, smaller businesses can be more disorganized or less sure about their planning. Often they're just trying to survive rather than grow, can't afford to pay much, can't pay cash up front, may buy impulsively, or lack the time, people, or money to follow through 100%.

We're not saying smaller businesses are bad—they're wonderful and the backbone of our economy. But don't *count* on making a big business out of small deals or customers.

> **Don't *count* on making a big business out of small deals or customers.**

What We Love about Big Deals

As you get off the ground, one of the best ways to double your other growth, without working more hours, is by closing bigger deals.

With bigger deals, you will (a) make a lot more money, (b) exert less effort, and (c) help customers become more successful. If you're selling to someone who's close to your Ideal Customer Profile, closing a $100,000 deal shouldn't be much more work than closing a $10,000 deal, and may not even take longer. So if it takes two to three times the time and effort—but if you get 10x the revenue and your customers get 10x the value, it's worth it!

Don't be afraid of raising your prices when selling to bigger companies with bigger needs. Bigger deals can take longer to close, but they're worth the wait.

The size of the deal doesn't determine the sales cycle length; that's affected by things like:

- Clarity in Nailing a Niche, especially becoming a need, not a nice-to-have, for executives
- The number of people involved in a buying decision (bigger companies means more people are involved, the decisions are more complex, and more time is required)
- Selling on value, not price, and with unique advantages customers can't get elsewhere
- Your ability to show believable proof of results

Also, bigger deals can lead to better customer results:

- *Better service:* You can focus customer service/Customer Success people on fewer customers, ensuring customers get the most value from your product.
- *More commitment:* As long as you're not selling to people who aren't a fit or aren't ready, bigger deals should lead to companies that have greater *need, commitment, and resources* to get the most from your product.
- *More cash upfront:* Working with bigger deals often means working with companies that have cash or funding, to *pay cash upfront for one- to three-year contracts,* so important for growing businesses!

The Best of Both Worlds

We want to be clear: We're not telling you to give up small deals. Use small deals to get started, and appreciate those customers and love them—but don't *limit* yourself to small deals by thinking small. Before the Internet, businesses ended up focusing on either lots of small, transactional customers, or on big customers and big deals. Now, companies can blend them cooperatively, building a customer base of small, medium, and large customers. The trick is in focusing on one as your primary business, while keeping the other(s) as complementary.

CHAPTER 16

Not Too Big, Not Too Small

Small deals can sink you, but so can big ones. Mark Suster envisioned customers as three kinds of animals—rabbits, deer, and elephants—and came up with the metaphor "Most startups should be deer hunters." For early-stage companies, he said to focus on the deer (good-sized deals) and avoid the rabbits (too small) and the elephants (the largest companies and deals, which are difficult to sell to and service, very demanding, and hard to make successful).

Mark wrote, "It's tempting on many levels to be an elephant hunter. If you manage to kill an elephant, it'll have so much meat it will feed you for a long time. But elephants are hard to catch, and they take whole teams of people to bring down. They take special tools. If you're not successful you may starve. And if you *do* catch them, it could be even worse. Avoid elephants in your early stages."

David tackled Goliath, but your life is not a myth. Be smart about the largest deals and companies that you can:

1. Realistically close
2. Realistically help succeed in a big way
3. And that won't kill you with new product requirements or service level expectations that take your business off course

WHEN YOU CAN'T TURN SMALL DEALS INTO BIG ONES

If you're doing lots of small deals with big companies but nothing's turning into bigger opportunities, something's off. It could be that you're not selling high enough; the product isn't a need for your customers or explained the right way to them, or perhaps you're just too impatient and the cake is still baking.

Figuring out how to improve this can be as simple as getting salespeople around a table to talk about what has and hasn't worked in turning small deals into bigger ones, then coming up with a new plan. For example, you might be rushing to pilot/trial too fast with bigger companies; it might be better to slow down and get more executives to buy in before kicking off a trial or paid pilot. Or, you might be assuming that the small deals at big companies matter. If someone at IBM buys a license or five of your products, it's unlikely their VP knows or even cares.

You can't assume that just because people are using your stuff in one part of a company that other people will automatically find out about it. Letting things bubble up on their own can take a long time—or not happen at all. Don't be afraid to take things into your own hands, systematically and explicitly asking for referrals, and when referrals don't work, outbound prospecting directly to senior executives at other divisions. There's a difference between being patient and being passive.

There's a difference between being patient and being passive.

Ignore Our Advice

If there's some problem you're seeing in going for bigger deals, then don't be afraid to ignore anything or everything we've said here, or in this whole book. Don't do something just because we said so, or an investor or some bigwig like Marc Benioff or your brother Bob said so. What Zuck does only works for Zuck. Always think for yourself, taking ideas and adapting them to your specific situation. Hey, if you're selling small deals as transactions and it's going well, keep at it! Or perhaps all you have experience in is small deals or more consumer-type customers. Use your strengths: Do more of what is already working.

It's a *lot* easier to triple down on something that's already working than to get it working in the first place.

IF YOU HAVE CUSTOMERS OF ALL SIZES

One time, I talked to a great entrepreneur/CEO, who at the time was doing a few million in ARR and growing quickly. His make-up of customers was split roughly three ways:

1. Big customers (Fortune 500/Global 2000 types)—not many, but each paying a lot
2. Small and medium-sized businesses, each paying four or five figures a year
3. A large group of very small businesses paying very little individually, but a material amount as a group

He asked me where I thought he should place his bets. On one hand, their largest customers were very important and were creating six-figure deals. On the other hand, they didn't represent the majority of revenue and were a ton of work.

He showed me his customer list, ranked by revenue. His largest customer, a Fortune 500 leader, was paying him $100,000 a year. I told him that I was pretty sure, given the importance of the problem he was solving and its impact across the enterprise, that this number-one customer could pay them at least $300,000 a year. The CEO turned to me and

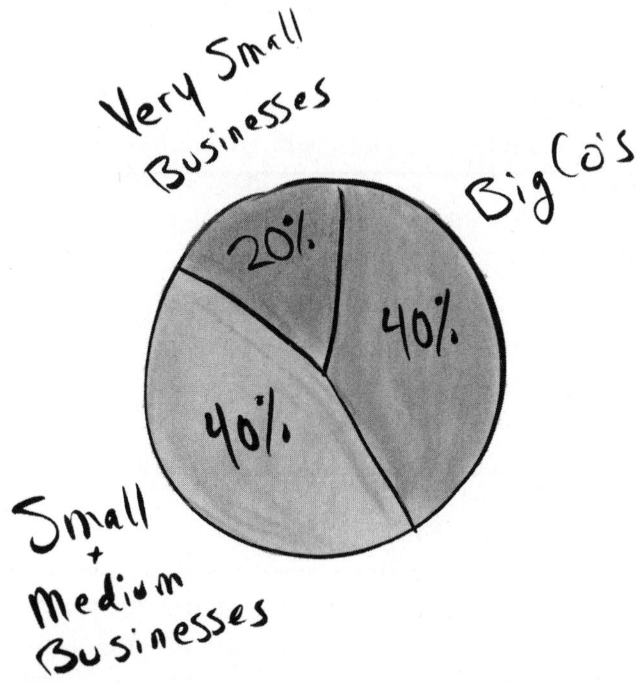

FIGURE 16.1 How much of your revenue comes from which different customer segments?

nodded his head. "Amazing! In fact, they told us the exact same thing the other day—that we were worth $300,000!"

Boom! That's me, Mr. Clairvoyant.

Actually, it wasn't very hard. Because *what he had with his SaaS company is something you may have with yours, too: an application that can be used by businesses of every size*. And if you do, you'll want to decide if you're selling a *tool*—or a *solution*.

It's not always obvious which way to go. And the 40/40/20 ratio you see in the chart above is surprisingly common. It's basically what we had at EchoSign. It's also basically what WebEx and Salesforce.com had, in the early years. It's what a lot of apps have that can be used by businesses of all sizes.

But once you are at even $1 million in ARR, you'll need to make a primary bet. Which segment do you put as your top priority in marketing? Which segment is the #1 orientation of your sales team?

If you have multiple segments with 10% or more revenue, you need to service them all in some fashion. Let them atrophy and you may regret it, if 12 or 24 or 30 months later, you're trying to find a layer where you can grow your business another 10%!

If you have multiple segments with 10% or more revenue, you need to service them all in some fashion. But one segment has to be number one.

But one segment has to be number one. And as you see this segmentation develop, you have to decide. Am I mainly DropBox, going for the mass market of smaller users to cover as much area as possible? Or mainly Box, going for revenue growth through bigger deals? Am I mainly like HubSpot (medium), or MailChimp (small), or am I Marketo (Big)? Maybe you could go any way at this time. At the end of the day, I think there are two main considerations:

1. *Understand that you can make 3 to 20x the revenue on a given enterprise customer with a solution sale versus a tool.* Having been a VP at a Fortune 500 company, I can tell you that getting me as a corporate VP to pay $100,000 for a web tool was basically impossible. It gets sent to Procurement, and by the time you are done it's hard to get anyone to pay more than $20,000 for a tool. There's never any extra budget for a six-figure tool to make the troops happier (sadly). But a solution? Solve my problem around billing? Around Customer Success Around CPQ? Well … you can get $20 million if you go the whole distance to completely solve a core enterprise business problem. Twenty million is what Salesforce gets at many large customers.

My point is that (relatively speaking) it's "easy" to get a six-figure contract in larger companies if you solve a real, painful business process problem. Those problems are very expensive to solve at BigCos. If I'm a VP in the Fortune 500, it costs me $200,000–$500,000 in people just to get anything done, and it takes forever. If you solve a true problem for me, and I have a $20 million budget, I'll spend 1–2% of that to solve my problem. Easy. Another tool? That's not on the list. The budget here has to be a rounding error if it's just a tool. $5,000 ACV is fine, and $10,000–$15,000 is maybe fine, for a tool. Above that, don't bother me, I'm a Corporate VP … I've got real problems to solve.

2. *You'll need a lot more people and processes (and features and software development) to provide a true solution.* You can't sell, provision, implement, and support a solution the same way as a tool, even if it's basically the same business process you are addressing. You'll probably need solution architects. You may have to fly there and go onsite. You may need account managers and a dedicated professional services team and sophisticated Customer Success managers. You may need a more sophisticated approach to techops and netops, and disaster recovery and enterprise-grade security. You may need your own CIO to talk to their CIO. And you may need more, and more expensive, sales people. DropBox didn't need anyone in sales, really, until they hit $100 million in revenue; then they decided to add solution sales. But Box doubled down early on this—and while they got to $100 million a little more slowly, they got to their first millionth *customer* more quickly.

An example of the difference: EchoSign was a tool that let you sign a contract on the Internet, and it's also sold as a very sophisticated solution that completely automates the process of creating, signing, routing, and managing millions of contracts made up of thousands of dynamic documents, automating hundreds of business processes for an entire enterprise. The two products share a core set of functionalities, but a very different set of edge features and support. The first is worth about $15 a month. The latter may be worth $1 million a year.

If you have a broad mix of customers, I'm not telling you which way to go. But I can tell you what the math says: It's easier to get to $100 million in ARR and an IPO on the backs of enterprise customers who can pay $100,000-plus a shot. After all, you only need 1,000 of them then to get to $100 million in ARR. To get to the six- and seven-figure price points, you need to sell a solution to a big problem, not just a tool.

It's easier to get to $100 million in ARR and an IPO on the backs of enterprise customers who can pay $100,000-plus a shot.

Don't fear the solution. Don't fear the Professional Services team, or the solution architect, or the sales engineer. Deep down, many of us would prefer to sit at our desks or in front of our iPads and watch the customers roll in with no human interaction. If you can get 1,000,000 paying customers that way, that's probably the way to go.

But whatever you do, don't do all the expensive work to provide a solution and then get stuck at a low tool price point; that's the kiss of death.

CHAPTER 17

Going Upmarket

So you have a good thing going already? Maybe it's time to push yourself on investing in salespeople, on pricing, and going after bigger, more complex customers.

IF YOU DON'T WANT SALESPEOPLE …

A lot of people have a desire to avoid having to hire salespeople. They have this question of, "Do I even need salespeople at all? Slack and Atlassian don't have any (yet). Can't I just do a Basecamp model? Can't I just have customer happiness officers who make customers so happy that they keep referring new customers, and people simply buy my product without me doing anything or having to 'sell' it?"

Well, maybe you can. More power to you. As long as there is enough momentum in your business to keep hitting your revenue goals without a true sales team, then by definition you don't need one … but you will probably want one. Maybe your goals are too low.

A lot of founders who haven't managed the revenue side of a business can be anti-sales. They see it as an unpleasant part of the business if they haven't done it themselves or worked with a great sales team.

"Isn't sales just a bunch of guys in a virtual boiler room, trying to get people to buy stuff they don't really need? If my product is so great, shouldn't it sell itself, so long as I have Happiness Officers answering questions and moving things along?"

Again, it has been done. But is it smart for you?

But the "problem" with depending on Happiness Officers is threefold: First: What works at the bottom of the market may not work as you tilt upmarket. Self-service (and almost-self-service) models can work well with Happiness Officers whose goal in part is to be customer support on steroids, that is, not just to be reactive but also proactive. Not just to respond to tickets but also to make sure customers are happy with the product and loyal to it. It's a great strategy for the bottom of the market.

What works at the bottom of the market may not work as you tilt upmarket.

While that will still work at slightly higher price points, say $99 or $299/month or even a $5000 annual contract value or so, in many categories above that your prospects will expect to talk to a true salesperson, or at least some of them will. A Happiness Officer can probably do a decent job here, but ultimately a salesperson is the best fit for someone who wants to talk to sales, especially if they're looking for your help in selling your stuff to their executives!

Second, and perhaps most important, Happiness Officers are great "Middlers." But they are not Openers or Closers. Middlers are smart, engaging people who love a product but have no experience in real sales. They don't know how to pick up a phone or send an email and prospect or find a possible sale. They default to, "If I talk to someone, then I'll mention something they could buy, and if my customer needs or wants it then they'll just buy it." They are ill-equipped, uncomfortable, and unpracticed in asking for the close. It's not easy to ask for money if you're not used to it. Professionals are much better at it than amateurs. "Amateurs" (those not classically trained in sales) don't know how to close. They wait and hope for the close to happen magically on its own. Sometimes it does. But you'll see that once you have someone managing a prospect who knows how to close, then a lot more deals happen, and they close more quickly.

Third: You'll make a lot more money with a true sales team. It's just basic math. As noted, more deals open and close when you have trained sales professionals working with your prospects or current customers. Just as important, sales professionals know how to maximize the revenue per opportunity, how to figure out the maximum number of seats that can be closed now and later. How to get a customer to buy a more comprehensive edition or set of services than they might buy without guidance. How selling a bigger deal upfront and charging more, rather than less, can increase the chances of Customer Success later because the customer is all in from day one.

Because sometimes charging customers less means they are less invested ... and makes it easier for them to quit halfway to the goal.

You may not care so much in the early days. But you'll quickly care once you have even $1 million or $2 million in ARR under your belt. Because leads are precious. If a great sales rep can turn a lead into $40 on average, but a happiness officer only turns it into $20 on average, and a sales rep can close 50% more often than a happiness officer, then, seriously, go pro. Putting true sales professionals on those leads is going to increase your revenue per lead by 300%—at least in the segment of your customer base where it makes sense to have sales professionals (e.g., $99–$299 MRR and higher).

Now, if you're still on the fence, because you're very "customer-focused" and believe customers are smart enough to figure it all out on their own, then, I get it. Trust me; you don't want a used car-type sales rep leading the charge here. But a great SaaS rep doesn't sell used cars. She sells a beautiful, gleaming Tesla Model S, or at least a shiny new Audi A4, metaphorically speaking. What I mean is, the customers already love your product. The sales rep's job isn't to lie, cheat, steal, or convince you that it's just "surface rust" on the '05 Impala. Rather, it's to be a trusted guide, a consultant, helping the customer through an often-complex evaluation and purchasing process to buy a product that generates a big impact for them. It's about learning, bonding, adding true, real value—and believing it, delivering it. Plus, it's about having the confidence to ask for the biggest possible check :)

The sales rep's job is to be a trusted guide, a consultant, helping prospects through an often-complex evaluation and purchasing process.

ADD ANOTHER TOP PRICING TIER

I've been fortunate enough to meet with many outstanding entrepreneurs building self-service SaaS businesses at the bottom of the market—a customer base made up of very small businesses and individual business purchasers within slightly larger companies.

By all means, if you can build a $100 million self-service SaaS business without a sales team, a Customer Success team, webinars, getting on planes, and all that—go for it.

Small customers are valuable, beyond any revenue they bring in. They can be champions for your company; they can refer others to your business. They'll often give you useful product feedback; they're willing to develop add-on ideas, code, features, and content for you. Small customers can be enjoyable to work with, satisfying to help, and they may seed larger deals.

For lead generation, it helps to have some free, easy, or affordable ways for prospective customers to kick the tires and get to know you. This could be a free or low-cost product, a free trial, or free content. For the first couple of years, Aaron dropped the price of the Kindle e-book version of *Predictable Revenue* from $10 to .99 to make it a no-brainer to buy. Losing thousands in book profits was worth it to triple the audience and help find customers for speaking gigs and five- or six-figure consulting projects.

For lead generation, it helps to have some free, easy, or affordable ways for prospective customers to kick the tires and get to know you.

But as I said before, don't expect small customers to drive a lot of *revenue*. As I mentioned before, no matter how hard I tried at EchoSign to drive up self-service freemium as a percentage of our revenue, the laws of this math and gravity held it back to less than a third of our revenue. Just as it is at Box and Yammer and many others that started as simple self-service models, before figuring out how to double their deal size (and then double again, and again ...).

If your product is 100% individual-focused, and you add *just enough features to sell to a team*, to tilt just *slightly* upmarket—you can grow your revenue, at least a segment of your revenue, by 20 to 30 times. Because deal sizes can go way up, and customers will stay with you much longer.

Virtually every self-service, individual-seat web service churns at a relatively high rate—from maybe 2.5% a month at best, to 3.5 or 4.0% a month or more in many cases. (There are rare exceptions.) Four percent monthly churn means you have to replace half your entire customer base *every year* just to stay flat.

FIGURE 17.1 Going upmarket can increase both Customer Success and revenue.

Now come up with a slight extension of that same product whereby some team or segment of an entire enterprise can use it together. Let's call it just five seats to start, instead of one. Maybe you add management-level analytics. And then some sort of collaboration. I'm not sure what it will be for you, but let's call it the most basic features necessary so that a team or a group will buy, instead of an individual user. Often it's around extra reporting features, administration, security, or configuration controls.

What you'll find is epic on the churn side. As the deal gets just a smidge bigger, your churn will drop by 50–80%, toward 1–1.5% per month. As you add more seats, the churn will trend toward 0% and eventually become negative: your customers will add more seats than they cancel over time.

Since SaaS compounds and is a long-term play, over three-plus years you'll be just so far ahead. That single-seat user that left after eight months might be gone forever. But that five-seat team edition sales customer is still there in year 2 and year 3, paying you, and maybe even adding seats.

Within a $30/month product, all of a sudden you've gone from a $240 customer lifetime value for the single-seat purchase to a $5,400

CLTV over three years—from the same customer, from the same basic core product—just with whatever additional functionality you needed for your team or enterprise edition. The math just gets better as you support slightly larger teams.

And if you create a higher-end level that's $50 or $100 or more per month, the math compounds even faster. Even if a customer isn't a fit for it, a side benefit is increasing the perceived value of the $30 product. For example, having a top package of $10,000 per month can make your $1,000 per month offer feel more affordable (a psychological principle called anchoring). Salesforce.com started with a $65 per-month/per-user product and eventually was able to create $125- and $250-per-month versions.

So what's my point? I'm not saying that if you are building a freemium or self-service product you should immediately *Go Enterprise*. (Although I've done that exact path.) What I *am* suggesting is that you at least think about adding a layer: If the one-seat freemium thing is working for you, add a Team or a so-called Enterprise Edition, even if it's just for an enterprise of five.

Think about adding a layer: If the one-seat freemium thing is working for you, add a Team or Enterprise Edition.

And hire a sales rep—or better yet, two—to actually talk to these customers and try to close them, to go beyond just customer support. If it works—just that little extra functionality, for that extra edition—you can dramatically increase your growth rate. All of a sudden, that same customer, that same lead, that same person who came by your website or app, all of a sudden is worth 20 to 30x more. Same effort to get them to your site or app. But 20 to 30x the return.

PRICING IS ALWAYS A PAIN

If you're struggling with nailing down your pricing, remember:

- Pricing is always frustrating and never perfect
- It's easier to start with higher pricing and then lower it, than to start low and raise it later

Getting your pricing right is often—if not always—confusing and frustrating. Many companies end up missing out on a lot of revenue by underpricing. Here are a couple of approaches you can use:

It's Easier to Get Started with "Bottom-Up" Comparative Pricing

First, take a look at what people are paying for products that are similar to what you're offering; This gives you a useful baseline for expectations. For example, most B2B SaaS companies charge between \$10 and \$60 a month for a general user. After seeing lots of services priced this way, buyers naturally expect similar services to charge a similar amount. You can charge more, but you'll need a justification for it, and users with compelling needs.

Come up with a few products or packages, guesstimate the prices, and bounce them off live prospects. There's no secret formula or seven-step magic system for this; just make it up as you go and see what works. (Hmm—the same way you "figure out life.") It won't take long to get the data you need, or to get a feel for what's working and what needs adjusting.

So that's not much of a new idea. Now for one that many first-time entrepreneurs miss . . . .

"Top-Down" Value-Based Pricing

If you have a good sense of the impact your product or service can have on customers, try pricing it backwards: first set the price, then figure out who'll need and value it enough to pay your price. In this scenario, your costs shouldn't matter. If you can tell that something is worth \$1,000,000 to an ideal buyer, and they're willing to pay for it, what does it matter if your costs are \$100,000 or \$10,000? Charge \$1,000,000!

> **Maybe anyone can use what you've got, but who would find it especially valuable? Who needs it?**

Maybe anyone can use what you've got, but who would find it especially valuable? Who needs it? What is the impact you can help create? What is the dollar value you can justify because of that impact? Rethinking this'll help you (re-)Nail A Niche ... working backwards from who the best customers could or should be.

These ideas can apply to your $50 general users—perhaps you should rethink that and charge $125?—and also to your $150,000 enterprise customers—perhaps you should really charge $750,000!

This only works when you're unique and people believe in your value and the expected results. Anyone can *claim* anything on the Internet—how do you back it up, so people believe you?

Another side benefit of this: When you imagine setting a higher price, it forces you to imagine how you'd deliver enough value to customers to justify it. For many of you, especially if you're too early to have much of a customer base, this "backwards"/value-based pricing approach is still useful, even as just a thought exercise that challenges how you think about your customers and your value to them.

Simplicity, Not Perfection

High-end pricing and deals get complicated. A complicated pricing structure may "perfectly" capture revenue, at least in theory, but in reality, complex pricing makes it harder for customers to buy, and harder to keep track of what has or hasn't been delivered. Confusion will slow things down—including when your champion has to explain the structure to the CFO or ultimate decision-maker.

Complex pricing makes it harder for customers to buy and harder to keep track of what has been delivered.

Balance customizing the deal with keeping it as understandable as possible. When you need to decide between simpler pricing and "perfect" pricing, go simple and don't be afraid to leave some money on the table in order to close the deal.

Don't Be Afraid to Experiment with Pricing

It's hard getting your pricing "right." And even when you do nail it down, markets change, you release new products, or your competitors come out with something that forces you to revisit how you price or discount.

Don't let the fear of losing a deal stop you from trying out new pricing ideas with prospects.

GOING FORTUNE 1000

By Mark Cranney
Partner, Andreessen Horowitz

One of the myths of SaaS and many online apps is that the products are so good, so easy to use, and so quick to deploy, that the product sells itself and you don't need salespeople. By now, hopefully we've helped puncture any illusion of this you've held onto.

Given the popularity of try-before-you-buy and freemium-to-premium models for SaaS, it's easy to see where that myth comes from. But as many startups discover to their horror, after they "land" users and try to "expand" to more departments in a large company or government agency, this is far from the truth.

But that's where the money is.

You have to learn how to go after and sell to companies who are hundreds or thousands of employees. And it's a new skill. Because selling an enterprise-wide deal is a lot like getting a bill passed in Congress. Decision-making in large organizations is a long, tortuous process due to legacy technology deployments, internal politics, entrenched home-grown solutions, sunk cost of integrations, account control by incumbent vendors, and the sheer size and scale involved.

In many ways, the purpose of enterprise sales is to *help customers get through their own internal buying processes*. Even the best and most popular product can't make typical enterprise buyers change the way they do procurement.

And just because a SaaS company has landed a Fortune 500/Global 2000 client doesn't mean it will *keep* that sliver of business, let alone upsell, cross-sell, or sell across more divisions spanning multiple geographies.

Doing *that* may require hiring salespeople who live across the country or the world, in addition to the inside salespeople who work at headquarters. It's precisely when the product *seems* to be selling itself that building out this sales team and process is critical: Stopping or stalling at that point could expose the company to the competition and lose the race to be number one in its category.

What Sales Is Really About

Some people think the sales force's job is to communicate value to customers. To these people, sales is about buying a bunch of search ad words, parroting a company's message, or manipulating or somehow compelling uninterested prospects into buying. *They're wrong.*

> **The true purpose of salespeople is to *create new value for customers.***

The true purpose of salespeople is to *create new value for customers*, especially when they are working for a startup or growth company that's addressing a new market or trying to solve a complex problem. That's why enterprise/SaaS sales requires a well-developed process and guidelines. Even though some of the advice I share here draws on my experience at Opsware, where we sold datacenter automation before there was such a thing, the principles remain the same even though the domains have changed. Whether entrepreneurs like to admit it or not, the new enterprise customer, and how they buy, is a lot like the old enterprise customer and how they bought.

Still, this kind of selling does require a different mindset for experienced salespeople. When I was at Opsware, sales reps would come back to me and say, "Look, there's no budget for data center automation at XYZ company." And I'd say, "Well, I'm going to give you one chance, because you obviously missed it in training, but if you ever come back and tell me that again, you're not going to be working here any longer." Because *of course* there was no budget for data center automation back then: *the market hadn't been established yet*. Our job was to go out there and show customers a different and better way of doing business.

Then I'd show the sales reps a long list of initiatives they needed to look for in companies, which is where the missing budget for datacenter automation could be found. Instead of competing with other products for the same budget, our product would be competing at the highest strategy level. That's creating new value for customers, helping them run their business in new ways that they didn't see or understand before.

The Three Things Every Enterprise Customer Wants to Know

Even though the enterprise sales process has many steps and stages, it ultimately has to answer three questions for the customer: why buy, why buy from you, and why buy now.

Customer Question #1: "Why buy?" The easiest way to help a potential customer answer this question is to identify their important initiatives. Every large company has strategic business initiatives that are always going to be funded and that are driving its IT investments. Once the sales and marketing teams have uncovered these initiatives (as well as the critical capabilities that need to be in place for the initiative to be successful), they can begin to define the unique value proposition.

The key here is to seek *first to understand* and then *second to be understood*. Listen first, sell second. The problem with telling a potential customer what you think they need before you understand what *they* think they need is that:

- You're basing your position on a known set of requirements from a broad base of companies instead of unknown specific opportunities.
- It positions you as more of a commodity play or just a vendor—as opposed to a partner who can help transform the way they conduct their business.

Customer Question #2: "Why buy from you?" No one knows more about your solution than you do, so you should be the one helpfully consulting with your target customer to craft what success looks like. By doing this, you're more likely to win the criteria-setting battle, because you're essentially *prepositioning and differentiating* your enterprise/SaaS product over that of your competitors. This helps block the competition, as you're helping the prospect learn to see the world, and success, through your lens.

Therefore, the sales team's job here is to help a potential customer define success in three distinct buckets: (1) business criteria, (2) architecture/scale criteria, and (3) feature and functional criteria.

This is also the best time to prepare messaging, metrics, and marketing to address three audiences: (1) enterprise-level (C-suite, senior vice presidents); (2) workgroup-level (VPs, directors, managers); and

(3) user-level (groups of individual contributors and their direct managers). Since most startups—and big companies, for that matter—spend most their messaging effort on the level 1 or 3 audiences, forcing your company to constantly see its prospects and customers through this three-level lens affects your win/loss ratio.

At this point of the sales cycle, there are many tasks that have to be guided by the project owner—usually the salesperson. This is where they show their value: by coordinating the right resource, action, or message—at the right level and at the right time—to determine success or failure. The best enterprise salespeople are coaches or entrepreneurs here, ensuring that prospects receive what they need, resources are rallied within the company, stumbling blocks are uncovered and avoided, and surprises are eliminated.

The best enterprise salespeople are coaches, ensuring that prospects receive what they need, resources are rallied within the company, stumbling blocks are uncovered and avoided, and surprises are eliminated.

This is key because your biggest competition isn't just other startups, perpetually licensed on-premise packages, home-grown solutions, or incumbent vendors. It's *inertia*. It takes a lot for a big company to decide and successfully implement a new solution. Enterprise salespeople often can't achieve that big account escape velocity, and they lose to *do nothing* and *no decision* more often than to any other competitor.

Customer Question #3: "Why buy now?" Once you've eliminated the competition and are on the path to technical validation, you have to turn the value proposition into a quantifiable business case. This kind of "ROI diagnostic" as a selling tool gives you three advantages:

1. It aligns and maps your product's capabilities, operational benefits, and financial value with the company's key strategic initiatives. This helps your enterprise-wide proposal compete for capital with all the other proposed initiatives, programs, and projects.
2. It improves visibility into the current operations environment, by providing a snapshot of operational inefficiencies and challenges.

Besides showing the company that you get what matters to them, this approach helps insulate you from pricing pressure.

3. It ensures that the plan for implementing your solution delivers on the most important business objectives first, which in turn ensures a shorter time to value.

If landing these bigger customers is new to your business, you're going to have to staff up with more customer-facing resources than you may have expected or wanted—professional services, customer support, and so on. Especially if you started out with some dream of self-service selling. Investing in these kinds of roles and people will pay off in securing and expanding these customers—and in getting the best marketing resource there is: happy customer references.

While new clients are great, the best place to sell something is where you've already sold something: adding more users or new services, or getting into other divisions. So don't obsess so much on getting new customers that you forget to invest in current ones. Including turning them into unassailable external references and advocates. Because good products—and even many great ones—don't sell themselves. You need champions who will help sell them for you.

Do The Time

The Painful Truth: It'll take years longer than you want.

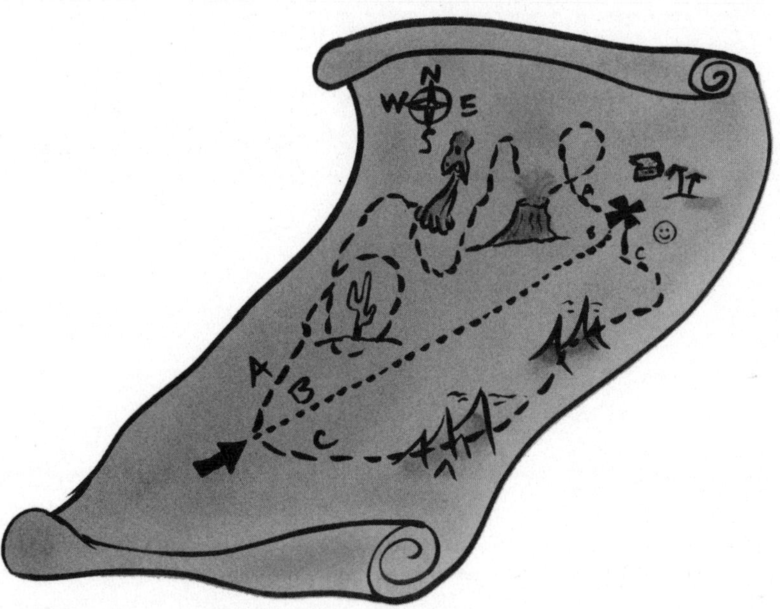

C: What you believe success requires.
B: What you hope happens.
A: Reality—if you're lucky.

CHAPTER 18

Embrace Frustration

Any expectations you have about how long it will take, or how hard it will be, are pretty much guaranteed to be wildly off. But it's worth it.

ARE YOU SURE YOU'RE READY FOR THIS?

One night I had dinner with the founder of a pretty successful web company and he asked me how long I'd worked on EchoSign. I told him and he nodded his head, "Yeah, same for me. It takes about seven years to get to exit." That's true in the software/SaaS business and it's true for many businesses and even career paths. You have to be ready for it to take years longer than you hope or want before you hit your big goals.

You may have heard that SaaS companies usually take longer than consumer Internet companies to get to $75–$100 million in revenue. But it's not always clear *how much* longer.

Let's look at some basic math: Assume it takes you a couple of years to get going and Nail A Niche, and then you grow 100 percent a year through $50 million or so in revenue (which isn't easy, mind you):

- Y1 revenue: $0
- Y2 revenue: $1 million
- Y2 revenue: $3 million
- Y3 revenue: $6 million
- Y4 revenue: $12 million
- Y5 revenue: $24 million
- Y6 revenue: $48 million
- Y7 revenue: $80 million

Having done extremely well, hitting $80 million ARR in Year 7—it took you seven years—you're ready for your IPO in Year 8. If you do well, but not quite as well as this, it can take a decade. A friggin' decade.

What about mergers and acquisitions? The challenge here is that in most SaaS M&A, unless it's trivial stuff, the acquirer wants to wait for some scale—they want you to have from $10 million to $20 million in recurring revenue at least. With the math above, that can take 5 or 6 years to get to a healthy exit as well. It took David Ulevitch 10 years from founding to clicking into hypergrowth and then selling OpenDNS to Cisco for $635 million. And that doesn't include the extra earlier years preparing to found OpenDNS.

Speaking as someone who's done a lot of M&A deals (as buyer, seller, and advisor), I'd say never count on selling your company. Selling a company, especially a tech company, is risky and complicated. It's like getting married but 10x more convoluted … and once it's done, you can never go back.

This math isn't new. Everyone used to talk about seven years to an IPO. The problem is that a lot of folks who are doing first-time startups, or coming out of the consumer Internet world, don't get it. In consumer Internet companies, you can think in terms of 18- to 24-month time frames. With companies that sell to consumers, it's a much faster business cycle: build, try to sell, pivot, and find a niche. Generally, you know very quickly if something is going to take off or not. There may be faster possible success, but with more risk to succeed or exit, since there's less of a template than in B2B.

That's not as true in a SaaS company. You have to be willing to Do The Time. It takes longer to get your team together, get your product right, Nail A Niche, and see your sales cycles take off. The feedback loops take longer.

If you're any other kind of company, this kind of time frame still seems to hold true: five to nine years to "make it," where you're making serious money that doesn't feel like it could disappear at any moment. Even big career, life, and income leaps can take that long.

The press earns more views from rare stories like "Johnny was 13 when he created an iPhone app, and made a billion dollars overnight." That's the Exception, not the Rule. When Slack raised $120 million at a billion dollar valuation, the press trumpeted, "Zero to a Billion in Less Than a Year!" What no one wrote about was that Slack had been started six years earlier (2008), and struggled for five years before their big breakthrough. And even after that write-up, they continued to struggle—although in this case it was to keep up with and sustain their growth.

You read these exciting press stories and feel a mixture of excitement first, and then depression: everyone's crushing it except for you ("compare and despair"). The media loves to build people up and then tear them down, but they rarely print the whole, balanced story. It's less dramatic that way, which usually means fewer readers.

You read these exciting press stories and feel a mixture of excitement first, and then depression: everyone's crushing it except for you ("compare and despair").

So get excited about these overnight success stories, but take them with a grain of salt—and be prepared to Do The Time for as many years as it takes.

You Need 24 Months to Get Off the Ground

I meet with great VPs of Sales and Product who are *ready*. It's time to go out on their own and start their own SaaS companies.

Awesome. I get it. I'd like to recruit you to be a VP at one of my companies, but I get it. Working for The Man can be a great way to make money in the interim, support your family, and get paid to learn. But no one who's truly ambitious wants to work for The Man forever. I mean, not really. If you're wondering if you should start your own SaaS company, here are three questions to ask yourself:

First: Are you prepared to give a full 24-month commitment to hit Initial Traction? Not 12 months. Not 18 months. But 24 months? Two *years?* Six months isn't enough. Twelve isn't. It's going to take you 9 to 12 months just to get the product right, and another 6 to 12 to get significant revenues.

Maybe an Instagram or a WhatsApp or a Pinterest can explode in just 12 months (though again, it took years of development and trial and error before they got to their "overnight" successes). You can't afford to expect miracles like that in business-to-business software, services, or whatever business you might be in. Can you *afford* to commit for 24 months just to get to something, to real initial traction? If not, you should pass. Slack went from $0 to $12M ARR in one year (2014). Whoa. But it wasn't *founded* on January 1, 2014.

Giving yourself 12 months to get to initial traction won't cut it. You'll quit. Just 12 months in, you won't have enough revenue to support yourself, if you have any at all. The honest truth is that most folks can't really commit for 24 months, because of financial or personal or other reasons. That makes sense. Nevertheless, you'll fail in SaaS if you don't commit to spending 24 months to achieve Initial Traction.

You'll fail in SaaS if you don't commit to spending 24 months to achieve Initial Traction.

Second: Are you able to commit to 8,760 hours a year? That's 24 hours a day times 365 days. I don't mean committing to being in the office 14 hours a day—that's not really necessary (that's for the Y Combinator kids). But can you really, *honestly* commit to obsessively thinking, worrying, and stressing about how to do The Impossible? Every … Single … Moment?

You'll be thinking of nothing but work, even when you are playing with the kids or having dinner with your husband. That's what it's going to take. If you don't have the mental bandwidth you should pass.

Everything in SaaS is insanely competitive. Because SaaS is so multifaceted, you're going to have to be the VP of sales, Customer Success, marketing, and probably product, too, in the early days. There's endless drama with paying customers. You'll almost lose your best logo accounts. You have to be intensely, painfully committed to do all this.

Later, there will be fat—once you get to $5 million ARR or so. It'll get easier in many ways as you grow (and harder in others). But in SaaS, it takes a long time until then; it's hard to get recurring revenue engines going.

Third: Will you Take the Leap? This is, perhaps, most important. If you keep a mindset that you're "just trying it out" but you maintain other options, it never works. "I'll try for a while and go back to Salesforce.com if it doesn't work," or "I'll do a lot of consulting while I see if it works," or "I'll raise $500K and see how it goes." This just never works, at least not for high-growth startups. Great founders Take the Leap. Not because they are crazy risk-takers, but because they see the risk and decide to go for it anyway. They know there will be many challenges—with funds, customers, family—but they decide to figure them out along the way. They have doubts. They have fears. They have money troubles. But they see The Future and believe in their own (eventual) success. If you aren't ready to Take the Leap, you aren't ready to do a startup.

What If You're Close?

Okay, what if you aren't *quite* there? You can't pass tests 1, 2, and 3 above, but you are close. Then take a pause—don't say no *yet*. Instead, go do some more homework. Do 20 customer interviews. Find a great cofounder who can pass the 3 tests, commit to 7–10 years and the overall 24-plus months to Initial Traction. You almost certainly can't do it alone; do that and then see how it feels. Even great founders that can see The Future sometimes need help. I did in both my startups. Twenty interviews and an amazing co-founder can be the missing pieces that really show you how to do your own SaaS startup.

Even great founders that can see The Future need help.

A Double Check: Are You *Really* Sure?

There's been one huge change in "entrepreneurship" over the past 10 years. No, it's not that it's cheaper than ever to do an Internet startup. That's not even true. When software came on a disk or a CD-ROM in the old days, it was even cheaper. You didn't even need a single server to start Microsoft, or Intuit, or Borland, or Lotus. Although distribution today is far broader, if not cheaper.

It's not that the web and tech are so much bigger, creating so many more opportunities. That's true, but even when tech was smaller you could scale very quickly. Inflation-adjusted, Lotus 1-2-3 did over $100M its first year and IPO'd in its second year. What SaaS company ever did that?

What's changed is the culture of entrepreneurism. Ten years ago, to be a founder you were a bit of a nut—a mad scientist, a crazy kook, someone who didn't realize the odds of success were 0.00001%. Someone so smart, so gifted, so bonkers, that they did something wild. Founders were a breed apart. You might have met some of them, but you could never imagine *being* one of them. Ten years ago, if you joined a startup post-traction, you were still taking a big risk. You were stepping out of an accepted career path and potentially taking a big hit; and you were definitely taking a big salary cut.

By contrast, today even a pre-traction entrepreneur is super-cool. Even being just a wannapreneur can make you feel cool. The risk is low, failure is fine, and you can always go join Facebook/Google/Zynga/Square if it doesn't work out. Joining a post-traction startup? No salary cuts necessary. And your resume? It's enhanced by that cool, hyperscaling startup, which is zero risk. That's okay by me, but I think that TechCrunch, Y Combinator, The Social Network, and so on have over-glamorized entrepreneurship.

My one piece of advice: You absolutely should not start a tech startup and try to raise money unless it's 100% clear to you that this is the best thing in the world to do. Why not?

You absolutely should not start a tech startup and try to raise money unless it's 100% clear to you that this is the best thing in the world to do.

First, your startup will almost certainly fail, and while that's okay, you won't really get any credit for it. No one will care about your failed startup that got no traction and that no one ever heard of. They won't judge you, but they won't care.

Second, risk-adjusted economics *suck*. If you are smart and driven rather than risk-adjusted, you'll make more money by joining a top web company, staying, and getting promoted. While the comp delta between a startup and BigCo doesn't seem huge at nonleadership levels, it really grows when you get promoted and into management.

Third, even if you want to do a startup, you're much better off joining an existing rock-star, super-strong team. Great startups need great teams, which are rare. Better to join one than try to start one from scratch, which is close to impossible.

Fourth, it's far, far harder than you can imagine. The highs are higher, for sure, but the lows are so low. Most people really aren't up for the lows and can't handle them properly, if at all. For example, are you okay signing a full recourse $750,000 promissory note to fund payroll when all the funding falls through (like I did at my first startup)?

While you'll have more "freedom" doing a startup, it's such all-consuming hard work, you probably won't appreciate it—at least not while you are going through it. It's hard to enjoy the view when you're glued to a screen.

Having said that, if it's your calling, go for it. I did. But that's really the only great reason to start a SaaS startup—the only logical reason, even though it is illogical. Passion is supposed to be illogical!

You have to see something the rest of the world doesn't see, be so confident in it that you don't see all the risk, *and* have nothing in the end that's "better"/higher ROI (all things considered) than doing a raw startup.

EVERYONE HAS A YEAR OF HELL

I once talked to a CEO who, clearly, was miserable. His business was doing $30 million and growing nicely. He was about to introduce a new product that he thought could be game-changing, and he had a strong team (according to him) that he truly enjoyed working with.

What was so bad? I don't know exactly. But what I do know is that he was experiencing what almost all founders experience at least once on the 7- to 10-year journey: the *Year of Hell*.

This is never the first year. As tough as that first year is, that's still an exploration. The potential is limitless, your long-term vision undiminished by short-term reality. You are learning, just trying to get something off the ground. You have a small, tight team. It can be incredibly stressful, full of drama, and have some near-death moments. But that struggle is … what it is. You make it, or you don't, and you're still in your hyper-creative period, figuring something new out, which is always stimulating.

No, the Year of Hell comes later. It usually comes post-traction and sometimes happens post-scale, like for the CEO above. It's that one year when it's just too darn hard on every level to keep slugging it out. You're just under assault on too many fronts.

This isn't a particularly profound insight, other than to say, trust me—it's part of the journey, and you're not doing anything wrong. Hang in there. I've talked with a lot of SaaS CEOs and founders, and almost all of them who've done it long enough have had a Year of Hell. If you're in your Year of Hell, you'll get through it. We've all been there.

My personal Year of Hell was 2008. The leads were there, the customer base was there, but we started to spend a lot of money, and it just wasn't clicking. It was a tough year.

FIGURE 18.1

The strange thing to me isn't that almost everyone has a Year of Hell. The strange thing is that when people get through it (if they do), most times the business does more than just improve; it Reignites and grows faster than ever.

That Reignition comes because the hell you go through forces you to you retool what was stuck. If you embrace it, and adapt, rather than keep doing the same old same old. David Ulevitch of OpenDNS had two different Year of Hell (lucky him). In 2010, just after returning as CEO, David had a Year of Culture Hell, because people were rudderless after a year under a prior, professional CEO. In 2012, he had a Year of Growth Hell because the company wasn't growing fast enough, and they had to retool the entire sales and marketing system, applying many of the same ideas we've already covered in prior sections of this book. In both cases, OpenDNS came out of the Hell Years stronger—first with energized people, and then with predictable, scalable sales systems.

If you keep at it in your Year of Hell, you'll see Reignition. A *reacceleration* of growth. It may be a full year after the Year of Hell (what we saw at EchoSign), but it does happen often. If you have good customers, decent product, a committed team, and you keep at it with 100% dedication, unless the entire market collapses (rare in true SaaS), you'll see Reignition, too.

Patience and dedication will see you through.

Don't give up. Do The Time and you'll see.

Don't give up. Do The Time and you'll see.

COMFORT IS THE ENEMY OF GROWTH

During your journey, at some point you'll plateau. It'll probably happen more than once, in sales, personal energy, or innovation. Everyone plateaus. You feel stuck and nothing seems to kick-start growth again. If it's a revenue plateau, it's often because:

- You've tapped out your networks and relationships.
- You or your business doesn't stand out; you sound like everyone else.
- You're overly dependent on a single person for a key function such as bringing in leads, closing deals, or engineering.
- The market or customer needs have changed, and changing the business feels impossible or impractical. You've hit a business model or market wall but aren't sure what to do about it.

Sometimes a business breaks this plateau and ends up growing by hundreds of millions of dollars. And others struggle, unable to break their slump. What was the difference?

In all of these cases, *comfort* is the problem: not as in the "relaxed and happy" type of comfort, but the comfort found in "doing what you've always done"—even when you've done it really well or even when it hasn't worked. Comfort as in "what is familiar, known, or taken for granted."

Unfortunately, comfort is the enemy of growth.

The irony is, *what's already worked best for you so far (what you're familiar and comfortable with) can be the enemy of faster growth*, because you become dependent, complacent, or just too busy to keep up.

The idea of tripling your prices, redoing your product, rebuilding a sales team, firing a revenue leader, and taking six months to find someone new, going for 10x as many deals, creating a whole new way to generate leads, swapping out sales automation systems, writing a book in your nonexistent spare time … these potentially game-changing initiatives feel impossible to get to with so many other demands on your energy. A drastic change might be required to Nail a Niche or get on the path to scalable growth along with the other lessons in this book.

A drastic change might be required to Nail a Niche or get on the path to scalable growth.

With any big change or investment, you're going to obsess with how long it'll take, how much it'll cost and whether it'll affect sales at all. *By definition* it's a big risk with an uncertain payoff, or else you would have already done it. Honestly, most people can't handle this much uncertainty, so staying with the devil you know is easier than "going for it."

In a bicycle race, when your bicycle tire's leaking air but not flat yet, it feels easier just to keep pushing. You don't want to lose time. It's hard for you to feel like it's worth stopping in the middle of a race, to get off the bike, fiddle with it, and finally fix it, before starting up again.

When your bicycle tire's leaking air but not flat yet, it feels easier just to keep pushing.

Likewise, you put off restructuring the sales team. Or firing the executive you know needs to go. Or rebranding and repackaging. Or doubling down on a target market, making the change from "What problem do you need solved?" to "We solve X problem, do you have it?"

You put it off until you end up in a Year of Hell, with your back against the wall with no other options, and you're forced to change.

It's the same reason employees will bitch and moan about their manager or their job, but do nothing about it—because it's easier (more comfortable) to stay in their job than to find a new one, confront their manager, or change their own attitude, at least in the short term.

MOTIVATION: HOW AARON REACHED ESCAPE VELOCITY

As we went over in Part I: Nail A Niche, I didn't reach a personal Escape Velocity motivation to grow my income and business until I got married and started a family, going from zero to 12 kids in less than five years (which is a whole 'nother story).

Because we grew the family fast, we needed our money to grow fast, too. We chose to grow our money to support our life, rather than fit our life into our money. That's *why* our money grew fast—I had an epic Forcing Function that I couldn't hide from.

Those who succeed in making the big leaps *find the motivation*—whether through drive or passion—to sustain them through the ups and downs of Doing The Time, or a Year of Hell.

You have to want something as badly as a drowning person wants air.

Without that kind of "I NEED to breath" motivation—from any mixture of ambition, passion, desperation or fear—you're going to keep falling back into your habits, routines, and comfort zone.

What are you willing to lose a limb for? What do you want so badly that you don't care about "how you look"—to friends, family, or employees—in order to get it?

If you can't *find* something that drives you to change your own life or your own contribution at work, you'll end up getting more of what you already have.

If you're reading this and are thinking "it makes sense, but there's nothing I want that badly"—dig into the next Parts VI and VII. The ideas around Forcing Functions are the main way I predictably motivate myself to do things I don't want—or am too tired—to do.

CHAPTER 19

Success Isn't a Straight Line

Overnight success stories make for great news, but how people achieve—and perceive—success can be complicated in reality. Have a plan, but hold it lightly.

THE ANXIETY ECONOMY AND ENTREPRENEUR DEPRESSION

It's important to understand why the nature of both real and *perceived* growth is changing because of the Anxiety Economy, and why change takes years longer than you want.

It's the Best of Times. It's the Worst of Times.

There's never been an easier time to start a business—even with less than $100.

Businesses are growing faster than ever.

It seems like every week another company's gone from nothing to $100 million in record time, or been acquired for $1 billion or some other huge amount.

While there will be ups and downs in the economy in the coming years, the overall trend of "easier to start, faster possible growth" will continue as we get more and more connected.

Yet there's also never been more anxiety, frustration, and depression—especially among CEOs and aspiring entrepreneurs.

Whether you're new to business or have been at it for decades, everybody struggles with the now overwhelming number of choices in what you can do; build, use, and ways to grow … that all keep changing constantly, such as:

- How should we market? There's inbound marketing, outbound prospecting, web scraping, Google advertising, video, 1,000 flavors of

social media, live events, app stores and marketplaces, conferences, and countless other ways to create leads.
- What should we build next? Software, an app, software-as-a-service, a product, a market, a media company … ?
- How do we communicate with each other and with customers? Email, phone calls, voicemail, Twitter, Facebook, direct mail, Instagram, chat, Skype, Quora, messaging apps, and dozens of other ways can work to update and communicate with people and prospects.

You can't do all of it, and do it all well.

Plus we're dealing with generational changes:

- Young people who expect big titles, high pay, and fast advancement, *now*.
- Companies who still expect employees to just come in and work like robots, without a voice or choice.
- Executives and salespeople who keep doing what they've been doing for the past 10 or 20 years … whether it works or not.

All this anxiety and uncertainty is one reason why growth and predictability keep increasing in importance. People want to reduce uncertainty.

Why for You (and Your Friends, Despite Their Pretty Social Pictures) Anxiety Is Growing

There are reasons why anxiety is growing, despite our relative luxury compared to billions of others:

- *What used to work now doesn't:* You can't rely on the growth of your business in the same way. Because of anxiety, overload, and inertia, people and businesses tend to resist change rather than embrace it with open arms. You just have less energy to deal with it. Until you can't avoid it anymore and the company is faced with a "How do we survive?" crisis. It's why a Year of Hell can trigger Reignition if you embrace difficult decisions rather than avoid them.
- *General overwhelm:* The number of new businesses, apps, and ideas published and updated every day is overwhelming. This is also true of the number of daily email, social messages, and alerts. There's no way any one person can stay on top of it all. It's mentally exhausting.

- *Decision competition:* The overload is making decisions more difficult for people to make—including your customers. They only have so much "decision energy." You're not only competing with other companies, but with *all* the other emails, messages, and texts they receive and decisions they need to make.
- *Reality distortion, or "compare and despair":* If you're on social media at all, and follow many news sources, you're bombarded with stories of other people's successes: in starting or growing companies, finishing triathlons, getting married, having happy kids, and so on. This generates a "Reality Distortion Field" in which everyone else appears to experience 95% success and 5% struggle. But your life feels like the opposite proportions, because there you are, working 95% of your day to solve problems. You start feeling like "everyone else is getting what they want—I must being doing something wrong." The funny thing is, everyone you're watching feels the same thing.

These issues have been around forever. But the Internet, mobile phones, and social networking turbo-charge them.

> **"We always focused on solving the unending problems in our companies, so we only saw issues. While we only saw from other companies the success they presented to the outside world."—Ken Ross, entrepreneur/investor**

These factors all work together. First, there's some change or struggle at work you're dealing with. But at the same time you're overwhelmed with messages and to-do lists, and with less energy to deal with them. Plus, everyone else you're watching online, in social media or the news, appears to be successful … it's a triple whammy.

This isn't a self-help message about, "Oh, you're not really struggling, it's all an illusion." These factors directly affect revenue growth. Because it's not just you—it's the same experience for your employees and customers. The Reality Distortion Field warps their own expectations and decisions, including whether they should work at, buy from, or stay with your company.

Remember three things when overwhelmed:

1. *Embrace your struggle, because it's real and not going away*. Everyone else has it too—even when it doesn't look like it. Use your struggle

as a fire under your butt to change things, rather than resisting it. Turn it to your advantage!

2. *Don't let "keeping up with the Joneses,"* whether friends or competitors, distract you from doing the important things you, your team, and customers need. Don't raise money, hire a ton of people, write a book, or spend money on a conference just because someone else did.
3. *Cut the "blah blah" crap from your communication*, to employees and customers. "Simple to understand, easy to act on," honest information that's valuable to the reader (not just the sender) will help cut through the clutter they're dealing with. Be blunt. Be honest. Be helpful.

Depression and Entrepreneurship

These problems can be a quadruple whammy for many entrepreneurs, especially in technology; early reports are showing that entrepreneurs are more likely to have a brain and/or emotions that work differently than the average person. A study by Dr. Michael Freeman, a clinical professor at UCSF (and an entrepreneur as well), was one of the first of its kind to link higher rates of "mental health" issues to entrepreneurship.

Of 242 entrepreneurs surveyed, 49% reported having a mental health condition. Depression was the top issue, present in 30% of all entrepreneurs, followed by ADHD (29%) and anxiety problems (27%). By contrast, only 7% of the general U.S. population rates itself as depressed. Yes, part of the depression is caused by the stress of running a company, but the study tried to account for that by also tracking mental conditions in close family members—which were also higher than the populace.

Here's a takeaway: If you say, or someone says, that you have a "mental condition" (whatever that means to them), don't automatically assume it needs to be "fixed". It can be both a pain in the ass and a fantastic gift—so *how can you work with it* rather than believe you need to eliminate it? Many of the most successful artists' minds worked differently from ordinary people—offering both extra benefits, like break through creativity, as well as extra problems, like soul-crushing depression. But often if you remove one you lose both. Something incredibly frustrating today can turn out to be a huge advantage in the future, once you see how it fits into the puzzle.

Trust us, our families think we are certifiably crazy (no joke). Which we are, in our own ways … and we embrace it. If we didn't, if we hadn't—we wouldn't be here writing this book.

For details and updates on that study, see www.MichaelAFreemanMD.com/Research.html.

MARK SUSTER'S QUESTION: "SHOULD A PERSON LEARN OR EARN?"

A mutual friend of ours is Mark Suster, past serial entrepreneur and now partner at LA-based venture capital firm Upfront Ventures, and writer of the popular blog "Both Sides of the Table." Enter Mark:

I often have career discussions with entrepreneurs, both young and more mature, who are thinking about joining a company. I usually try the old trick of answering a question with a question: "Is it time for you to learn or to earn?"

Let's face it: If you're thinking about joining a startup that has already raised, say, $5 million (as the director of marketing, or as product management manager, senior architect, international business development lead, etc.), the chances of making your retirement money there is *extremely* small. That's okay. Not every job you have is supposed to be your big break. It's okay for that to be a job where you *learn*.

Yet people often ask me whether I think a company is going to be a big hit. It's clear that they're confusing *learn* with *earn*. So here's a simple calculation I do for them: okay, you would own 0.25% of the stock. They raised $5 million in their B round. Let's assume that the company raised it at a normal VC valuation and gave up 33% of the company and thus $5 million/33% = $15 million post-money valuation. If you never raise another round of venture capital (a big if), and if your company is sold for the normal venture exit ($50 million on average for the 200 or so that get sold annually), then what is your stake? $125,000? Yup. Simple math would have answered that, but people rarely do the calculations or think about them.

Let's say that it took four years to exit—that's $31,250/year. Now … these are stock options, not restricted stock, so you'll likely be taxed at a short-term capital gains rate. In my state (California), that averages around 42.5%. So after tax you'd make an extra $18,000/year; and that's in a *positive* scenario! Also, this ignores liquidation preferences, which actually means you'll earn less.

Now let's go *crazy*. Say you get 1%, you sell for $150 million, and it's in three years (e.g., you won the lottery). That's an after-tax gain of $287,500/year for two years. Not bad. But, wait a second … stock vests over four years. You didn't get acceleration on a change of control? Sorry, we'll have to either cut your earnings in half, to $143,750, or you'll have to complete two more years at whichever BigCo that bought you to earn it all. Either way that money's earned over four years—so it's $143,750/year for four years.

Don't get me wrong. This isn't shabby money. Most people would *love* to make that much in four years. But don't confuse getting stock in a company with retirement. Given that a decent home in an expensive area such as Palo Alto or Santa Monica will set you back $2 million, it's hardly riding off into the sunset. It's why Jason says "the risk-adjusted economics of starting a company suck."

I'm not trying to depress you; I'm just trying to be realistic. If you want to *earn*—and by earn, I mean the chance to buy your house outright—you have to start a company or join as a senior executive. Or you have to hit the lottery and be an early middle management player at a place like Google, Facebook, MySpace, or Twitter. Let's be honest: how many of those are created per year in the entire country? One? Two, max? I spoke with an investor recently who told me that 1,500 deals get funded every year in the United States; 80 (5.3%) eventually sell for $50 million, and only 8 (0.5%) eventually sell for $150 million or more.

So when the Stanford MBA, the ex-senior technology developer, or the former Chief Revenue Officer of a company is calling me and asking my advice on their next gig, you can see why I start with, "Are you ready to earn or to learn?"

Are you ready to earn, or to learn?

For most people it's *learn*. I only emphasize the question because I find it much more helpful to join a company with realistic expectations. My advice is often this: Make sure that what you get out of working at this company is one or several of the following: a great network of talented executives and VCs, more responsibility than your last job, specific industry or technical skills that will help you in what you do next, or a chance to partner with companies that will increase your industry relationships, and so on. Learn now to earn later.

When I was CEO of my first company (where I admittedly fucked up everything before I figured it all out), we initially calculated for people how much their options were eventually going to be worth. This was in 1999. A company called Ventro, with only $2 million in revenue, was trading at an $8 *billion* valuation. It was easy to do these calculations. Over time I realized that this created a rotten culture.

Later, I took to telling people the following: "Join BuildOnline because you think you'll get great experience. Join because you like the mission of what we're doing. Join because if you do a good job, we'll help you punch above your weight class and work in a more senior role. And if you ever feel in the year ahead of you that you won't increase the value of your resume and you're not having fun, then go. Join because we pay good, but not amazing, salaries. Stock options are the icing on the cake. They'll never make you rich. Don't join for the options."

Obviously you should take only jobs that you enjoy and that let you be passionate about coming to work every day. That's a given. Don't blindly join a company without knowing *why* you'd join or asking the right questions.

A friend recently called to ask for advice on becoming the CTO of a startup. He'd be employee number three. The company was being spun out of a larger company. I asked him how much of the company would be owned by the parent company and how much would be owned by management. He hadn't thought to ask. When we next spoke, he'd found out that the CEO had about 5% and there was no management option pool in place. My advice was … *run!* I said, "All the hard work is ahead. Why start the game with a company that has a structure that's likely to fail?"

Another talented young man called recently to talk shop. He had an offer in New York, another with a well-known startup in the Bay area, and a third offer with a startup in Los Angeles. He also has his own company, which he'd started six months earlier. He's not even 21. He wanted to know what to do. I told him that he needed to decide whether to learn or to earn. He's young enough to do either, but you need to know why you're doing it. I advised against the LA job because it was a bigger company and his role would be pushing paper from one side of his desk to the other. If you're going to learn, then at least go work somewhere exciting. If it works, you can stay and grow for the next five years. If it doesn't, you'll have done three startups by age 26. And you'll be ready to earn.

On the other hand, at sub-21 you have the ability to swing for the fences and try to earn, if you're so inclined, and if you think you have the skill set and the idea. When you're 40, with three kids and a mortgage, this is much harder.

Now, for the *earn* part. My friend is a very talented executive. He went to Harvard Business School and has worked at three prominent startups and two well-known big companies. He's worked in the United States and internationally. He's in his early 40s. Whenever he calls me, he must think I'm a broken record. I always say, "Dude [I live in SoCal now!], it's time to *earn*. Stop dicking around with another number-two job (he always gets offered the number-two position). It's time for you to be in the driver's seat. Either start a company or go somewhere where they need a CEO."

If you really want to earn, you need to be among the top three or four leaders in the company. It's best to be a founder. Very few people can do this. It's a rare skill. Be realistic about your skills, background, and ideas.

I'm not all about the money; I think working in a startup can be an enormously rewarding experience. I wouldn't recommend it otherwise. But you need to match your talents, age, skills, ambition, and economic situation to your current reality. At a minimum, be realistic about the outcomes. And make sure you ask yourself, "Am I here to learn or to earn?"

Match your talents, age, skills, ambition, and economic situation to your current reality.

WHEN A STRAIGHT LINE ISN'T THE SHORTEST PATH TO SUCCESS

> Having a good heart isn't enough. You need to learn how to make money to grow your organization, whether it's for- or non-profit.

As discussed in the Nail A Niche section, Avanoo is a company that is going from a first sale to $5 million quickly. Along with cofounder Prosper Nwankpa, Daniel Jacobs took a roundabout journey to founding the company—including pit stops with orphans, artists, and Hari Krishnas.

Daniel always wanted to make a difference in the world. He used to believe (or hope) that a good heart and honorable values would be enough to create a movement that made a difference.

Now, he says he's learned the hard way that regardless of how meaningful an organization's vision and values are, it's not going to exist unless its founders embrace money. Including how to market, sell, and predictably grow.

Before founding Avanoo, from 2006 to 2010 Daniel had started and run a "philanthropic technology company" called Everywun. Everywun was a volunteer platform that businesses used to give their employees ways to earn points for volunteer work. Employees could get points, for example, by planting trees, feeding kids, or fixing malaria in Africa. Those employees could redeem those points for very specific goodwill outcomes, like "use 50 points to feed a child for a day." Businesses paid Everywun to use the service, as an employee benefit. It was a do-gooder's dream.

But then the recession hit, and in 2010 Everywun failed. Daniel felt he'd hit rock bottom.

"I'd devoted all of my life, practically every ounce of energy, for six years, believing that I would grow something that would make a powerful, sustained impact on the world. Then it was gone. And there was a big void. It felt awful, terrible. But I also saw in that void an opportunity. When I was working on that business, I couldn't touch any of the people I wanted to serve. Technology sat between me and the people I wanted to have as part of my community. But then when the technology was forced out of the way, I had the opportunity to be of service in a different way: with my hands, with my heart, as an anonymous helper on the ground."

He gave away all his stuff and went off traveling in South and Central America for a couple of years.

He worked on an Argentine organic farm run by a Hari Krishna group outside of Buenos Aires. In Cordoba, Argentina, he mentored entrepreneurs and served as a foil for Mormon missionary friends. In Santiago, Chile, he lived, and made art, with street artists.

Eventually, he landed in an old Guatemalan mountain town. He helped build houses for single, middle-aged women who'd adopted orphans to live with them, so that the community could avoid having a single institutional-style orphanage.

In 2012, Daniel was in this town, surrounded by kids who had so little but who seemed happy. It didn't make sense to him, because kids in the United States have so many resources, but so many behavioral problems—and don't seem nearly as happy. "It struck me: I'd come to help the kids here with material resources, but people back home had just as much of a need, but of a different kind. I wondered, is it possible to support people in transforming from the inside out, in ways we can measure? And show that a transformation actually happened?"

This was an exciting question to him—exciting enough that he spent more than a year researching it. And the research led him to partner with an old friend he'd met when he was 17, Prosper Nwankpa. Together they founded Avanoo.

Daniel's Lesson—and Aaron's

Don't obsess about getting to success so fast that you ignore your inherent interests, those "whispers" in the back of your head that you usually ignore as being impractical—you know, pretty much anything that isn't about your to-do list or your immediate career and home concerns. Anytime you say, "I'd like to do X, but I can't because of Y" imagine what it would be like if Y were not in the way. How can you pursue dreams you had when you were younger, such as moving to another country, making art, writing music or poetry, having kids, or adopting?

> **Don't obsess about getting to success so fast that you ignore your inherent interests.**

Those larks and quirks may be what end up helping you to success faster in the long run. Or at least they can help you stand out as a unique and interesting soul. Explore the whispers first, and then later you'll find ways to bring them into your business life.

I never thought of myself as an artist, but a few years ago, I started messing around with crayons, then colored pencils, then pastels—and later I ended up drawing all kinds of sketches for my work, including *Predictable Revenue*, and the art in this book.

It might be tech news, your social feeds, or even this book that make you Compare and Despair, thinking you have to go big or go home. You may feel that working in consulting, services, a small business, or whatever you do isn't big, fast, or good enough.

Ignoring what others say or do, *any* business that works for *you* is perfect. You may need to explore to find out what the hell that is. And along the way, like Daniel and me, maybe you'll change your mind about how important faster growth is to you. Maybe it'll be a much bigger, or a much smaller, deal than you previously thought.

We're just saying *if* and *when* you decide you do want to go bigger, there are ways to do it.

CHANGE *YOUR* WORLD, NOT *THE* WORLD

Something you hear all the time in Silicon Valley is, "We're going to change the world!" and "We're revolutionizing the world of [insert mission here]!" Great. We understand that's exciting and that you want your mission to be meaningful. But our sense of what truly changes the world is the people who developed the polio vaccine, radio, food refrigeration, electrical systems, or inspired millions into nonviolent revolution. If you're making a web-based sales tool, invoicing solution, mobile document syncing solution, travel app, or a new way to share pictures with people ... maybe not so much world-changing.

Look, it's very important for you and your team to have meaningful work. It's not that these aren't great things, it's just that the world would get there one way or another without them. There are reasons Sergey Brin is working on autonomous cars and Elon Musk on unlimited solar energy.

What you *can* do is make Your World better by appreciating all the tangible ways you're already helping the people you work with, serve, or inspire:

> **Make Your World better by appreciating all the tangible ways you already help the people you work with, serve, or inspire.**

- *You can seed new companies and new opportunities for the rock stars on your team, and create a virtuous cycle of innovation.* When I look back at the first startup I cofounded, the management team has since spun out three new innovative venture-backed startups.

- *You can create real, new jobs for people.* Truly creating new, good jobs—not just poaching engineers from other startups, which is a zero sum jobs game—but great new jobs that didn't exist before, including jobs that provide for employees to support their families.
- *You can help buy people homes.* Money is always nice, but making people enough money one way or another to buy their first home is a good thing. David Ulevitch is proud that selling OpenDNS helped his people; beyond making many of them millionaires, it helped a lot of them pay off debt, such as outstanding student loans.
- *You can advance the careers of many.* Startups, if they are successful, are career accelerators for folks with smarts and chutzpah but who may have imperfect or lean resumes. You can create great managers out of people who might never have managed—make highly successful salespeople out of raw enthusiasm, make heads of support and success and more—where, without your startup, that opportunity might never have existed. And they will then go on to play leadership roles at other great companies. People on your team will go on to create their own startups, small businesses, nonprofits, and consulting practices as well.
- *You can seed other great companies and startups.* I am not convinced Salesforce is changing the world, truly. Close, but not quite. But it has helped create scores of other successful companies. Without Salesforce, EchoSign would not have reached initial critical mass, would not have made it.
- *You can make a great journey.* Startups, companies, or teams don't last forever. They grow, one way or another, or they die. But you can make a great journey. You get only so many trips in life. Having a great one is something everyone takes with them, forever.

Wherever you are in your journey, one thing we've learned in both startups and Fortune 500 companies is that, risk-adjusted, it's probably less lucrative to do a startup. And startups aren't even any more nimble than the best teams in Big Cos. But in a startup, it is easier to make Your World better and see it grow and happen day by day.

Embrace Employee Ownership

The Painful Truth: Your employees are renting, not owning, their jobs.

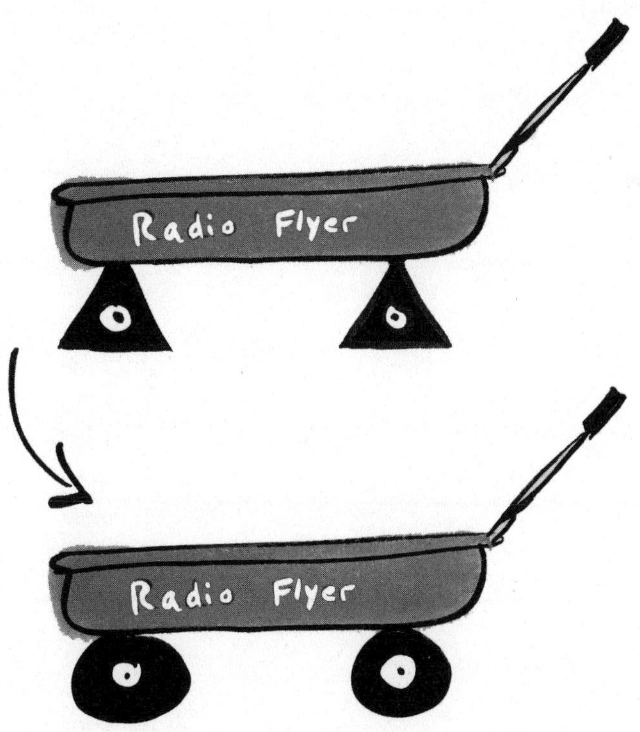

CHAPTER 20
A Reality Check

You're passionate and committed to what you do, which leads you to forget that many others aren't, or that they haven't learned yet how to execute as you do.

And they won't, unless you embrace Functional Ownership.

DEAR EXECUTIVES (FROM AN EMPLOYEE)

Dear Executives:

I enjoy working for this company. I like the people here, the culture, and I believe in the product!

I want to succeed here—in big ways. And make a name for myself. I want to contribute. I want to grow here and build my career further with you. I want to help the company, but I'm not always sure how.

I frequently get frustrated. It's hard to get time with you to have real conversations. I feel like you don't listen to me or the other employees—we have ideas, too. I've tried to share mine, but after the third time where nothing happened and no one cared or listened, I just gave up.

It's so hard to change anything here (even little things), and I don't know where my career is going with you, or have any confidence you even care about it or me.

In other words, while I make decent money here today, I don't feel valued—and that makes me feel like I don't have a future here. So I am only motivated to do the minimum here to get by, rather than going above and beyond—because, what's the point? I use my extra time reading up on topics like finding dream jobs, starting a business, and online marketing.

I am only motivated to do the minimum here to get by, rather than going above and beyond—because, what's the point?

I can often feel trapped in my role, not allowed to try anything new or experiment. Rather than feeling trapped by my day job, I want to use it as a springboard to discover what else I can learn and how I can make a bigger contribution. The more I learn about other parts of our business and market, the more ways I can contribute.

I know I need to perform in my "day job" (what I was hired for), but aren't there ways that I can also keep learning in other areas, including in making the company more money? Don't look at these other interests as distractions from my role, but rather as possible complements.

The career path here seems like a mystery, or worse, arbitrary, in which executive favorites get all the attention and promotions, even when more than a few don't seem that great, and some are even disasters.

DEAR EMPLOYEE (FROM THE EXECUTIVES)

Dear Employee,

So you want to be successful in your career. Maybe you believe right now that you deserve a promotion or a raise. Or you're just bored at work. Maybe people don't respect your (great) ideas, or listen to you. Maybe you think that you're not getting a fair shake from either the owners or perhaps even the customers. Maybe our management systems are just broken and defeat our people's best efforts (though we can't admit that publicly).

Because … the truth is, while we like you as a person and think you're swell, and you're doing well in your job, that's the minimum. We don't see how you're going out of your way to contribute in other ways. (And all those side projects you're working on don't count. What, you think people here don't know about them?)

Here's the deal. If things aren't happening the way you want, it's time to take charge of your own destiny rather than believe it's the fault of "other people" such as your manager, owner, or team. Don't blame others for not recognizing your greatness. If you wait for people to recognize or discover you, here or anywhere, chances are you'll be waiting a lo-o-ong time. The time will never be perfect. The opportunity will never be perfect. You have to work with what you have—as frustrated or defeated as you feel.

If you wait for people to recognize or discover you, here or anywhere, chances are you'll be waiting a lo-o-ong time.

A company is *full* of people who need things. Products launched, marketing campaigns run, sales closed, employees hired, customers serviced, and bills paid. There will always be innumerable problems to solve; *pick one and do something about it*.

You must be able to do this without sacrificing results in your "day job"; what your current manager, team, and job description expects from you. If you can't deliver on what we hired you for, we're unlikely to trust you to deliver on anything else. An owner doesn't deliver results only when it's convenient.

If your reaction is "How do I do that?" then, well, *that's the whole point*, because we can't tell you. If we knew, we'd already be doing it. How can you improve the business in ways that we don't see or that aren't practical yet?

If your reaction is "I've tried to do that, and keep getting shot down!" then the best we can say is, *find someone who will believe in you and coach you here*. Even if you have to do it privately, since it might not be your manager. You can't wait for the company (or anyone) to figure this out for you.

If you're unsure where to begin, start by talking to us and other employees. What problem needs to be solved, what function needs an owner, or who wants to help you?

There is no magic recipe to follow, where someone can just "tell you what to do." You have to practice figuring it out on your own—this is part of taking the initiative! Remember: so many of the success stories around you are part of the Reality Distortion Field, and they leave out most of the undramatic (and thus boring) bits about the daily struggle, from which 98% of success comes from.

We know you've got unbelievable potential, *so stop talking about it and show us by taking the initiative*. Put down your smartphone and Instagram; get out from behind your computer. We want you to succeed here as badly as you do.

P.S.: "DEAR SENIOR EXECUTIVES, DON'T GET LEFT BEHIND" (FROM THE CEO AND BOARD)

Dear Senior Executives,

I get that you're an expert in your area, with a long track record of success. I know you're looked up to as an industry expert, invited to talk, write, and speak on panels. But that success is now getting in the way of your own career growth. I get that you're an expert in your area. But I need you to also be an expert in how all our functions work together to grow revenue. I need you to know how our sales, lead generation, Customer Success, recruiting, and ownership culture work. What are you working on doing that the board will appreciate?

I know this is *in addition* to keeping us on top of trends in your own area, such as:

- **In IT**, the world of SaaS software is changing the needs of your group and how technology is built, sold, and maintained.
- **In marketing,** now it's all about data, analytics, and metrics—more than just creativity and branding.
- **In sales**, its metrics, role specialization, and predictability, more than just relationships, channel partners, and forecasting.
- **In human resources**, it's about employee engagement, satisfaction and development, more than just benefits and compliance.
- **In manufacturing or development**, it's about faster time-to-market, agile creation, and demand fulfillment.

I know we have set ways of doing things, but don't let them trap you into inertia or excuses:

1. *You can't wait for more people and budgets to happen* before you can evolve and adapt. There is always a way to move forward with the time and resources that you already have.
2. *Embrace faster decisions:* Nothing happens until a decision is made. Are you avoiding making an important decision (or keeping it in committee indefinitely, or hiring a McKinsey . . .) because you're afraid of making the wrong one or looking bad?
3. *Don't punish new ideas*. When a salesperson intentionally tries a creative new technique but loses a big deal or blows up a customer, do you punish them for failing or reward them for trying? It's not a loss as long you learn. Save stronger action for people who (a) make the same mistakes repeatedly, or (b) lie.

If you punish your employees for trying new ideas (or just ignore them), they'll stop trying.

4. *Get your hands dirty—say "I," not "we."* Do you think "we" should start a blog, start prospecting, or come up with a new vision statement? Kick off the grunt work yourself first. You'll set the example and learn more about what "it" will take to work.
5. *How can you and your team increase revenue?* Maybe no one else cared before how HR, procurement, IT, manufacturing, or accounting affected revenue. But I need you to understand what growth requires, so you can help. *At a minimum* you can teach our sales teams to be smarter about how *your function works at customers*. And the closer you can tie your area to financial results, the better for your career and responsibilities.

If you're feeling left behind already, or burned out, you have a chance to remake yourself. What trends do you want to learn about, what interests you?

My uber-point: Yes, you've overcome big challenges in your career to get here. What's next in your area, and how it can help revenue growth or customers? Because if you can't evolve the way you're thinking or running your team, you're going to be left behind.

ARE YOUR PEOPLE RENTING OR OWNING?

What if employees always knew what they needed to do next, without having to be told or managed all the time?

As an executive, it's impossible to implement new growth ideas as fast as you want to, as fast as is needed, unless your people embrace them. Otherwise, you're stuck in the mud. It could be specializing your sales roles, creating bigger enterprise packages or smaller SMB products, pivoting, going freemium, running away from freemium, changing culture, whatever.

How dependent is your team on *your* ideas, motivation, and execution? How often do they come up with *their own* new ideas, and take the initiative to figure them out?

Do you feel like you constantly have to step in and fix things for employees, tell them what to do, answer the same question time and again—or do they take initiative?

What would happen if you took a two-week vacation, unplugged?

What would happen if you took a two-week vacation, unplugged?

How can you help employees go above and beyond their job description—not in hours, but in *initiative*? In feeling like and acting like *owners*. How often does a nonexecutive come up with, and execute—out of the blue—something that increases leads, sales productivity, or customer retention?

Owners don't need to be managed. They don't sit around waiting to be told what to do—they do it. Because when they own something, emotionally, when they *care* about something, they *take care* of it.

How can you help employees go above and beyond their job description—not in hours, but in initiative?

Look, if most sales managers complain their salespeople don't prospect enough, then it's not the salespeople that are the problem—it's the *system* of prospecting that needs to change. This is why specializing sales roles works so well. Got it? Okay then …

Likewise, if most CEOs and executives wish their employees took more initiative and acted like owners, and then *it's not the people that are the problem, it's the system of management that needs to change*.

It's not the people that are the problem, it's the system of management that needs to change.

Because the truth is, your employees are *renting their jobs:*

- How do you treat a car you own versus a rental?
- How do you invest in a house you own versus a leased apartment?
- What's it feel like to babysit others' kids, versus having your own?

Your employees don't *act* like owners, because they *aren't* owners. Not really.

When you hear "owner," do you immediately start thinking about *Financial Ownership* (equity, commissions, ESOPs)? If Financial Ownership, combined with your typical goals, responsibilities, and recognition was enough to systematize things like learning, actions, initiative, results and decisions—then you and every other manager would already have teams full of people acting like owners and mini-CEOs. But you don't.

Because Financial Ownership for employees is icing on the cake.

Financial Ownership doesn't consistently create both the *Functional Ownership* and the *"oh shit, it's really all on me" moments* of 100% responsibility that inspire people to go beyond the bullet points of their job description.

Delegation isn't true ownership. Employees need *Functional* Ownership, to *own* something, to learn how to *act* like owners.

Employees need *Functional* Ownership to inspire owner-like behavior.

Functional Ownership

Someone has Functional Ownership, and the emotional commitment that comes with it, when they, as a single person, *clearly and publicly* own a slice of how the business works, whether it's the P&L for a billion dollar division or the office refrigerator cleaning routine. He or she is 100% responsible for it, including its results, related decisions, and improvement.

People support what they help create—the size of what they own doesn't matter as much as the reality of their ownership. Including an *inability to hide* from that responsibility, which is why shared responsibility tends to create pointed fingers.

So, Functional Ownership is a key piece of the motivation puzzle here. Then, combine it with inescapable deadlines and Forcing Functions (which we'll get to later in this chapter) … that's when predictable magic happens.

First of all, there isn't "one thing" that makes all your wishes come true, like some kind of magical sparkly-purple unicorn. And if anyone claims there's "one thing" that will fix all your problems, they're bullshitting you or themselves.

But Functional Ownership can be life-changing for:

- Employees who want to take their contributions to the next level, but haven't been sure how.
- Executives who keep looking for ways to predictably motivate and energize people.

It's not going to work for everyone. You'll always have Complainers and Clockers, in addition to CEO-types and Careerists (we'll describe those further on). But if you directly manage 10 people, and even one more acts like an owner, it can be transformative. If a manager can go from having zero to even one, or from one to two "employees acting like owners" on their team—*wow*.

Even If You Can Get By Today, What about Tomorrow?

Change is unavoidable. So are you going to react to changes in the market or get ahead of them and help create the changes yourself? If your employees wait around for orders rather than taking initiative on their own, growth will *always* be a struggle, because you're going to be responsible for the whole burden.

Are you going to react to changes in the market or get ahead of them and help create the changes yourself?

There's no better way to do this than to develop more owners, and continuously frustrate them with uncomfortable challenges that drive learning. Yes, by definition you and your people *should* feel frustrations when getting outside your comfort zones. As long as it's new frustration from new problems, not from the same ones that never get solved or evolved.

You're Not Cloning Yourself

No one will ever be *you*. Their job is not to sell like you, create like you, or lead like you. Sometimes they'll be worse than you at things, sometimes better, but never the same. Everyone has a Unique Genius that they can bring to work and use to make a difference there.

Everyone has a Unique Genius that they can bring to work and use to make a difference there.

By not tapping into the ideas, energy, and motivation of your employees, without creating systems that *challenge them to get off their butts, out of their ruts, and make things happen*, you're wasting their potential and your time.

This isn't some kind of one-sided sermon on why you should treat people well; give them love, kumbaya and so on, because employees can be half of the problem. Most wait to be told what to do. It's what they've been trained to do since they were young, in school and most jobs—"do what you're told" and "just follow these 10 steps to pass the class and get the reward." They're impatient for those rewards—including unearned ones. They get bored fast, complain, and expect you to keep them challenged and babysit their needs. And that's just the good ones :)

CHAPTER 21

For Executives: Create Functional Ownership

Let's break down how you start and create functional Ownership in your teams.

If you're an employee and this stuff doesn't interest you, feel free to skip ahead to Part VII: Define Your Destiny, which is just for you.

A SIMPLE SURVEY

It's best to start out with a fresh pulse check on the morale of your teams. If you have any moral or trust issues, you need to know about them in more detail, or else they can derail everything else. Employees that don't trust management don't listen, care, or follow through. If they don't feel the company is investing in them, they're not going to invest in helping the company.

A Simple Survey: Six Questions

1. *Context:* What's your role? Who's your manager?
2. *Likes:* What do you like about [working here | your job | your manager | our product | how we sell ...]? Please include details or specific examples.
3. *Dislikes:* What don't you like about [working here | your job | your manager | our product | how we sell ...]? Please include details or specific examples.
4. *The twist:* If you ran things, what would you do differently? Please include details or specific examples.

5. *Catch-all:* What else is on your mind? Anything else we should know?
6. *Optional:* How do we contact you if we have follow-up questions about your answers?

Notice how by focusing the "Likes" and "Dislikes" questions, you can target any specific or general topic.

You want *honest* feedback from people, and so you need to make it optional, but not required, to include their identifying information.

You want honest feedback from people, and so you need to make it optional, but not required, to include their identifying information.

Now, if you're sending this to one or two employees/partners, obviously it won't be anonymous. They may not be 100% forthcoming. Do your best to reassure yourself and whoever is taking this survey that the answers will be used only to improve the business, not against them. Right?

Why You May Not Want to Send It

It's natural for people to have a fear of getting honest feedback from others. It can feel easier to hide, but it's better to find out now than in the exit interview.

They might say something critical about you and the business, and that never feels good. If you find this fear's stopping you from sending this out, focus on how (a) you will have people saying many positive things, too, and (b) if there are problems festering beneath the surface, it is better to find out about them *now* and deal with them, rather than remaining ignorant and allowing them to grow into a bigger time bomb that will explode someday in your face, probably at the worst possible time.

Your Job

When you get this information back, you need to act on it, even if a first step is acknowledging that you received it. Ideally, in the announcement or survey itself, publish the date by which you'll acknowledge you've received the answers.

If you don't acknowledge your respondents quickly, you're reinforcing any feelings of "I knew this was pointless, they never listen to us or do anything anyway."

Tips

- To get honest feedback, consider asking an outside person to act as a neutral party.
- Don't survey more often than you can communicate back what you have received and reviewed, and can act on something and show that you listen.
- Pick one or two things to focus on to fix each time so that you can prove your progress quickly.
- Have a team or employee meeting to review problems, suggest ideas, volunteer owners, and come up with Forcing Functions.

Don't try to fix or respond to or improve everything at once.

"NO SURPRISES"

Changing a company's culture can be hard. That's why there are probably thousands of books and millions of articles written about it. How many of those ideas have created any impact at your company? It's challenging to create cultural change—cultures and people are made up of habits, and habits are hard to change.

Let's begin with one simple idea, transparency: If you stick with developing it, transparency will help to increase trust, inform employees, and move things forward quickly. Because once you get the ball rolling with a first few "wins," it's easier to keep up the improvements.

Why People Hate Surprises

First, consider how many happy surprises happen at work or with money. Can you think of any? Our guess is they're much rarer than unhappy surprises at work.

Customers hate surprises from salespeople. Salespeople hate surprises from customers. VP Sales hate surprises from their salespeople. CEOs hate surprises from their executive team. Boards hate surprises from the CEO.

How can you create a culture of "No Surprises"? Consider what it would take to eliminate surprises.

It'd force you to improve how your company runs internally: how teams such as marketing, sales, and customer support work, communicate, and improve together. Let's take just customers: how can you make sure customers aren't surprised by proposals? Product changes? Downtime? Personnel changes?

What it would take to eliminate surprises—across employees, customers, investors, and the management team?

How Far HubSpot Goes

Even when it was a private company, HubSpot shared with everyone company financial information normally carefully guarded by execs: details on the cash balance, burn rate, P&L, board meeting decks, management meeting decks, and strategic topics. Their goal was to support smarter behavior and better decisions.

They only protect information when (a) it's legally required, or (b) it's not completely theirs to share.

Where to Begin

Walk the halls and ask employees about their priorities. What do they feel blind about, and most want to know? Whether or not you think it's needed or helpful to them to know, consider how they may be kept out of the loop.

Or if there's a main challenge you're dealing with—yes, especially a financial one—begin by sharing updates on it or other top issues, in person, by phone, web, and email, whatever line of communication is *easiest to maintain*, because you have to keep it up, as regularly as possible for the first few months. Over time, regular updates will evolve to change style and pace, but in the beginning, you need to establish that you are serious about keeping everyone informed. If you have a board, turn board presentations around and use the same one for a regular company update.

This helps prevent "surprises": Employees who normally feel left out of the loop will be more engaged and have a better feeling for areas where they can contribute.

Over time, regular updates will evolve to change style and pace, but in the beginning, you need to establish how serious you are about it.

Example: Financial Transparency

Do you keep your finances mostly secret? If so, why? Is there a specific business reason to keep them secret, or do you keep them secret out of habit? To learn how to help the company make money, employees need to also learn how the company makes (and loses) money today, and why. Educate your employees on your finances.

You don't need to begin by suddenly springing (or dumping) the complete information on everyone. Make whatever you share helpful to people.

Educate your employees on understanding finances.

Example: Career Transparency

Are there proven career paths in the company that people can look forward to? How are promotions or job changes decided? Are new job openings publicized within the company in addition to outside the company, and are internal people allowed to apply? If not, why not?

Example: Sales Transparency

Do you have a sales process? Why not update it a bit, and then begin to share it with prospects, so they can see the roadmap you and they should follow to determine if there's a fit or not here?

For example, here's a simple outline of a process that aligns both buyer and seller:

1. *Initial "Are We A Fit" call:* Determine if this is a waste of time or not, before moving forward. This may include a first simple demo to the

buyer, so they can decide if a next call is appropriate, and who to invite from their team.
2. *Demo or discovery call:* Include several people from the buyer's team, including a decision-maker, so again we can make a decision whether a deal is worth pursuing.
3. *Proposal:* Lay out the terms so the buyer can see all the details regarding how it would work to meet their expectations, pricing, options, and terms. Offer alternatives—honestly presented!—to the seller's products (including "do nothing" or "competitor 1") to help the buyer make the best decision.
4. *Executive buy-off:* The decision-maker gets all questions and objections answered. What would it take to get them excited for the project?
5. *Finalize terms:* The word "negotiation" implies a "win-lose" situation for most people, when in reality, both sides are trying to finalize the details in ways that make sense for each other.
6. *Sign contracts (or paperwork):* Both sides celebrate today, and then get back to work tomorrow on delivering on the promises made.
7. *Kickoff/implement/begin:* The customer on boards the new product or service.
8. *Track success:* Help the customer measure and gauge their results to date, and how successful the project has been compared to their expectations.

Do you see how this kind of joint buyer-seller process can help both sides navigate their way to a successful outcome?

FUNCTIONAL OWNERSHIP

The previous two sections were about setting your people up for success in whatever comes next. But if you got stuck in doing (or avoiding) them, you can skip them for now and jump in here.

There's an enormous difference between *being* an owner and *helping* an owner, just as there's a difference between *owning* and *renting*. When someone owns something emotionally, the way they think about it, work on it, and commit to it is far deeper than when they're just a part-time player. When they can dabble. It's like the difference between being a parent and being a babysitter.

Answering the question "Who owns marketing?" is easy if you have a VP of Marketing. And usually, they own everything in marketing, with all important decisions being made or affirmed by them.

But who runs the blog? That's not the VP Marketing, unless they are a one-man marketing team and run everything themselves. Whoever runs the blog on the team should *own* it. *That means the head of marketing would defer to that person on decisions about the blog*, which could include decisions about the visuals, rhythm, format, content, and style. And that person would own it and be 100% responsible for the metrics related to the blog.

Rather than having people coming to you with options all the time and asking you to decide, they are coming to you for advice when they need it and then *they* decide. It's made an enormous difference in the management load at Carb.io to have decisions spread out across the team, rather than funneled up (and bottlenecked) at the top.

Remember, we're concerned with two kinds of ownership (well, what we truly care about is emotional ownership, but that's a side effect of implementing these others):

1. *Functional Ownership:* Who owns which responsibilities—Sales? Leads? IT?
2. *Financial Ownership:* Who are the equity owners of the company? How are commissions made or profits shared?

Executives often have both. But many employees have neither, or have only token amounts.

Financial Ownership's important, but it's more complex, and normally an incentive for people to exceed at their regular job rather than go beyond to improve the company. It's easier to compensate employees for what they *are doing*, then what they *could* do. Functional Ownership at the employee level—how we define it—is less common.

To encourage your people to take charge of their lives and be more entrepreneurial, they need to own something, *anything*, even if it's the kitchen refrigerator.

To encourage your people to take charge of their lives and be more entrepreneurial, they need to own something, *anything*, even if it's the kitchen refrigerator.

At Carb.io, ownership of different subfunctions has been divided up across the team, not by rank or title, but by interest—volunteers—and logical fit:

1. Software product and roadmap (Patrick, Product Management)
2. Website (Alec, Account Strategist)
3. The "Nail A Niche" Program (Rob, Account Strategist)
4. The Product Handbook (Patrick, Product Management)
5. Fundraising: Collin (CEO)
6. Initial inbound lead response: Jeff (Associate)
7. Outbound prospecting (Patrick, Product Management—yes, a product guy prospects: How else would he know what to design?)
8. Application sales: Kay (Account Executive)
9. Services sales: Shaun (Lead Coach)
10. Lead generation: Aaron

Each person has a main job plus one to three smaller side projects they own, which may or may not be related to their main job.

Five Aspects of Ownership

Not everyone is a natural go-getter, and you're not going to magically create a team of Richard Bransons or Elon Musks. But change their environment, and you can move some people's Go-Getter Needle from a 5 to a 7.5 with:

1. *Single, public ownership*—The CEO can't hide. Everyone knows who's ultimately responsible. For a function or project, who is the single owner everyone recognizes? Even if there's a committee or partnership involved, *one person* is the designated final decision-maker, which is not determined solely by seniority. An executive can be responsible for the whole puzzle (marketing), but others can own individual puzzle pieces (internal meetings and systems, playbooks, content, events, tools, reporting, campaigns, career path ...).

   Being an owner doesn't mean you have to do all the work, but you are responsible for seeing it gets done, whether it's by you or others.
2. *Forcing Functions*—The CEO has obligations they can't hide from, like payroll. Public, specific deadlines drive progress like nothing else. What works better to get fit: (a) signing up for a gym membership or

(b) announcing to your friends that you're going to run a marathon? Executives create Forcing Functions all the time: starting a business, raising money, taking on debt, or announcing a launch or publication date. The trick is pushing this down and across the organization, applying it with employees so that they have that same feeling of "having to meet payroll" too (the next section goes into the details on how).

3. *Decisions*—The single owner makes and lives with all decisions, but gets advice from people as needed. Decision-making is a skill that gets easier with practice. People only get better at decision making when their boss lets them make decisions on their own, and then learn from the consequences.

People only get better at decision making when their boss lets them make decisions on their own, and then learn from the consequences.

4. *Tangible results*—CEOs have inherent business results they can't ignore, like sales and cash flow goals. With an employee owner, what results are important to them and their domain, and how can we measure them? How do we know if this is working or not? What metrics, third-party ratings, or milestones can we use to measure progress?
5. *Learning loops*—CEOs with boards of directors have a system to help them gauge results, receive feedback, avoid blind spots, and get pushed out of comfort zones. Internal owners need the same things. Functions must be delegated, not abdicated to people.

An Example

While I (Aaron) came up with most of the original content around the "Nail A Niche" topic, Rob Russell owns our Nail A Niche programming, such as workshops and customer workbooks. So:

1. *Owner:* Rob.
2. *Forcing Functions:* Usually these are committing to dates (a workshop, webinar, publication), or delivering the content as part of a bigger customer onsite. There's nothing like announcing an event date to energize people!
3. *Decisions:* Rob decides where, how, and when standalone events will run, the format and order of content, and how to evolve it.

4. *Tangible results:* For events, net promoter scores can be measured, as well as attendance and sales (if relevant). Customers rate their experience with the workbook.
5. *Learning loops:* After workshops or other chances to share content, Rob gathers feedback from both customers and Predictable Revenue employees (like me).

Now, as an example, I'm going to create a Forcing Function for Rob right now, by telling you—the reader—that you can download a copy of our latest Nail A Niche workbook and read related articles at www.FromImpossible.com/niche.

On the day I wrote these words you're reading now, that link didn't exist. But by typing these words out, there's now an inescapable, public deadline to make it happen. (Rob, you're welcome!)

Start with Three Questions

1. *What needs an owner?* Make a list: What's on your plate that you'd like someone else to own? What other things are in need of focused Ownership?
2. *Who should the owner be?* With a few most important functions, who is the person who will own it? They can volunteer, be designated, or be selected by group consensus.
3. *What's the initial Forcing Function?* The owner, with help as needed (or being challenged by a manager, as needed), should come up with what will be delivered next, and by what time. Keep up the Forcing Functions and they will keep driving everything that needs to get built: results, decisions, and learning loops.

> **When you have a Forcing Function deadline that someone can't hide from, it drives everything else to get built as they go: results, decisions, and learning loops.**

Get Started Even When You Have No Idea What to Do

If you want your people to start picking these ideas up, but someone's just plain stumped, then their first Forcing Function can be to find something to own (by a specific date). "On June 5th, I'm going to announce what I'm owning." This can include making the rounds with the team to find the right project.

Then, the next Forcing Function could be to come up with another Forcing Function! "On June 12th, I'm going to announce what I/we're going to do next."

Execs: Let Employees Decide

Every time an employee comes to you for a decision, you're stealing a chance for them to practice their own decision-making. You're teaching them to depend on you.

> **Every time an employee comes to you for a decision, you're stealing a chance for them to practice their own decision-making. You're teaching them to depend on you.**

First, decide together if it is something that *requires* your decision or authority. If it's not required, then make it their decision, *even if they don't want it!* New responsibility can be exciting and intimidating. Decisions determine destiny. Owners need to improve their decisiveness and confidence, which comes from practice and coaching.

So as often as you can, find opportunities for them to make more of their own decisions, and live with them. One rule: they have only to ask for *advice* from someone else before they make it.

If what they decide "fails" or just doesn't work out, don't punish them. Punishment will teach them never to take another risk. Help them by coaching them on what to learn from the experience, so they can do better next time—and make sure there's a next time.

When you make a decision for an employee, you're robbing them of a chance to practice it themselves, to learn. Even if the decision ends up being a painful one, making mistakes is the cost of doing something new—especially when learning how to be entrepreneurial.

Push decisions down, to develop your people and reduce bottlenecks at the top.

How Does Functional Ownership Develop People?

As employees keep up the momentum in owning projects and creating Forcing Functions, they'll continue to pick up the habits of successful Ownership. Some will learn quickly, others slowly. Owning means:

- Learning how to deliver results, not excuses. When you're a CEO with a payroll to meet, you learn quickly what a waste of energy excuses are.

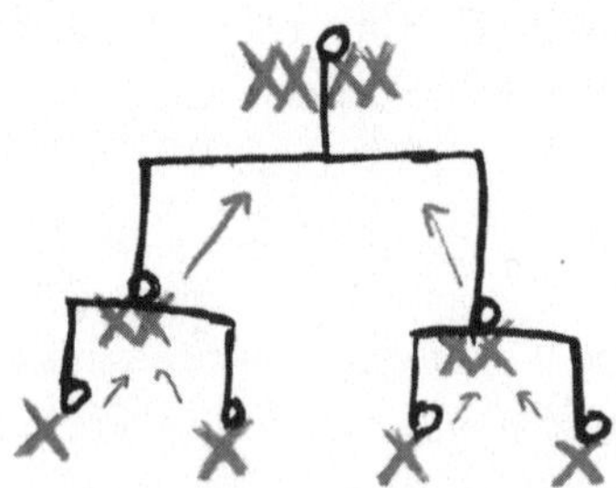
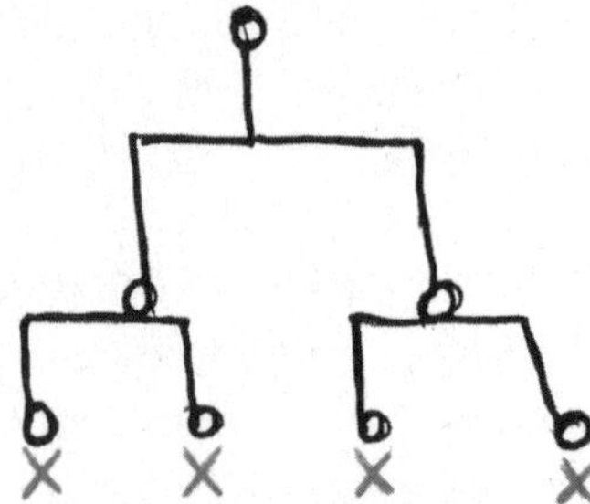

FIGURE 21.1 Push decisions down to avoid executive bottlenecks and develop your people

> **When you're a CEO with a payroll to meet, you learn quickly what a waste of energy excuses are.**

- "Asking for advice, not the answer," and gaining confidence in yourself, your ideas, and initiative. How did you end up in your current role? It was probably because you've always followed your own intuition and desires, instead of happening because other people thought you should do it or would be great at it.
- Making decisions as the authority, not deferring to others—and then avoiding responsibility for the results.
- Getting used to being uncomfortably honest and transparent, including dealing with problems now rather than pushing them off. Does someone on the team need to go or change? Is there a problem with a new product, leads, or sales that no one wants to admit because it'd cause an embarrassingly painful reforecasting for the CEO and board?
- Embracing and taking appropriate credit for your successes and responsibility for failures, and not denying or hiding from either one. And honestly giving credit where credit is due—again, whether people contributed or screwed up.
- Learning how to grow, improve from, and get used to inevitable disappointments and failures. If you're not failing, frustrated, or disappointed almost every day about something, you're too comfortable.

> **If you're not failing, frustrated, or disappointed almost every day about something, you're too comfortable.**

- It means learning about sales, decisions, and customers' success—whether with external customers or internal ones—such as identifying a problem with the fridge system, selling a team on why change is needed, and ensuring change happens.
- It means developing self-awareness. As an owner, when you step into 100% responsibility for something and stop making excuses, then all that's left is *you*. For some, it's liberating; for others, it's frightening. You are the only person in your way; you're the one who can make the most of your opportunity at work and in life. Hate your boss? Change your own attitude, or change jobs—but don't complain or make excuses about it.

Ownership isn't about how "big" or "small" something is, as long as it's important to someone, and is appropriate to the owner (not too easy, not impossibly challenging). It can mean owning the fridge, the company blog, the phone system, fun team-building events, an internal wiki, a product launch, a multimillion dollar product line, or a conference.

Discover the latest case studies and examples of how other teams Embracing Employee Ownership at FromImpossible.com.

Now Do This ...

After reading this section, get together with your people and talk about how you're going to apply this at your team or business.

Take what you like, leave what you don't.

CASE STUDY: HOW A STRUGGLING TEAM TURNED INTO A SELF-MANAGING SUCCESS

Lou Ciniglia managed a 13-person national sales team at TheLadders. *This is an example of how he created Functional Ownership on the team, transforming results. Enter Lou:*

I was a new manager, and my team was struggling with several issues.

- Few people ever hit quota.
- Little communication from executives—we were the last ones to know about comp or pricing changes.

- No career path.
- People were regularly laid off without warning.

Beyond my team, the whole company had communication and trust issues. Executive management was very busy and tight-lipped. Sales and marketing never talked. No one knew what was going on. Directives from top leadership would change regularly without warning. Frustrations went unacknowledged and festered. Trust in senior leadership was nonexistent. So whatever the company or executives said or directed, without the trust of the team, they were being ignored.

We didn't yet have a defined sales process, hiring system, or understanding of what was required to make a rep successful. There was no predictability.

TO TURN THINGS AROUND

First: Two-way communication. We had a very top-down, command-and-control management approach here. The first thing we did was start communicating more often and more quickly with the team and actively listening to what they had to say and the changes they wanted, rather than thinking of their comments as complaints.

Second: Functional Ownership. Instead of creating and managing the new sales playbook by myself, I delegated the work to a volunteer who wanted to own it. They led the team in creating the content, we worked together on the format, and they trained themselves. It became an example for other teams in our company to emulate.

Instead of creating and managing the new sales playbook by myself, I delegated the work to a volunteer who wanted to own it.

Third: Transparency. We focused on transparency when decisions needed to be made, how our strategy to get there would be impacted by each one of the participants, and our commitment to it. Including goals, quotas, and comp, transparency helped the team feel engaged and energized—because they knew what was going on, and how they could contribute. Money, comp, and possible changes to them are sensitive topics. We were able to work through it successfully by being very upfront and honest about even these sensitive topics, and explain the process from the business's perspective. Being transparent before any changes happened made it a much simpler, smoother process for people. No one likes surprises at work.

Fourth: Meetings. Within weeks, my team began hosting their own meetings. Every single week someone from the floor hosts the meeting, creates an agenda, and includes people from within their team who are excelling in certain areas of the sales process. They include other people from the organization who can knowledge-share with us. "The old Lou" used to run the meetings as if they were all about him: his agenda, his system, and his expectations. And those meetings probably sucked for the team.

Now they create an agenda that's important to them. So they invest more energy in making it effective, and we get more variety.

Now that our team's actually hosting its own meetings, building their own sales playbook, and training each other in it, it's basically a self-managing team.

Competition in the Team

Another challenge that we originally faced was having a lot of reps who kept their best secrets, well, secret. We've changed the whole team attitude to "We're all in it together" rather than "If you win, I lose." People are constantly helping each other.

Team Leads

One of the other changes that helped bring the team to life was the promotion of team leaders within this organization.

We were a team of only 13 people, but we had a couple of people who said, "I want to take on a new challenge. I want to push myself, to stretch myself, and learn a little about leadership." And we've created opportunities for people to take on extra responsibility, particularly for tasks I don't need or want to do anymore, such as basic training of new reps.

We considered paying extra to the team leaders, but decided together against it. The people who volunteered to take this on are doing it not for pay, but for experience. They're excited about gaining some business acumen, maturity, or experience.

But How Are the Numbers?

You might be wondering: If everyone's doing their own thing, are they more motivated or are they sloppier? Coming in late, or goofing off?

Too much freedom can create chaos. Did this experiment in freedom and empowerment end up hurting sales instead of helping?

If everyone's doing their own thing, are they more motivated?

The results that we've produced as a team have been impressive. We actually had some milestones last quarter that had never been hit on either individual or team levels. We can't share actual numbers, but here are two big milestones we saw happen.

- First, we originally wanted to be able to identify, hire, and promote new hires quickly. Our last three new hires exceeded their quarterly target significantly in the first three months onboard, which had never been done before. It sent an unmistakable message that "Hey, we've got something here that is *really working*."
- Second, as a team, we had a record number of reps exceed their quarterly targets over the past three months. So, yeah, this change in team culture and my management approach made a huge difference in the sales numbers.

How It Affected My Ability to Lead

Having a more self-managed team means I've been able to get an enormous amount of time back. First of all, I can do a lot more one-on-one coaching and developing each person. Even with 13 people, they don't feel like I'm too busy to give them dedicated attention.

Instead of having to focus on minute team details and assembling weekly KPIs (which my team leads do), I had more time to focus on the strategy of our department and work with other organizations within TheLadders.

And our team and people have been in the limelight much more, because of our success and new methods. Success has added a lot of energy to the team.

All the new teamwork and ownership totally re-energized the team. There was a constant buzz here that even visitors commented on. There was a life, energy, and positivity to the team that was obvious.

CHAPTER 22

Taking Ownership to the Next Level

More on Financial Ownership, moving people around, and understanding how to work with different types of employees.

FINANCIAL OWNERSHIP

A *complement* to Functional Ownership is Financial Ownership. We touched on this in Part III: Make Sales Scalable, in the section in Chapter 13 titled "Jason's Advice to CEOs: Put Nonsales Leaders on Variable Comp Plans, Too."

Not every employee is a fit for Financial Ownership (or Functional Ownership, for that matter). For those who are, there are infinite ways to pay employees in ways that are related to results. However you do it:

1. *Provide a meaningful (to them) stake* or Financial opportunity. If it's too small, they won't care. It could be through bonuses, profit sharing, equity, commissions, variable comp plans, or other avenues.
2. *Train employees* in what Financial Ownership means: How does the stock or commission plan work? If a person is confused about how it works, the ownership doesn't help! Whoever designed the Financial structure will vastly underestimate how complex it may appear to salespeople and employees. Earning 10,000 shares of stock might sound like a lot to a new employee, but they may not understand that it's only 0.01% of the company, and can easily end up being worthless depending on strike prices and liquidation preferences.

3. *Publish accurate results* so that employees know exactly where they stand in relation to their compensation and ownership, and see the "cause and effect" on their finances. What were the revenues this month? Attrition? Collections? Accomplishments and disappointments?
4. *Educate employees on business, financial, and sales basics* so that they better understand what drives revenue, profit, and growth, and can get a handle on where they can best make a difference in them.
5. *Involve them* in helping decide how Financial Ownership should work at the company. Give them a voice and respect it, whether it's related to how programs work across the whole company, or specifically with that single person.

When your company is newer, growing fast, or going through a transition, compensation and Financial Ownership programs may need to change, and change, and change again until you nail it down. The more you involve your people in the process of transition, even though it might slow the process down, the better the result for the company and all its stakeholders.

The more you involve your people in the process ... the better the result for the company and all its stakeholders.

Remember, *No Surprises*: unless it's an unforeseen bonus, no one enjoys getting a new comp or profit-sharing plan sprung on them out of thin air.

MOVE PEOPLE AROUND

You need to shake things up with yourself and your people: both (a) where people physically sit and (b) what they do for their job. Your office manager. Your top salesperson. A great collections person. A product manager. Maybe you.

We understand why you think this is a terrible idea at first glance. When an employee excels at a job, you want to keep them there.

You feel a little (or a lot) dependent on them, because you simply trust them to get the job done. And it's hard to imagine someone else doing it as well or even better. It's easy to see what you could lose by moving them. And hard to see what gains you might get from exposing them to other parts of the business. Look, if you're going through intense growth or change, maybe you shouldn't move people around until things settle down.

But otherwise, here's the paradox. By keeping them doing what they do best (today), they'll excel in that job (today). But if they get stuck there, at some point it's going to stifle them and you'll miss out on who they could become and how they could contribute in even bigger or broader ways.

If you have an office, a simple way to do this is to simply change where people sit every three or four months, including moving employees so that they sit next to new people. Don't change desks so often that people always feel unsettled, but often enough to ensure healthy variety for everyone. By sitting next to new people, everyone's networks, culture, and learning will be broadened and strengthened. And this is *simple*.

At Salesforce, I obsessed over the seating chart and how to sit new people next to veterans, and center team leaders with their subteams.

Have multiple people in one vertical division (like Financial Services) sit near each other while that industry is nailed. Once the learning slows down, break that group up and move employees to sit with experts from other industries, to learn from each other.

If there are remote workers in your company, find a way to get them together in person. However well Skype works, there's no replacement for face-to-face meetings.

There's no replacement for face-to-face meetings.

Other Ways to Shake Things Up

- At in-person events, ban employees from sitting or talking to teammates, rather than meeting new people
- Internal social media sites and wikis
- Job rotation
- Apprentice, mentoring, and shadowing programs
- Pull a Freaky Friday executive switch, such as having the heads of sales and marketing switch jobs for X days
- Bring nonessential employees to customer visits
- Have employees conduct interviews around the company to identify problems and suggest solutions

Get employees to understand how the *whole* business works, not through slide presentations or reading, but by *experiencing* it. Your employees will develop empathy for others' functions. Have more powerful internal and customer conversations. Or at least appreciate how they fit into the big picture.

THE FOUR TYPES OF EMPLOYEES

If you're all excited about the prior chapters and how you're going to get everyone on board and fired up with this new idea, hold on! Not everyone's going to embrace them. And that's okay.

As an owner, it's unfair and unrealistic to expect every employee to want the same things you do, in the same way and at the same time. And it's not the way to get the most out of them.

Not everyone is meant to be an owner or an entrepreneur; sometimes people are meant to be helpers. Someone needs to enter the data, punch the clock, dig the ditch, or follow up on the reminder. And even in those jobs, there is honor, variety, and a place for individuality and ideas.

You will have, you should have, variety in your workplace. Appreciate it and work with it, rather than trying to fight it. Help people find their individual strengths, desires, and genius, to work together as a group of talented individuals, not clones. Yes, even in what you may believe are clonelike jobs, like data entry, support, or in call centers. It's not the job that defines people; it's your culture, management, and expectations.

Help people find their individual strengths, desires, and genius, to work together as a group of talented individuals, not clones.

To help you focus your energy where it can make the most difference, we've laid out four (+1) types of employee attitudes. These aren't unchanging personality types, but a snapshot of how people are thinking and appearing to others at any one time.

We are not categorizing employees by how they think and feel inside their heads, *but only by how they appear to others, based solely on their actions* (or lack thereof).

The Four Types (+1)

Axis 1: Motivation (Ambition + Passion): What's the total amount of energy regardless if it's from ambition or passion that an employee demonstrates?

Axis 2: Agitation (Frustration + Communication): This isn't how agitated that person gets, but how actively and *constructively* they *agitate for change*.

1. *Mini-CEO:* This is your natural internal entrepreneur, who isn't afraid to take charge of a program and push it forward. They are naturally frustrated by most everything, because they can see how much better it can be and want to act to make it so. These employees can be a pain to manage but can also create big breakthroughs. They may or may not be long-term employees, depending on how far they can take the opportunity they have with your business.

   What to do: The bigger the challenge you can give these employees to bite into, and room to maneuver with it, the better. Being

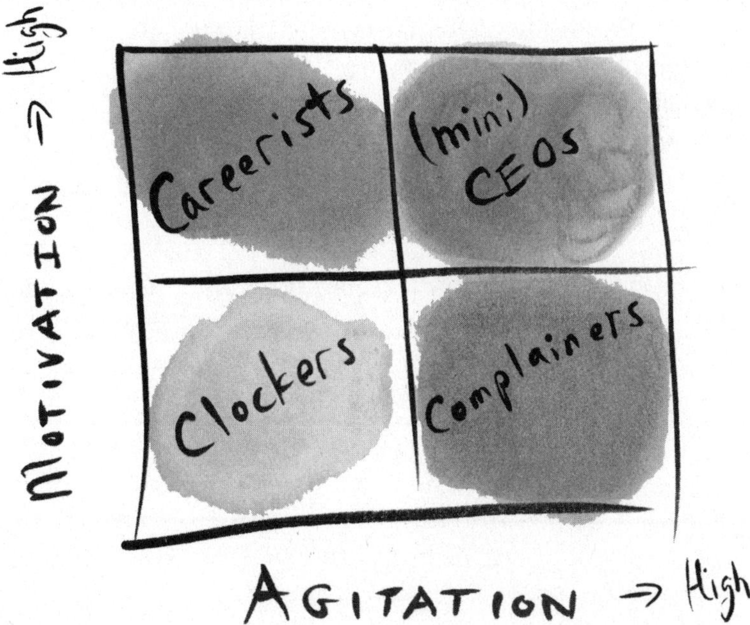

FIGURE 22.1 The four types of employees (excluding the Toxic/Liar type)

independent spirits, they may resist what they perceive as a waste of time or nonsensical, like complex budget planning, consensus building, and so on. Rather than demanding they comply, spend the time to educate them on why they are important.

2. *Careerist:* These are people who are content to climb the career ladder. Capable. Problem Solving. Trusthworthy. Dependable. Usually easy to manage. Once they have a lot of experience, or are senior at a big company, they are in danger of turning into clockers, unless they regularly refresh themselves.

   What to do: They mostly self-manage, as long as you keep up regular goal-setting and progress conversations, coming up with new opportunities for them to own, and challenging them where and when they need a push.

3. *Clocker:* Someone who is there only for the paycheck, clocking in and out and doing little else. A single parent who needs to get by and just pay the bills, and has no extra energy. A senior person who's just doing their time and keeping below the radar. A twenty-something struggling to pay rent, but putting all their extra energy into side passions like yoga classes, consuming hours of YouTube, or date-app surfing. Clockers are valuable to keeping things running, but don't expect anything extra out of them until they come to you asking how they can contribute more.

   What to do: Clearly define job expectations, and don't avoid hard conversations about meeting them. Check in occasionally to see if and when things change, and they either want to leave or are ready to tackle more.

4. *Complainers* are great at identifying problems, but either don't know how to fix them, make excuses, or are just plain stuck. They get just as frustrated as a CEO, but while a CEO will doggedly persist in finding a way to improve things, complainers … don't.

   What to do: There's nothing you can do for a real complainer except nod, smile, and do your best to solve the "actual" problem. "The leads I get are worthless" could be a real problem, or a complaint. You have to dig for truth to know. Every complaint doesn't need to be resolved, or resolved right away.

A fifth type: Toxic. A small percentage of people are sociopaths, psychopaths, chronic liars, or just plain toxic. They are abusive to work with or for. There's nothing you can do to change them. You can either (a) suck it up, or (b) quit, to find a nontoxic manager or team. If you manage one, you need to find a way to get them out of your company. If you work for one, get out.

There's nothing wrong or right about any of these types. It helps to better gauge what expectations you should have with them. Expecting a Clocker or Complainer to act like a mini-CEO is just going to annoy them and frustrate you. Expecting a Toxic person to start telling the truth or stop making excuses will result in chronic disappointment (in work or in love).

Who to Focus On

Everyone is important, but in your own expectations on pushing people to grow, focus on the CEOs and Careerists. It's ultimately up to that person to Define Their Destiny, if they want to move themselves from category to category. Encourage them, hope for it, but don't *expect* it.

Channel Frustration into Motivation

In these types, how an employee is feeling inside isn't what matters to the team. We're observing only how those internal feelings manifest in their behavior.

Mini-CEOs and entrepreneurs, usually, are obsessively frustrated or even angry with their career, with changes that aren't happening fast enough, or because they haven't figured out the right way to solve a tough problem. But they channel that frustration and anger into action, and that's the big difference between mini-CEOs and Complainers.

Do you channel your frustration and anger into figuring out how to change? Or do you let it simmer and fester inside, without doing anything about it?

You may be the one frustrated at work, with compelling ideas on how to fix things but if no one there knows about them, or you can't sell the ideas, it doesn't matter. The greatest idea in the world is worth nothing unless it leaves your head or the pages of your journal and is wrestled into a form and action that inspires others.

PART VII

Define Your Destiny

The Painful Truth: You're letting frustrations stop, not motivate, you.

CHAPTER 23

Are You Abdicating Your Opportunity?

Hi, employee. There's always someone or something you can blame when you're not getting the recognition, excitement, or results that you want: a manager, a job, the market, teammates, the CEO, HR....

But you can't control them. You can control only yourself. And you can't wait around for the perfect opportunity to drop into your lap. Stop waiting for someone else to fix it, and use your frustrations to motivate you to Define Your Destiny rather than letting others define it for you.

YOUR OPPORTUNITY IS BIGGER THAN YOU REALIZE

When we ask executives, "What do you wish employees knew?" they answer that employees *have way more opportunity than they realize to make an impact in the business, their careers, and their lives*.

Employees: you wait around for others to tell you what to do, to help you, or to motivate you. You're letting yourself become dependent on others, and that's not going to get you to your goals.

How often do you catch yourself saying "But"? "I want to get promoted/be recognized/earn more/become a manager/but ... "

- "... I don't know what to do to get ahead."
- "... no one listens to my ideas."
- "... I don't have a college degree/MBA/certification/award."
- "... I'm not an exec favorite like Bob, who can do no wrong."
- "... I don't have the budget/money ... "
- "... I'm not talented at selling/marketing/product/speaking/and so on."

- "… I'm too busy/I don't have the time … "
- "… I'm just here to pay the bills, because what I really care about is X, Y, and Z."

These are all examples of how you aren't defining your own destiny—you're letting others shape it for you. How you're boxing yourself in with these constraints.

There's a difference between (a) giving up in the face of challenges and (b) *using them* to motivate yourself to be more creative, to push for change, to find a way forward—*no matter what*.

There will never be an ideal time, opportunity, or idea—there will *always* be challenges. Owners and entrepreneurs succeed despite them, not without them. Even in baby steps. A step is a step, no matter how small.

It's Easier to Dream Than to Do

How much do you daydream about being promoted, recognized, richer, or inspiring to others? Or reading about others who are doing it?

Compare that to how much effort you spend on making those daydreams happen. Clocking hours at work doesn't count. What are you learning that's important to your goals—and not just through watching videos or reading books, but by doing it? (The best way to learn how to market or sell is to … market or sell.) How are you contributing *beyond* what's expected at work, or from customers?

In any job or career—you have a golden opportunity *now*, to do more with what you've got than you realize. For example, even if you're working for a toxic manager, you're learning the ins and outs of what doesn't work or spotting toxicity at work. If you *pay attention* rather than blaming them for everything. You can do a lot with that in the future. Great managers know greatness because they've seen crap management, too. And next time you'll be smarter about looking for and accepting a job.

It's useful to envision success, and get clear on what that looks for you. But when you let "dreaming replace the doing," you're in trouble.

It's fun to dream about success. Making it happen—and keeping it going—is a lot tougher. And far more rewarding.

If you're working on a career, just like starting a business there will be a Year of Hell while you Do The Time, times when you feel like it's never going to happen. Which is why so many people give up on dreams too early, and too often.

It's easy and fun to dream about success. Making it happen—and keeping it going—is a lot tougher. And far more rewarding.

Start Where You Are—*Today*

Most employees have an unconscious dialogue: "I'm going to do well at my job. And by doing that, at some point I'll be recognized and promoted. Eventually I'll be a senior executive. With the money and respect I deserve. I'll have enough money for a house, my family, and retirement. I'll be able to live happily ever after."

There's nothing wrong with this, but it misses out on something: Having a job, even climbing the career ladder may seem like a safe bet. But there will always be ups and downs in the economy. Layoffs, restructurings, recessions. You can't depend on jobs to always be there for you, paying you what you want or need.

By acting like an owner/entrepreneur at work *now*, it can help prepare you to be one later on. It's hard to create financial freedom by working for others—but often even harder to do it on your own if you're not prepared.

Another unconscious dialogue is "I'll make a difference here when the right moment comes along. When I get the right manager. When I see the right opportunity (etc.)." In other words, when someone or something comes in to save or help you, *then* you're going to do it, rather than *you* making it happen, regardless of how hard your culture or manager makes it to do so. You give up too easily.

Take charge of and define your destiny *now*—regardless of your circumstances. There's always something you can do to take a step, even when you have no time, money, or energy.

HOW TO EXPAND YOUR OPPORTUNITY AT WORK

You can use the same lessons throughout this book to help you with your personal opportunity. Because that's where you begin, let's call it "nailing a personal niche" in the company, in what you're interested in and can be great at, and then creating leads and opportunities for yourself, specializing your time, looking for fewer, bigger ways to make an impact, doing the time, and so forth.

But here's a quickstart:

1. *Make a list* of what you want to do or what most interests you—whether it's related to business or not. Then add to the list at least three ideas around revenue that you could or *should* be interested in, such as "Learn how to sell" or "Learn copywriting." From this list, can you see any ways to learn any at work, to get paid to learn what you want to learn or do anyway?
2. *Read the "20 Interviews" section again in Part 1: Nailing A Niche.* Use the same approach. Interview people in your company, as well as partners, prospects, or customers as needed. Can you find a problem that requires you to learn or do something from your list? What problem do you want to solve? If it's not something that your leaders care about, how can you reframe it from a "nice to have" into a "need to have" for them?

Can you find a problem that requires you to learn or do something from your list?

3. *Find a mentor, coach, or champion* at your company to ask for advice, who can support you and will be painfully honest with you about the areas where you need to improve (everyone does).
4. *Create a Forcing Function* to come up with something tangible to deliver (a prototype, an analysis, a presentation, a blog post, a talk, an event ...). If you aren't sure what that is, first pick a date and tell some people you're doing "something" on it. There's no better way to pull yourself forward in life or business than to publicly commit to doing something specific by a deadline, even before you know how you're going to do it.
5. *Do The Time*, repeating steps 1 through 4 (especially the Forcing Function step) over and over and over and over again ... because, chances are, it's going to take a lot longer than you want or expect to turn any idea first into proven results, much less recognition, career, and money. Keep updating your "want to do/learn" list to keep yourself interested.

Remember: the whole point here is that executives (at least the confident ones who aren't threatened by others' success) *want you to take the initiative and make the most of your opportunity*. It makes their jobs much easier! As long as you don't go rogue . . . .

Go to them for guidance and mentorship, not hand-holding for every little step. Holding your hand at every step makes more work for them. Make it easy on them and others to understand why your idea or project is important, how it'll work, and your plan.

Make sure—to borrow an idea from Nail A Niche—to go back again *and again* to put everything in terms that matter to others. Don't make it all about you! Why should they care? What's the benefit to them? Why do they, the business, or customers *need* it?

Embrace Frustration

I'm frustrated most days. It's the nature of pushing for change—or being pushed. If you look at your frustrations another way, is there an exciting opportunity there instead?

Make a list:

1. What's most frustrating to you at work?
2. List the worst parts, all the "cons"
3. How could you flip it to be a positive? In the future, looking back, what was so great about this situation?
4. Now list some pros about it—what can turn this into an opportunity?
5. What baby step can you take *today* to take advantage of it?

Do this regularly, to practice turning your resistance to change (frustrations) into embracing opportunity (excitement).

YOU NEED SOME HUMDRUM PASSIONS

"Do what you love and the money will follow" is something people who already made it say to people who haven't. Besides, it's not even true. There are millions of people who do things they love and make no money. How many people get rich working at nonprofits?

Likewise, any version of the advice "Never do it for the money" is ridiculous. At least change it to embrace money too, such as: "Never do it for *only* the money." Or "Do it for the money, and do it honestly." Or "Do *whatever* needs to get done to support my family, without shame (or pride)."

100% *yes*: Develop your personal interests, explore your passions, and improve your art. And not *only* for the money, when you can help it. They can balance you out, add joy, human connection, make you more unique, and expose you to unexpected people, adventures, and successes. There's an endless list of reasons to do and develop your interests, "just because you want to." It's how I started sketching and writing.

But here's where people go wrong, with a belief that "if I just keep working on my art/writing/code, someday I'll be discovered or magically make more money."

Money does *not* automatically follow passion. How many starving artists and writers are there versus the number of rich artists and writers? How many aspiring social media stars are on YouTube or social channels, compared to those who can support themselves from their acting?

Pursuing passions doesn't mean you'll make money. And it doesn't mean you won't make money. They're *different*, and can be complementary. Money and passion are like water and food. You need both, though you can last only a few days without water (money) while you can go for weeks without food (passion) ... even if it's unpleasant.

Money and passion are like water and food. You need both, though you can last only a few days without water (money) while you can go for weeks without food (passion) ... even if it's unpleasant.

You need to (a) explore your interests and passions while also (b) learning how to create value and create money.

Learning how to create money's not unlike learning to play the guitar—a few people are born naturals, but most learn through diligent study and practice. And many never bother learning, ignoring it completely.

Frankly, it's often easier to bring your passions into your current job (boring or not) than it is to bring money into your passions. We'd argue that you can find passion, meaning, and impact in *anything* you do—whether it's cleaning houses, writing software, or working at a bank—if you look for it.

Anyway, no matter how passionate you are about what you do (or who you're with), some days will be incredible, some boring, and some awful. Especially when you aren't making enough money at it.

No matter how passionate you are about what you do (or who you're with), some days will be incredible, some boring, and some awful.

In the blogosphere, "Follow your passion" is usually misunderstood as, "Quit your soulless job to follow freedom, art, and wine on the beach, changing the world, surfing, and yoga on your own terms."

Yeah, and how much do 99% of those international, beach-lounging, yoga lifestyle, work-from-home-in-my-underwear people actually make? Except for a small number of standouts, much less than you probably assume. We aren't against beach yoga, and as for the ones doing it—great for them! The problem is *when you read those sexy stories and assume you're failing, or think that you need to quit whatever you're doing to start from scratch*, or buy into a overnight success pitch. Because 95% of you shouldn't make such a drastic change, and instead need to take *what you're already doing* and dig back into it, build on it, and expand on it.

Remember that those successful people whom you're following (including ourselves) still have plenty of problems. It's just more fun to write about how awesome life is than to share the sucky parts—especially on social media where your friends are watching. It's embarrassing to write "I'm doing yoga on the beach in Bali, but after a few months it's not that great, and I want to go back to a job where I see friends every day and can rely on a stable salary."

Here's the point: to learn how to create money for you, your family, or a business, there are several seemingly boring, humdrum passions you need to nurture that are just as vital, honorable, and important as any "sexy passions" such as food, fashion, motorsports, travel, romance, and art.

For example:

- Creating financial stability and choices for your family.
- Marketing and selling products, yourself, and your ideas.
- Saying "no" to people, ideas, and opportunities that threaten to overwhelm you.
- Spotting problems that others would be willing to pay to solve.

- Finding new ways every month, every week, and every day to learn in your routine job, and learn something new (avoiding the Grass Is Greener trap).
- Learning outbound prospecting, and how to drum up business.
- Communicating clearly in emails, speaking, or messaging.
- Creating and maintaining relationships: authentic curiosity about others, impeccable honesty, small talk, eye contact.
- Connecting with people, making small talk, having conversations—not just via email, texts, or social media (or dating) apps.
- Building your confidence by taking on new challenges, and "going for it," then—whether you succeed or fail—learning and try, try again.
- Exiting toxic situations whether with a manager, business, or customer.
- Having the hard conversations with coworkers or customers that you've been avoiding, even when it scares the heck out of you.

These passions aren't sexy, but they're examples of what you need to do to make as much money as you want, doing what you love. Work—every day—to find passion in what you do, including in making customers successful, learning how to make money, and managing people.

Questions

- What skills do you want or need?
- How can you get paid to learn and do it *now*?
- What baby step can you take *today* toward doing it?

Nurture a passion(s) in something you already do.

Get good at these kinds of humdrum passions and they can take you anywhere in life, to an epic career with or without your current business, or off pursuing your sexy passions, making your friends jealous by posting pictures and videos from your Costa Rican surfing art trip. So, now:

- Pick an important life or work goal.
- What are you doing about it, or need to, to reach it?
- How can you get paid to learn and do it here, wherever you are right now?
- What baby step can you take *today* to move forward?

YOUR COMPANY ISN'T YOUR MOMMY OR DADDY

The whole movement around making employees happy is well intentioned, but it's also unintentionally distracting people from what actually creates revenue *and* enduring fulfillment.

Happiness is a funny thing. It's transitory, often coming and going on a moment's notice. And happiness today can be the enemy of happiness tomorrow, if you let it make you complacent.

We don't believe anyone really understands it, regardless of what the studies say.

A company is responsible *to* employees, not *for* employees. It can create the conditions for your fulfillment: a safe work environment, no assholes, fair pay, career opportunities, and an honest culture. But it can't be responsible for *making you* happy—just as it can't be responsible for keeping you entertained or interested.

Your company isn't here to make all your boo-boos go away. To keep you entertained. To praise you at every turn, or avoid calling you on your shit, because they don't want to upset you.

Are you bored? *You* are just as responsible in making things interesting for yourself as the company is in helping you find a good fit. Boredom usually comes from a lack of learning. Don't wait for the company to figure out what you do: What can you do to take charge of learning on the job, so you can effectively get paid to learn?

Hey, it's *your* life, and only you can solve your problems, as much as you'd love someone/something to come in and save you—a big deal, an investor, a producer, a spouse, the Universe, a big bet, or family. Including matching your life to your finances (or vice versa), or finding purpose and passion in your life and work.... it's all on you, guys and gals.

You *need* a support system. You *need* to find people that believe in you. But *depending* on them for advice is different from *being dependent* on them for answers.

People hope easy answers and instant results will make them happier, which they do ... for a few seconds or minutes. Easy come, easy go. Fulfillment, a more enduring form of feeling good, comes from using all your talents and growing through challenge.

Fulfillment, a more enduring form of feeling good, comes from using all your talents and growing through challenge.

There's a paradox in which happiness often comes from unhappiness. The company's job is to create a supportive environment. Extra vacation days and ping pong tables can create temporary happiness, but being supportive also means *challenging* you, pushing you to improve yourself as a person, to better build enduring happiness. In that way, actually, the company *should* be like a parent.

BACK TO FORCING FUNCTIONS: HOW TO MOTIVATE YOURSELF TO DO THINGS YOU DON'T FEEL LIKE DOING

Everyone struggles with motivation. Well, maybe except 0.1% of us who are mutants like Elon Musk. But that's not me. I am very, very human. And like you, I suffer from procrastination, perfectionism, confusion, and erratic motivation.

What, you say? "Aaron, you went from 0 to 12 kids while publishing multiple books, grew your income by leaps and bounds, released a Predictable Revenue software product, while (usually) working 20–30 hours a week. And you say you get confused and are erratically motivated?!"

I might look like a mutant from the outside, but I've learned some tricks to work around my limitations, and I've seen them work for others. And remember, with all the external success you see, I have just as many problems as you do – and probably more!

I often love what I do and what it does for my family, but not every day. Even if you love what you do, it's going to suck some days.

I do struggle weekly with parent-entrepreneurship, dealing with:

- *Authentic busy-ness:* With lots of kids, whom I love playing with, and a growing business that must keep growing, I'm always tired: physically, emotionally, and mentally.
- *Overwhelmed:* I'm conflicted about what to spend time on, with so many irons in the fire at home and work.
- *Resistance:* Fear, doubt, uncertainty, perfectionism—I experience them all.

Like you, I have bills to pay—which somehow keep growing as fast as my income!—and still bigger dreams to chase.

As I mentioned before, if there was one thing (though there's never "one" thing) that has propelled my growth and bulldozed through my busyness, confusion, laziness and so on—it's that I create constant and challenging Forcing Functions for myself.

They are my source of predictable motivation.

How I Motivate Myself When I Am Tired, Confused, or Don't Want to Do It

Have you heard of the popular way of creating smart goals? Use SMART as the acronym for Specific, Measurable, Assignable, Realistic, Time-related goals.

Well, the acronym doesn't work for me. My mind simply doesn't function in a way that has me writing out these goals and then keeping track. And the busier and more overwhelmed I am, the harder it is to focus on anything other than the top one or two priorities—once burned into my brain with concrete dates that I never have to refer back to (like the due date for this manuscript).

What works for me is creating Forcing Functions made of up simple ASSes:

1. **A**nnounce to others that you'll create a …
2. **S**pecific Outcome, by a …
3. **S**pecific Date

If you're an overachiever, you could probably combine the two approaches into SMARTASS goals, but that's too much for me.

Yes, that was a joke. Look, you can have serious goals without being so serious all the damn time! Just change the acronym to SAS if you want a safe-for-work acronym.

Or keep it super simple: tell some people what you'll do, and when you will do it.

> **Tell some people what you'll do, and when you will do it.**

This doesn't mean announcing "Hi everyone, I'm going to beat my quota this quarter by 10%." Make your stated goal as *inescapable* as possible, with something you have total control over, that will help lead to the results you want: "Hi, everyone, I've scheduled two CEO group breakfasts for October 1st and November 3rd that I'm going to host."

Remember the example of (a) telling people (or yourself) you're going start exercising more, vs. (b) signing up for a marathon and announcing it. It's the same principle.

It's especially effective with events, which I've used time and again, and what Jason has used for his big SaaStr Annual conference (SaaStrAnnual.com). Announce the exact date for an event—even before you have the details nailed down or feel ready.

The announcement of a date will get your brain working on the challenge even before you mean to. *It'll propel you.*

Don't let the panic stop you. The best way to deal with any fear or panic is to *get moving* and take one more step toward your deadline.

I've seen these work for anyone. My wife, Jessica, says they're the best way she's found to propel herself into getting important but not urgent things done, that otherwise get pushed aside with the daily hustle of a big family.

Don't Assume Motivation Will Find You: You Must Find It

Especially when I'm tired, motivation hides. It cowers. It runs away. It doesn't just come to me. Motivation is attracted by action. Ninty percent of the time I don't start working after I'm motivated. It's only after I start something—a workout, writing, drawing sketches—*then* motivation shows up and keeps me going.

As excited as I was about writing this very section, I resisted writing it until my fingers started moving. Because as I write these words, I'm on an airplane to visit clients, tired, and sad from saying goodbye to my wife and kids. What I want to do is read a book or watch a movie on the plane, but I have an inescapable deadline with my publisher to meet.

What's in Your Control?

A goal is something you're striving for: "Have 100 people show up at an event on April 20" or "Lose 10 lbs. by August 1." You can announce it, but you don't have *100% control* over it. If you're new to this, start by designing Forcing Functions that are 100% in your control, that you can't hide from.

GOAL	Not 100% in Your Control	100% in Your Control
Run faster	3:30 finish	Sign up for a marathon and tell your friends *Next Level: hire a video crew to film your journey*
Self-managing team	People make all the decisions without asking your advice	Go on vacation totally offline, with only an emergency hotline to you
Double growth rate	Create X qualified leads per month through paid lead generation	Invest in a lead generation budget and product, with regular board or exec team updates
Maximize company growth	Grow from $1M to $10M, or $10M to $100M	Raise money from professional investors
Launch new product	X Customers buying the product	Commit to attending or launching a conference where the product will be announced
Publish book	Book sales	Announce publication date.
Double personal income	Create average monthly income of $60,000	Sign lease for $17,000/month house

Agree to give a talk someplace—even before you know what you'll present.

More examples:

- Agree to give a talk someplace—even if you don't know what you'll present.
- Announce you're going to hold a training session to teach people about one particular industry.

FIGURE 23.1 Don't let yourself chicken out ... go through with it in *any* way you can.

- Specialize people's roles so that prospectors prospect, and closers close.
- Raise sponsorship money for an event or publication that isn't yet complete.
- First publish a Kickstarter page, and then raise money through it.
- To learn a language, buy a one-way ticket to that country.
- To limit your smartphone use, switch to a dumb/flip phone.

Technically, Forcing Functions don't *have* to have a specific date—like raising money from investors. But when you're exposing your people to this for the first time, you'll want to start with specific dates. They work.

In Review

1. Pick a date (often two to three weeks out, unless it's a *big thing*).
2. Choose what's going to happen on that date.
3. Tell other people about it!

Tips

- You know you're doing it right when your Forcing Function makes you flip between feeling anxious and feeling excited. That means you're challenging yourself.
- Do everything possible to avoid chickening out. You may find yourself coming up with very creative excuses to bail out of your commitment.
- When it's done, and you wonder "what's next?"—then sit down and *come up with another Forcing Function*.

May the Force be with you!

SALES IS A LIFE SKILL

What descriptions do you think of when you hear "sales" or "salespeople"? Most people say "aggressive," "fake," and the like. Even my wife says "greasy." Why can't we begin associating more words like *helpful, sincere, expert, noble*, and *honest* with people who sell?

Because "selling" isn't just for salespeople. To Define Your Destiny, to accomplish *anything* in work or life, you need to know how to *sell*. To sell yourself, your ideas, or your stuff.

To accomplish anything in work or life, you need to know how to sell.

Getting a job or promotion, getting buy-in from coworkers on a new project, inspiring people to volunteer, finding distribution for a film, getting press, raising money for a nonprofit, raising venture capital, starting a company, recruiting people … these all require "selling."

What's one thing people like Gandhi, Mother Theresa, Elon Musk, and Richard Branson have in common? They are examples of people who are superb at *selling*.

Selling can be noble in business too. The skill of selling brings money into companies while inspiring customers to adopt new practices, of inspiring change in others. People who sell (including entrepreneurs) are on the frontlines every day; they are a company's most important point of contact with customers!

Can you imagine what a company would be like if *everyone* there could sell effectively and honestly, whether to customers or internally? A lot of great ideas are stifled because employees have them … and have no idea what to do with them. A lot of customers don't get what they need, because employees on sales, support, or success teams are afraid to "sell" the customer on something they might need.

For employees who aren't salespeople, let's use a new "ABC."

Your primary goal should not be to close a deal, but to help your "customers" solve problems and realize success.

A New ABC

Alec Baldwin gave the greatest sales rant of all time in the movie *Glengarry Glen Ross*. In it, he reminded the team to "ABC = Always Be Closing." (Search YouTube for "glengarry alec" to find it; it's the best investment of seven minutes you can make). But it exemplifies a "Sell something to someone whether they need it or not" approach.

The best kinds of sales are when both parties win. You make money, they get a problem solved, and you both feel good about it. So, here's an alternative ABC if you're new to selling:

A. **Ask questions:** Listen more than you talk. Insightful questions make it easy to have conversations with customers or prospects, learn about their problems, and know what solution will help them best. People won't be ready to listen to you until after you've listened to them.
B. **Be Honest:** About why you're doing this, and what your personal story is. In being curious about them, their situation, and what they care about. What you're passionate about. Why you think they should or should *not* do this. That you're new and don't know the answers, but that you know where to get them.
C. **Customer Success:** If you stay focused on *what will help your customers succeed*, you can't go wrong. That doesn't mean only selling them on what they ask for—because people don't always know what

they need. Become an expert in what you do, and you will guide people in helping decide what's best for them. Through experience, you'll learn how to challenge people to get out of their comfort zone, to make a decision and move forward—even when at first they're uncertain or resistant.

Other Tips on Keeping Sales Both Real and Really Effective

- *Practice:* The only way it gets easier, and you get better, is by doing a lot of selling. And as you gain experience, it'll become easy to identify when you should challenge people on their beliefs: "You should/should *not* do this for these specific reasons ... "
- *Pleasant persistence:* Do you find yourself saying, "I sent them a message and they didn't respond, so they must not be interested"? Following up, repeatedly, is *vital*. Not optional. Required. Who says they even saw or read your note? Don't be afraid to follow up on your follow-ups; just do it in friendly ways. The only way you'll be annoying is by actually being annoying.
- *ABT, "Always Be Testing":* The best way to learn is to try it out and see what happens. You can't whiteboard your way to success.
- *ABL: "Always Be Learning":* If you close zero out of 10 opportunities, step back and figure out what needs to change.
- *Take "no" as information, not criticism*: If people aren't buying, look at is as market research. Are you targeting the right people with the right need, right time, and right message? What needs to change to improve?
- *It's a numbers game:* The more swings you take, the more possible hits you get. The more you sell, the more practice you get and the more chances you have to fall down and learn.
- *People buy on their time, not yours*: Don't be desperate or needy.
- *How to ask "hard" questions*, such as finding out if they have the money to pay for it: *just ask them*: Pretend you're asking about the weather, "Is it raining where you are?" "How would you pull together the budget for this?" Get help in crafting better questions and role-playing to practice.
- *It's a multistep process*: Read the next section!

Don't be afraid to follow up on your follow-ups; just do it in friendly ways.

SALES IS A MULTISTEP PROCESS

By Steli Efti
CEO Close.io,

Whether selling is old hat to you or makes you nervous, a few simple questions can help you and your customer get to the truth and reach an agreement faster.

So you have a deal on the table. It could be a sale, pitching executives on a new initiative, or even raising money. Whoever you are selling to, let's call them the prospect or buyer, and assume at this point they're interested. But, you're not sure how to take this across the finish line to close it, and get it signed. Let's help you:

- Figure out the roadmap of steps it's going to take to close the deal.
- Discover major red flags and issues that will slow it or sabotage it, while ensuring it's a good fit.
- Educate your prospect through all the steps he or she will have to take to make the deal happen.
- Help your prospect imagine and visualize a future where he or she has become a customer of your idea, product, or project.
- Uncover whether there is no real "buying intent" (are they honestly serious?).

How? Simply ask this question: "Dear [*executive/investor/potential customer*]: Now that you know what I'm doing and I've answered all your questions, it seems we're a good fit. Would you agree? And if so, what are all the steps we have to take to help make this happen?"

Then shut up and listen.

If the prospect says something to the effect of, "Well, I'm not sure ... " or, "Well, we can't buy for three years because we're locked in the current contract ... " then, you're in trouble. This means they're not serious about buying. Walk away. Then retool the product, or try a different customer. A serious buyer will work with you to figure out a way around their roadblocks.

In all other cases, you have to put on your investigative hat and keep following up with questions until you both reach a point where a deal can happen.

Put on your investigative hat and keep following up with questions until you both reach a point where a deal can happen.

Here's what a typical conversation should look like:

You	"Dear prospect. What will it take for you to buy our [product/program/idea]?"
Customer	"Well, I would have to show it to my boss and some colleagues and see what they think."
You	"Great. How do you typically get feedback? Scheduling a meeting? This week? Next week? Do you make a presentation—or how does this typically work?"
Customer	"Well, we have a weekly standup meeting, and that's when I will present this."
You	"Awesome. What happens when your boss and teammates really like the idea and want to move forward?"
Customer	"Then we would schedule a follow-up call with you and the key people to get our questions answered."
You	"Makes sense. Let's assume we have a great call and I can answer all questions to the team's satisfaction and we're all happy to move forward. What happens next?"
Customer	"Well, then it would have to go through legal." [This is the point where most people would stop asking questions and feel happy about what they have learned. That's a mistake. Keep asking questions until you get to the finish line.]
You	"Of course. How does this process typically work for you? Have you purchased something similar to our product in the past six months, and can you describe to me what we'll have to do to make the process as smooth as possible?"
Customer	"Yes, we'd have to run through a few higher-ups, then the purchasing department and ethics committee."
You	"Oh, interesting. Could you describe this process a little more?"
Customer	"Well, Purchasing usually takes a couple weeks to review, and if it looks good, then they move it on to Ethics, who have the final sign-off."
You	"Great. But *then* we're in business, right?"
Customer	"Yes!"
You	"Great. Let's say we get started. How will you know this project is successful? What will be most important to you?"
Customer	[Explains what they need to be successful with you . . .]

Now you know what it will take to make this happen. You have a roadmap to:

- Forecast accordingly
- Identify roadblocks
- Decide if you really want to pursue the deal
- What Customer Success looks like

After this conversation, which of course never goes quite as perfectly as the one above, you'll have a much clearer plan for moving forward.

The takeaway—people new to selling don't realize how many steps it can take. Learn everything you can about the buyer's steps and what it takes to get *to their end*—which is past signing the deal and projecting forward to the point where "the customer is successful."

If the words and phrases here don't feel right to you, don't throw this away. *Try it* and plan on finding your own phrases that fit your style along the way.

CHAPTER 24

Combining Money and Meaning

Fulfillment comes from applying your "full self." Are you treating work as something completely separate from life? Or is life interfering with your work? Combine them to make the most of both. Work can enhance life, and life can enhance work.

MEANING GONE WRONG

It's cool now for people to expect their work to be purposeful, to be meaningful. As it should be. And Meaning Snobs can go on and on about how meaning is more important than money, or how impactful their gigs are ... and that's great.

The truth is, putting meaning first, second, and third on your list of priorities won't make you money. For Avanoo's Daniel Jacobs, building a meaningful business didn't take off until he put money first, realizing that without being able to create predictable revenue or funding, nothing he created—however inspiring or meaningful—would last.

Putting meaning first, second, and third on your list of priorities won't make you money.

Luckily, there are many ways to make money meaningful. There's nothing like the fear of seeing your kids go hungry—or a payroll date coming up, or visiting people in dire need, or struggling to raise money for your nonprofit project—to get you over your hesitation in bringing in sales in new ways and see new meaning in money.

Here's one test you can run to see if someone's using "meaning" as an excuse to stay comfortable and avoid growing.

Imagine one of your friends, for example, one who means well and wants to help people but who pretty much just shares inspirational quotes all day or posts pictures of himself or herself being spiritual or edgy. Maybe they volunteer weekly or monthly. Now imagine this friend saying, "I'm going to create a $1 million organization to help/fix/address [*insert cause*]."

Can you see that person—or maybe it's you!—actually *doing* it? Can you see them walking the walk, jumping in and embracing the idea of putting money as a top priority, a necessity to support the mission? (Assuming integrity is a given.)

It's easier to hide and pretend that the "money stuff" (or whatever else you need to change) isn't important. No guts, no glory—and no risk of failing. Breakthroughs often require you to let go of your ego, and egos can be harder to break down than bad habits. Pride often interferes with taking the leap to grow.

Breakthroughs often require you to let go of your ego, and egos can be harder to break down than bad habits.

This is just one example of why we resist change: it forces us to admit that we could be wrong, or makes us feel we're not as good as we think we are, or that we don't know as much as we thought we did. It's easier to avoid facing those truths; including telling yourself and others that say money is a nice-to-have. Remember, comfort is the enemy of growth.

In your case, rather than telling yourself "you can only work at a job with meaning," maybe instead it's a belief that you need to stick purely to software, and avoid creating professional services. Or you're afraid of raising prices. Maybe you can't accept help from others. Or believe standardization is impossible. Are you sure you're a need-to-have on your team, rather than someone who's surprisingly replaceable? You could believe that you're VP-level talent trapped in a manager-level role. Or that you're above average (which is statistically impossible) and deserve a break for being special. That you're going to be magically discovered …

This is why successful entrepreneurs care more about the brutal truth than about being right or looking good. They take responsibility for results, not intentions. It boils down to this: "Is this working?

If the answer is yes—great, do more. Is the answer no? Then don't blame other people; instead, ask what can I do, what needs to happen, to fix it?"

Use crises to motivate you to embrace the change, as painful as it may be, rather than avoid it. And if you don't have a crisis, get creative with manufacturing one with Forcing Functions that drive you to grow anyway.

And if you just can't find something that'll drive you, or find the courage to keep creating challenging Forcing Functions, or spend the years needed to Do The Time … maybe you should give up on your current goals and find some smaller ones.

Try starting with what you're already doing. Don't assume that meaning will come only from quitting your job and finding some exotic new occupation. Or that you'll feel purposeful when you're helping homeless people, volunteering in Africa, or are inspiring X million people.

Don't assume that meaning will only come only from quitting your job and finding some exotic new occupation.

There's nothing wrong with those goals, but start by finding more meaning in the *little things* you already do every day: talking with a customer, giving someone a helpful idea, writing something (whether anyone else cares or not). Getting feedback from a coworker. Getting coffee with a teammate. Fixing a bug. Coding a new feature. Learning how to better organize your workspace. Talking with an angry customer and saving the relationship. Breaking through a creative block. Or just breaking something. Getting your reports and dashboards to finally work. Learning from a spectacular failure. Finishing your daily sales or activities goal.

WHAT'S YOUR UNIQUE GENIUS?

How can you make unique contributions to the business and team? What would make your job more fulfilling? How can you stand out from the crowd?

Unique Is Good Business

It's hard for companies that sound the same as every other business in their field to stand out. And it's the same for people: to succeed in your

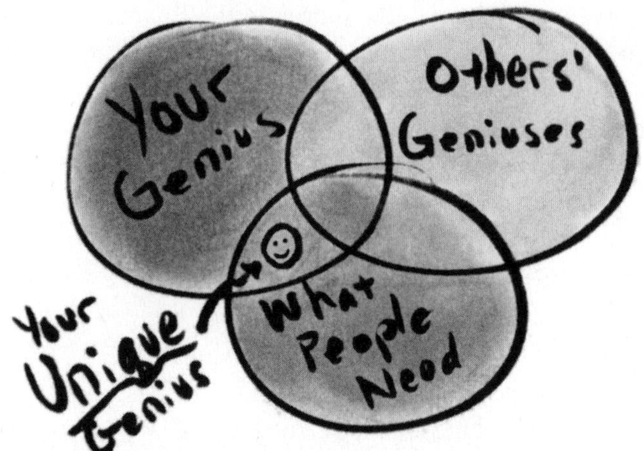

FIGURE 24.1 You have one, even if you don't appreciate or understand it yet.

career, you have to stand out. Discover what makes you different, learn how to express (market) it, and apply it in a way that solves others' problems, whether they're coworkers or customers.

> **Discover what makes you different, learn how to express (market) it, and apply it in a way that solves others' problems.**

Does your resume cover 100 different things you can do? Chances are you're sounding generic and vague to others, so they don't "click" with why they should hire, promote, or recruit you. How do your executives perceive you—as someone to watch or as a face in a crowd?

Being different and unique can create buzz.

Being different and unique can take courage.

A great brand (personal or business) repels as much as it attracts. Because it stands for something. And when you stand for something, no matter what it is, many others are bound to disagree.

Instead of thinking about all the stuff you *could* or *should* do, what do you *want* to do? Rather than thinking about many talents and skills you have, what problems or goals do you want to apply them to? What do you *want* to do or create, that you would be proud of?

> **Instead of thinking about all the stuff you *could* or *should* do, what do you *want* to do?**

Uncovering Your Unique Genius

Once you ask the question, "What is my Unique Genius?" your mind will begin trying to answer it. Here are some questions to help you figure out how to better combine money and meaning.

> **Once you ask the question, "What is my Unique Genius?" your mind will begin trying to answer it.**

- What do you want to learn about, if you could learn about *anything*? List at least 10 things, and then pick the top few.

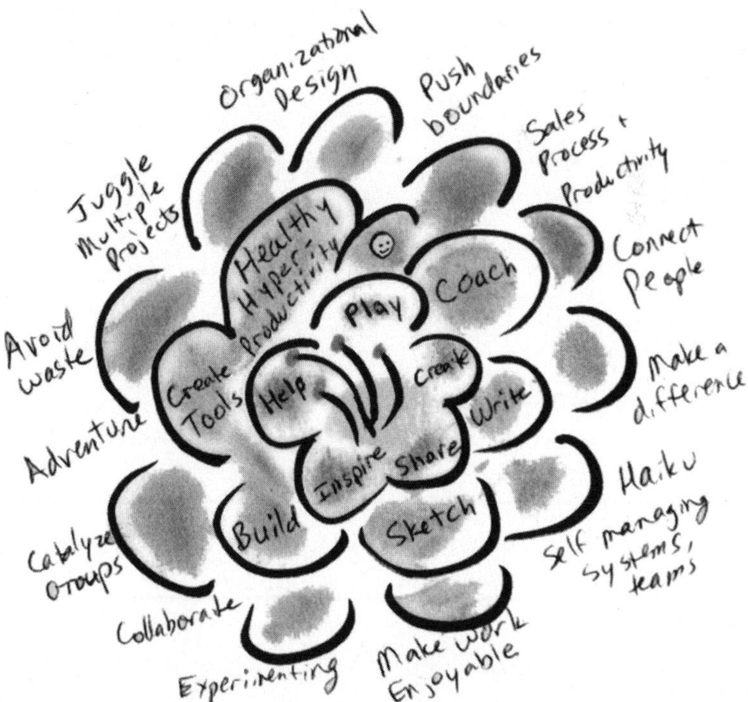

FIGURE 24.2 List out all your interests (you don't need to make it pretty).

- Imagine having more money than you could ever spend, so you don't need to work. You take a few years to lie on the beach, and then get bored. What would you want to do, if you could do anything? (This is usually something that helps others or that makes a difference in the world.)
- Ask coworkers or customers the question, "What's the one thing you hired me for, or would hire me for?"
- Complete this: "If I could help anyone/any kind of person, I would help . . . ." Or, "If I could have any kind of customer, I would have . . . ."
- If you could start a project that wouldn't fail, that is assured of success, what would it do? Who would it help? What about it would make you proud?
- Who are you jealous of, and why? What would you have to learn, do, or have in order to not be jealous of them anymore?
- What have you been the most successful at so far?
- What frustrates you that you would like to personally help fix in the world? Especially something that you deal with *personally or daily*.
- What parts of work do you enjoy most? What *daily activities* do you like to do?
- What do people keep coming to you for help with, to ask your advice on?
- What do you secretly love to do, or love about yourself?
- If you're in a bookstore, what section do you go to first? What's your ideal book to read (or write)? What if you stick only to the business section?
- What would it take to make your work so enjoyable that you'd do it for free?
- What do your friends see as your strengths?

Apply these questions to your job today:

- What do you like, and not like, about your job today? Your company? How can you increase what you like, and reduce what you don't?
- Is your manager or work environment irretrievably toxic? If not, what needs to happen to improve it? How can you kick that process off?

- With what you want to learn, how can you make it relevant to your work? For example: If you want to get paid to speak, or inspire people through speaking, how can you begin doing it for your job?
- If you want to help kids, also try imagining those kids as grownups who you work with in some way today … How would you help them as adults?
- If you want to change the world or people, how can you make the same change happen in your team, business, or market?

You can find downloadable worksheets and other free resources at FromImpossible.com/unique.

IGNORING REAL LIFE DOESN'T MAKE IT GO AWAY

In 2015, Amazon was publicly embarrassed by a *New York Times* article that said the company's work practices included "85-hour workweeks, annual staff culling, executives encouraging underlings to sabotage one another, employees weeping at their desks." And that female employees who had suffered miscarriages, stillbirths, or sickness were expected to either remain productive or be punished.

Now, we gotta take all this with a grain of salt. The *New York Times* and its writers, like all media businesses, is naturally going to take whatever ugly stories they can find, and embellish them as much as possible while remaining true to the facts, because it attracts readers. With any company that hires 100,000-plus people, you can find pretty much any story you look for. And as far as the news goes, drama brings in far more readers than happiness. People love to read about others' problems, yet never post anything about their own, instead sharing pictures that show how great their life is.

Pretending you or your team don't have kids, aren't exhausted or sick, or that "everything's fine" doesn't make it true.

> ***Everyone*** **at some point ends up living with challenges they can't just simply sweep under the rug.**

Everyone at some point ends up living with challenges they can't simply sweep under the rug, and that will affect him or her at work …

Babies
Teenagers
Death
Sick family members
Depression
ADHD
Cancer
Debt collectors
School
Severe anxiety
Addiction
Divorce
Breakdowns
Abuse
Sleep deprivation
Lawsuits

All of these are a part of life. Life happens. So … how can you integrate life and work, even when you're being dealt a crap hand?

You Can Integrate Work and Life

How? Start by setting the example. Don't be embarrassed to admit you have problems. Keep it simple, without having to make a big deal or drama out of it. "Sharing" is about *informing*, not whining.

If you show other people how to be honest with personal challenges, and not feel judged or punished, it lightens the situation. And it stops others from wondering, "Why's Bob been so distracted and absent lately?" so they can focus and adapt, too. It can help prevent unhappy surprises later. When people are honest with each other, a solution can be found to help everyone win.

If you show people how to be honest with personal challenges, and not feel judged or punished, it lightens the situation.

The Golden Rule Always Applies

Lastly, you don't—and shouldn't—share everything. Some things should remain private. If you're having problems with your significant other, don't blab about a private matter without their permission. Respect the other person: How would you want them to treat *your* privacy?

You don't—and shouldn't—share everything. Some things should remain private.

You can say nothing, or keep it vague: "I'm sorry I've been distracted. I've having personal problems that have been a real drain on me, and I don't know how long they'll last."

If You're Struggling with Juggling

Having a lot of time and money can make growing a business easier. But don't let a lack of either be an excuse to do nothing. A baby step is better than nothing; you can't take one that's too small. A lack of money or time can force you to be more creative with what you do have, if you look at it like a challenge. It's one reason I've limited myself to (usually) 20- to 30-hour workweeks, and using less than $100 to start each business.

Just because you have a tough or horrible challenge doesn't mean you have to give up on your goals.

Even if you work part-time or "part-energy"—you can still make progress, as long as you find ways to set aside some time each day or week, or even year to focus. And keep setting or resetting goals. When you wander off track, get back on.

It might take you 3 or 10x longer than someone who can work full time or raise extra money, but you can get there.

AARON: HOW THE HELL DO YOU JUGGLE 12 KIDS AND WORK?

Paul Heill wrote, "I see you're a dad of 12! WOW!!! How the hell do you do it man??? I have two with another on the way, and am stressed out."

We have 12 kids (so far …), from a newborn to 17. The most physically and time-consuming part of being a dad has been having a new baby. So, while 12 kids may sound like a lot, I cheated by skipping the whole infant stage with many of them:

- I had two of them "from scratch" with my wife, as babies.
- Two are from my wife's prior marriage.
- Four adopted from China and one from East Los Angeles. It's a lot easier, physically, when the kids can dress, eat, and go potty by themselves.
- Our newest is a baby we adopted domestically at birth.
- Plus a teen daughter originally from El Salvador, and her baby.

Also, three of our kids have or had physical challenges—like our six-year old son Maverick, whose elbows and knees don't bend—but they are mostly correctable, and we all just adapt, so it ends up being not as big a deal as you might assume it would be.

Trust me, when I hear about a family of two parents—with no extra help—who have had four, five, or more kids all biologically, I think "How the hell do they do *that*!?!"

Juggling

Jump in with both feet, and figure it out later.

- *I jump in with both feet, and figure it out later*. Another adoption? We need twice the house for twice the rent payment? Let's do it, and figure out how to pay for it or make it work later. Sometimes there are painful bumps to this approach (like having to be late paying rent), but it's always been worth it.
- *It's gotten easier as the family gets bigger*, and the kids have more people to play and work with. It's also easier as we've adopted children beyond the toddler stage.
- *We hire a lot of help*. One au pair. Two nannies during the week. A housecleaner. One grandfather lived with us for a year. A grandmother comes once in a while for a few weeks. Uber serves as backup transportation for older kids.
- *I block out important things on my calendar:* Monday dates with my wife. The whole day of Wednesday for writing. A couple of mornings a week for exercise—when I'm not writing a new book. Tuesday, Thursday, and Friday are for phone calls. These calendar blocks tend to evolve every six months.
- *I stick to, but not rigidly*, that 20–30 hour workweek. Typically three days a week are 4 to 5 hours of actual work, and two days are 6 to 8 hours. Some weeks it's a lot more, if I'm traveling or have a big deadline. For example, during many weeks of creating this book with Jason, it's often been more than 30 hours a week. Some weeks are less, if we have something intense going on at home like a new adoption (the paperwork and appointments tend to take a ridiculous amount of time).

- *My other job (and 168-hour workweek):* When I'm not "at work," I'm a full-time dad. I vaguely remember what it's like to "relax" as a dim memory :)
- *I trust my wife*. And she is super organized at running the family calendar, our nannies, meals, and activities—all while creating her own books and SpyGirlHigh.com. She wasn't born that way, but was forced to learn time management as a single mom. She runs the family and does almost all our paperwork. I make all the money (for now). She does want to make money through her own business in the future.
- *I stopped exercising*. For about four years, all I did was Dad-aerobics. My exercises include the Trampoline Jump, Baby Press, Pillow Fight, Grocery Carry, and Furniture Move. So I'm still moving around every day!
- *Our kids do zero to two activities a week*. And most activities are within easy driving distance, like a music lesson at home, or a dance class nearby.
- *Being present*. When I work, I work. When I'm home, I'm home. When I eat, I eat. I rarely read or check my phone while I'm eating (with others). When I'm with family, I do my best to be attentive to them, looking my kids in the eyes—whether playing or disciplining them. I'll check email or texts in the evening, but quickly, when I take a break. I rarely work at night. I'd probably write at night if I could stay awake, but that never happens.
- *I usually have multiple, major Forcing Functions at work*. I commit to doing things before I know how I'll get them done: writing a new book, merging my company, committing to a paid keynote address, or selling a new kind of product or workshop such as the newest one, a Predictable Revenue Certification program (PredictableUniversity.com). Having clear deadlines cuts through my other busyness clutter.

Money

- *The motivation* (and sometimes desperation) to keep money growing fast, and far beyond anything I'd ever made before, has come from having a growing family. It's been the ultimate Forcing Function. I'm never comfortable, but always fulfilled.
- *The methods* I used in the first several years are the same as in #1 Nailing A Niche, #2 Create Predictable Pipeline, #4 Double Your Deal-size, and #5 Do The Time. In 2015, after cofounding Carb.io,

and now that our software company is growing, I've added focus on the others #3 Make Sales Scalable and #6 Embrace Employee Ownership.

- *I always have a 10x thing in development* such as a book, merger, or product. They usually take 6–18 months to launch. I'm always investing in my future, even when it's years out.
- *I work to find trusted partners* on projects, so I'm not doing everything alone.

Kids

- *Everyone is always "my kid" or "my son" or "my daughter."* And that's what they are. I never use the words "stepfather" or "my adopted son/daughter."
- *I play a lot with my kids.* I play with them, rather than watch them play. I take them on motorcycle rides, whether they can ride their own motorcycle, or if I have to stick a smaller one on the cycle in front of me. Trampoline jumping with everyone. Card and board games. Forts. Legos. Cooking. Pillow fights. Hide and seek. Minecraft. Creating funny videos with them.
- *All our kids go to different schools.* It might sound crazy that few of our kids attend the same school—they're scattered at schools all over Pacific Palisades and Santa Monica. But any extra driving work is *far* easier to handle than when a kid doesn't fit a school.
- *I'm wary of electronics.* Electronics today make it easier than ever to create amazing things—or to sit alone watching videos or social feeds while life passes you by. We minimize them with younger kids. We push the older ones to use electronics to create, not just consume. I am much more liberal when the kids are using them to play with each other (it's been great bonding for them when not overdone), or if we're watching classics or musicals. This is an ever-evolving challenge.
- *The kids play with each other a lot.* And also fight. Either way, they're interacting with each other rather than needing parents all the time.
- *Trips.* It's been really fun taking one of the bigger kids with me on speaking trips. When she was 10, my daughter Aurora even helped me onstage to keynote the first Sales Hacker Conference. Any *Predictable Revenue* or From *Impossible To Inevitable* events will be kid friendly.

Challenges

- *Less guilt.* As much time as I spend with the family, frequently I feel guilty about not being there even more. Especially when I travel. So I look at it this way: when I need to work to pay the bills or create financial stability for my family, work *is* family time. You gotta pay the bills.
- *I have as many challenges and frustrations as you or anyone.* But they're better challenges than they were when I was younger.
- *I'm far from perfect.* My wife says I'm the calmest person she's ever met. It's hard to ruffle me. But I can get mad. Like when my 10-year-old snuck up behind me, while I was working on something important at home, and slammed a heavy pillow into the top of my head, hard enough to hurt my neck. I've yelled at our kids and judged them unfairly.
- *Living paycheck to paycheck for years.* I violate all the sensible financial advice from money experts and my family (which really upsets them, but what are you gonna do?). Whatever we make (and more), I invest in the family or business. Years ago I was so anxious about spending all or more than we made, including exhausting my savings and adding credit card debt. Now I've gotten used to running down to almost zero cash every month or two. And spending our savings or taking on debt was worth it for very important investments in the business and family—adoptions, new business programs, private schools for some kids, vacations (yes, these are investments), nannies, and help.
- *One-on-one time with each kid, regularly.* This just doesn't happen enough. Even a walk or bike ride alone, or going out for breakfast. Each kid needs some time alone with one or both parents.
- *Avoiding Roommate-itis.* Even with the fun chaos we have at home, my wife and I can get into routines, or just be busy, and forget to stop and connect with each other. When we start feeling like roommates, we amp up our own alone-time or do little daily things like leaving notes for each other, touching, talking, and going out on dates. We both look forward all week to Monday evenings, our Magic Mondays—our regular, jealously-guarded date night.
- *Tiredness.* I'm always tired. Physically. Emotionally. Mentally. But when there's a choice between resting and doing something important, I keep choosing the something fun or important.

- I would like to post more on my personal blog PebbleStorm.com, but it's not a priority—yet.

The Bottom Line

In 2007 I spent a lot of time envisioning what I wanted to create with my life. I was still single. I wasn't thinking at all about kids. It had never occurred to me I'd have or want a big family.

I thought I wanted fulfilling work. And to make as much money as I wanted, doing what I loved.

Almost 10 years later, I've seen the impossible become inevitable. I just never expected family to be the main driver of both the money and the fulfillment and fun I wanted.

Though, even with all the growth, I can't see slowing down anytime soon in work or family. No comfort here, yet! Among other goals, my wife and I want to inspire more families to adopt and help kids who are alone in the world. I can't tell you how many people say "I've always wanted to adopt, but … [insert reason]."

Just do it.

When you're pursuing anything vitally important to you, you can figure it out. If you stick to it, especially through the times that feel like failures. Even if it takes you years longer to get there than you wanted, and in totally unexpected ways.

When you're pursuing anything vitally important to you, you can figure it out when you embrace the challenge and growth rather than avoid it.

About The Authors

JASON LEMKIN is a serial tech entrepreneur and venture capitalist, who founded the biggest community on the planet for SaaS entrepreneurs: SaaStr.com, and has invested in SaaS companies worth collectively in excess of $1.5 billion. Jason was CEO of EchoSign, and led it from $0 to $100 million+ in revenues and a sale to Adobe. He is married with two kids, runs every single damn day, and loves anything related to Hawaii.

AARON ROSS is married with 12 children (mostly through adoption), loves motorcycles, and keeps a 25-hour workweek. He's a keynote speaker and best-selling author of *Predictable Revenue,* called "The Sales Bible of Silicon Valley," based on an outbound prospecting system that's created more than $1 billion across Salesforce .com and other companies. He's cofounder and CRO of Carb.io, a Pipeline Automation software company, and cofounder of PredictableUniversity.com.

For More, Including Videos, Extra Material, and Updates, Visit:

FromImpossible.com

Index

Note: Page references in *italics* refer to figures.

go to

10	9	17	2

slash

14	9	4	4

pw

1	10	6	3